THE
FRIENDSHIPS OF WOMEN
WORKBOOK

THE
FRIENDSHIPS
OF WOMEN
Workbook

Dee Brestin

Cook Communications

OTHER TITLES BY DEE BRESTIN
Books

We Are Sisters

A sequel to *The Friendships of Women* that looks at the wonderful bond between biological sisters and also, sisters in Christ. Small group study included.

My Daughter, My Daughter

An amazing faith story in which Dee and coauthor Lori Beckler parallel the lives of well-known contemporary women with the lives of biblical women. For example, Kathy Troccoli, whom God is using to save the unborn, is compared to the Hebrew midwives. Sandi Patty who is a leader in song, but fell, and is being restored, is compared to Miriam. Small group study included.

Bible Studyguides Exclusively for Women

The following in-depth guides look at topics of interest to women and look at books of the Bible from the perspective of women. Women like to share their hearts, and these guides will help you bond and find applications very relevant to your lives. Detailed descriptions at close of this workbook.

The Joy of Women's Friendships	*A Woman of Insight (Ecclesiastes)*
The Joy of Eating Right	*A Woman's Journey through Luke*
The Joy of Hospitality	*A Woman's Journey through Ruth*
A Woman of Joy (1, 2, & 3 John)	*A Woman's Journey through Esther*
A Woman of Value (Proverbs)	*A Woman's Journey through 1 Peter*

Most Scripture quotations are from the *Holy Bible, New International Version*®, © 1973, 1978, 1984 by International Bible Society. Used by permission of Zondervan Publishing House. All rights reserved. Other Scriptures are taken from J.B. Phillips: *The New Testament in Modern English*, (PH) Revised Edition, © J.B. Phillips, 1958, 1960, 1972, permission of Macmillan Publishing Co. and Collins Publishers; *The Living Bible*, (TLB) © 1971, Tyndale House Publishers, Wheaton, IL 60189. Used by permission; *New Scofield Reference Bible, King James Version*, (SCO) © 1967 by Oxford University Press, Inc. Reprinted by permission; *King James Version* of the Bible (KJV).

Editors: Pamela T. Campbell, Jane Vogel
Cover Design: iDesignEtc.
Cover Photo: Matt Orthober
Interior Illustrations: Guy Wolek
Recommended Dewey Decimal Classification: 301.412
Suggested Subject Heading: FRIENDSHIP; WOMEN
Library of Congress Catalog Card Number: 87-62482
ISBN: 0-89693-432-2

9 10 Printing/Year 05 04 03 02 01

Faithful Woman is an imprint of Cook Communications,
Colorado Springs, Colorado 80918 Cook Communications, Paris, Ontario
Kingsway Communications, Eastbourne, England

TO MY DAUGHTER, SALLY

At eleven years of age, your gift for intimacy has blessed our family with immeasurable joy. May you be strong, my darling, and open to God's pruning; and may you so abide in Christ that your gift flourishes, bringing warmth and redemption to a cold and hurting world.*

*Sally was eleven when **The Friendships of Women** *was first released. At the release of this workbook, Sally is married. She and her husband are studying and sharing their faith in Krakow, Poland.*

CONTENTS

ACKNOWLEDGMENTS

I am so thankful to my friends who responded honestly as I probed them with questions about their friendships with women. Some of their answers were very personal, and sometimes a pseudonym was used. A special thanks to the women from Sonrise Bible Studies. Luci Shaw, Madeleine L'Engle, Win Couchman, and Margaret D. Smith have shared wonderful stories and comments with me. My friend Sara Andreesen combed through my manuscript repeatedly and offered helpful insights. My editor, Laura Bush, worked with me on the original manuscript, and Pam Campbell, encouraged me and guided me with the workbook. Both women were of enormous help! And the inspiration for this book came from the women who have nurtured me through their gift for intimacy as I lived in Wisconsin, Illinois, Indiana, Washington, Oregon, Ohio, North Dakota, and now, in Nebraska. You are part of me, and part of this book.

Permission to use excerpts from *Song for Sarah* by Paula D'Arcy granted by Harold Shaw Publishers, Box 567, Wheaton, Illinois 60189.

Permission to use excerpt from "On Friendship and Homosexuality" by Letha Scanzoni, Sept. 27, 1974 granted by *Christianity Today*.

"Perfect Love Banishes Fear" and "Salutation" from *Polishing the Petoskey Stone*, ©1990 by Luci Shaw. Reprinted with permission of Harold Shaw Publishers, Wheaton, Illinois.

Permission to use excerpt from *Being a Christian Friend* by Kristen Ingram (1985) granted by Judson Press.

Permission to use excerpts from "The Unexpected Gift" by Isabel Anders from *Partnership* (Jan/Feb 1984) granted by Mrs. Anders.

Permission to use excerpts from *Just Friends* by Lillian Rubin (1985) granted by Harper and Row.

Permission to use cartoon from *And Then We Were Women* by Steve Bjorkman.

Cover photo by Matt Orthober of Photos by Matt, Egg Harbor, Wisconsin.

INTRODUCTION

Hundreds of thousands of women have read Dee Brestin's groundbreaking book, *The Friendships of Women*. Letters poured in from the United States and beyond. She understood them, they wrote, and helped them to understand themselves:

> *I read thoughts of my own and feelings of my own that I have never heard anyone put into words.*
> Vicki Presley, Conyers, Georgia

> *Thank you for expressing feelings that I have felt and wasn't sure I should feel, for helping me understand my own need for friendship, and for seeing the dark side as well as the good.*
> Pat Stevenson, Anderson, Indiana

> *I feel like you understand the relationship that I've been trying to explain to myself and others for fourteen years.*
> Julie Hines, Defiance, Ohio

If you have already read *The Friendships of Women*, don't let that stop you from going through it again. Friendship is vital to your life, and it is a wise woman who wants to do it well! What makes this book different from the original book is that you will have an opportunity to journal your way through the entire text aided by probing questions. Charles Swindoll says: "Thoughts untangle themselves as they go from the lips down through the fingertips." Journaling your reflections on the text, as well as on corresponding passages in Scripture will increase your understanding of yourself and your friendships. Journaling is also a powerful tool of the Holy Spirit in life application. You may choose to use this book as a daily devotional.

This workbook is also perfect for small group studies. If you've done this study in a group before, doing it again with individual workbooks will be like walking down a lovely street that you have driven down before. You will see so much more, and have so much more to share.

HOW TO USE THIS WORKBOOK

As a Personal Devotional
I recommend that you divide each chapter into five quiet times. These should be completed in a week, and if you miss a day or two, you can make them up on the weekend. You will find questions in the **Warming Up** section which are geared toward breaking the ice in a small group. You can do these or skip them, as you choose.

Pray before you begin each day and ask the Lord to teach you something for that day. Read the text and corresponding Scripture with an expectant heart. Journal honestly. Underline anything God impresses on your heart. In the back of the book you'll find a list of suggested reading materials for women. Reading some of these books simultaneously in your leisure time will enhance your learning.

As a Small Group Participant

Small groups of women can be immensely powerful in helping one another find strength in God—or, they can degenerate into coffee klatsches. What kind of group will yours be? If you are diligent about filling out your workbook, and sensitive to how the spirit is leading you to share and minister to the other women, you can help make this group one of the most intimate, powerful, and life-changing groups you've ever known.

God can use your gift for intimacy mightily in this group. Listen sensitively to the other women. Be ready to meet needs and show love in and outside the group. Keep confidences. Pray for the other members.

As a Small Group Leader

You may have a designated leader. The value in this is that she may take more responsibility in shepherding the women: writing notes, calling absentees, and following up on those who are hurting. However, a group can do this together and take turns leading this study, as the study is virtually self-facilitating. Simply read the questions with the exception of those marked: **For Personal Reflection Only.**

With the exception of ACTION ASSIGNMENT ON THE SPOT the sections marked ACTION ASSIGNMENT should be done outside the group.

If your group is a Time-concious Group which meets for less than sixty minutes, discuss only those questions marked with a ⌛.

Place chairs in as small a circle as possible. Space inhibits sharing.

Be willing to pave the way for honest sharing by making yourself vulnerable.

Draw quieter members out by going around the group occasionally and asking everyone to share, giving women the freedom to pass. If you have a monopolizer, the following may help her:

Pray. Pray not only that she will see her need to control how much she talks, but for the needs in her own life that cause her to want to talk so much.

Minister to her one-on-one through notes and visits. Often, excessive talking is a plea for attention.

Try to sit next to her instead of across from her. Frequent eye contact encourages her to talk.

Ask to hear from those who haven't shared or have only shared once. Go around the group.

If the problem persists, talk to her, gently, one-on-one. I have said something like: "I'm concerned about our group being lopsided in sharing. You and I are very comfortable sharing—but Lisa, Sharon, and Annie seem hesitant to speak up. Can you think of anything else we could do to help them?"

Your most important responsibility as a discussion leader is to be a vehicle for the Holy Spirit. Don't teach, but encourage the women to share. Keep the discussion on track, and be sensitive to God's leading.

Start and end each meeting on time.

Write notes and call absentees. Let the faithful know they are appreciated. The main reason women drop out of a group is because they don't feel valued.

May the Lord be very near to you as you study and share, and may He make your friendships deep, satisfying, and strengthening in Him!

Chapter 1
From Girlhood On, Gifted for Intimacy

PERSONAL PRAYER

Quiet your heart before God. Before you begin to read and journal, become aware of God's presence!

- Sing a praise song to Him, or praise Him for some of the qualities you value in Him such as His love, His faithfulness, His power, or His mercy.

- Confess and turn from anything that might keep you from hearing Him.

- Ask Him to teach you something and to help you meet with Him every day. (This might be a good time to divide this chapter into five quiet times for the coming week.)

WARMING UP

Remember! If you are a Time-concious group, discuss only those questions marked ⌛ throughout.

1. Spend some time getting acquainted by each sharing:

- Your name
- A little about your life—Do you have a family, a job, a ministry?
- One hope you have for this group

If your group has been meeting together for a while, share:

- One way that women in this group have ministered to you in the past

- One way you think you could help this study to be spiritually life-changing.

GROUP PRAYER

- Before you begin to discuss together, quiet your hearts before God. Whoever is leading the discussion should ask for the Lord's help for herself and for all the women as they share and interact.

When Elliot Engel watched his wife and her best friend say good-bye before a cross-country move, he found that their last hugs were so painful to witness, he finally had to turn away and leave the room. He said: "I've always been amazed at the nurturing emotional support that my wife can seek and return with her close female friends. . . . Her three-hour talks with friends refresh and renew her far more than my 3-mile jogs restore me. In our society it seems as if you've got to have a bosom to be a buddy."[1]

THE CLOCK RADIO clicks on, mercifully playing "When Morning Gilds the Skies" instead of today's market prices for hogs and corn in Nebraska. I shift under our electric blanket, curling my perennially icy feet against my husband's sleep-warm body. I peer out at the illuminated digits: 6:55 A.M. I hear our new puppy whimpering, eager to be lifted from her box, and the timed coffeepot gently perking. Soon we will all be up, showering and dressing for work or school. But for now, I snuggle down, hoping to enjoy a few more moments of the morning's soft darkness.

Reality breaks through with the piercing jangle of the telephone. My hope and covers are abandoned as I rush to still its persistent ring. I have little fear of evil tidings as I anticipate the voice of one of my daughter's fourth-grade friends. I am not disappointed.

"What is Sally wearing today?" Michelle inquires.

"She laid out jeans and her pink sweater," I answer cooperatively.

"Oh." Michelle sounds disappointed. "I was going to wear sweats. Is she bringing her lunch?"

"She's not planning to."

"But hot lunch is baked fish and beets today," Michelle argues plaintively. I ask Michelle to hang on as I discuss these vital issues with my sleepy daughter. It is decided. Sally will bring her lunch and Michelle will wear jeans.

REFLECTION

2. In the opening quotation, Elliot Engel commented on witnessing emotional support between women. What are some specific ways you have witnessed this?

_____

_____

⧗ 3. Dee described an early morning phone call from Sally's friend. What are some specific ways you have witnessed the desire for connection between little girls?

_____

_____

_____

LITTLE GIRLS ARE CLOSER THAN LITTLE BOYS

As the mother of two sons in college and one eleven-year-old daughter,* I can testify that the friendships between little girls differ from the friendships between little boys. I had no inquisitions at dawn when the boys were small.

The boys had friends over frequently, but they seemed more absorbed in their activity than in each other. One friend, whether he liked roaring up and down the driveway on a Big Wheel or playing football, seemed as good as another.

Sally is much more likely to sit face to face on her bed with a friend, whispering and giggling. They are absorbed in each other. When Sally and her friend Gwen were six, they would often hold hands.

Sociologist Janet Lever indicates the differences I have noticed between our sons and daughter are typical. Girls, for example, tend to feel most comfortable with a single best friend; boys prefer to play on teams. Lever reports:

> There is usually an open show of affection between little girls, both physically in the form of hand-holding and verbally through "love-notes" that reaffirm how special each is to the other. Although boys are likely to have best friends as well, their friendships tend to be less intimate and expressive than girls. Hand-holding and love-notes are virtually unknown among boys, and the confidences that boys share are more likely to be "group secrets" than expressions of private thoughts and feelings.[2]

Do you remember? I do.

_____

*Our family has grown since the original edition of _The Friendships of Women!_ We have two additional daughters, adopted from orphanages in Korea and Thailand. Friendship is a vital part of their lives—making me suspect that it isn't just little girls raised in America who are consumed with friendship.

When Donna Rosenow and I were in fifth grade, we took turns walking each other home after school, even though our homes were a mile apart. A standing joke occurred when we reached the door. "Now I'll walk you home!" Then we'd laugh and turn to walk the mile through the tree-lined streets of our small Wisconsin town. When we finally did part, our giggling and chatter resumed right after supper as we monopolized our respective telephones.

Girls are more demanding, empathetic, and confiding in their friendships than boys. They are closer. Zick Rubin, author of *Children's Friendships*, has noted: "Girls not only have a much stronger need for friendship than boys, but demand an intensity in those friendships that boys prefer living without."[3]

REFLECTION

4. Think back to your own childhood. Did you have a strong desire for connection? (Did you pass notes, dress alike?) If so, give examples.

_____

_____

_____

When our daughter was nine, she received the following note in the mail from her friend, Gwen.

TO SALLY
CHEK ONE—YOU HAVE TO
Do you like me????????????????????????
       Yes, and you're my very best freind_____
       Your a good freind_____
       sort of_____

       NO NOT AT ALL!!!!!!!!!!!!!!!!!!
       COME ON NOW TELL THE TRUTH!!!!!!!!!

I showed Gwen's questionnaire to our eighteen-year-old son, John. I was interested in a male reaction. He read it over, brows furrowed, several times. Gwen's thinking was so foreign to him that he had trouble understanding her meaning. When he finally did, he said, "Good grief! Who cares?"

We do. As women we have mellowed, and we have increased in subtlety, yet we still empathize with Gwen's questionnaire. We care about our feelings for each other.

The marketing departments of two card companies, American Greetings and Hallmark, would appreciate Gwen's note. They've been studying women, zealously, for years. Their surveys have given them a preponderance of evidence that women, like little girls, care intensely about their friendships with one another. Armed with this knowledge, these card companies developed extensive lines of friendship cards targeted directly at women. With one of their cards I can tell another woman how much she means to me, I can encourage her when she's down, and I can congratulate her on a job promotion or even a divorce. You won't find a card line like this for men. "Men's friendship cards" would be a financial disaster.

NOTE: At the writing of this *Workbook*, Sally is eighteen. She is still receiving affirming notes from friends, as is typical of our sex! The following note, from her new friend, Shelli Henniger, was written in five different vibrant marker colors, and Sally has it proudly displayed on her bedroom door.

REFLECTION

5. Think back over the last few weeks. Can you think of some specific ways women have given you emotional support in the form of notes, hugs, words, gifts, or prayer? What did they do? How did it minister to you?

_____

_____

_____

6. Think of a few specific ways you have ministered to other women emotionally in the last few weeks. What did you do? What motivated you?

_____

_____

_____

Little girls and big girls are closer. They are also crueler.

LITTLE GIRLS ARE CRUELER THAN LITTLE BOYS

Little girls, studies show, have a tendency to go straight for the jugular. Judith Bardwick tells us, in *Psychology of Women*, "Girls do not kick and bite" (though I do remember a few hair-pulling, nail-scratching sessions with my very dearest summer playmate, Barbara), "but the verbal slings and arrows they hurl at one another and their merciless vendettas are often far more piercing."[4]

"Patti and I were very popular in fifth grade, and we enjoyed the power of popularity," reminisced a twenty-year-old woman. "Lynette wanted desperately to be a part of our circle. She would write notes to us asking if she could play with us at recess. Patti and I would exchange glances and then give Lynette either the thumbs up or the thumbs down signal."

After his first years as an elementary school teacher, a young male told me how shocked he was by his inside look at the world of sugar and spice:

> *I have problems on the playground with boys and girls—but they're so very different in character. The problems with the boys are competitive ones, involving a disagreement over rules or fair play. I step in, referee, and basically, it's over. The disagreements between the girls, however, become intensely personal. Two girls who have been arm-in-arm the day before amaze me by suddenly turning on each other and screeching cruel and revealing insults in the earshot of all. The wounds may not heal for months. Girls completely drain me. Give me the problems with boys any day!*

Girls have a tendency, more than boys, to draw a close, intimate circle and leave others out, hurting them deeply. Do we change when we become women? Do we stop throwing darts?

I'll be showing you the dark side of our gift for intimacy in chapter three, as reflected in the world of college sororities and even, sometimes, in the world of women's Bible studies. We've become more discreet than we were as children: we choose gossip and betrayal over screeching on the playground. When one successful career woman heard I was writing a book on friendship and women, she said, with deep cynicism, "Those two words don't go together." Perhaps Solomon was thinking of this dark side of our nature when he said: "I found one upright man among a thousand, but not one upright woman among them all" (Ecc. 7:28). Some women have been so wounded by other women that they no longer pursue friendship with their own sex.

Other women have withdrawn because they no longer want to endure the pain of parting—and parting is increasingly common in our times. Becky expressed it like this: "Every time I get close to a woman she either moves away or gets a job. I feel betrayed."

Using our gift for intimacy may bring pain to our lives. But stifling it is not the solution. Kathleen tried that when she moved from Virginia to Ohio. She told herself, *This is it. I'm not making any friends because it's too painful when we leave.* "And that year," she commented later, "was the worst year of my life."

The scriptural models in this book will give you insight in controlling and tolerating the pain our gift brings. When God gives us a gift, He expects us to use it. And we have a gift. It isn't just evident in little girls; it is evident in women.

FOR PERSONAL REFLECTION ONLY

■ In what ways have you experienced intense pain in your friendships of the past?

_____

_____

_____

_____

■ Pain is inevitable in relationships because we all have sinful natures. Instead of dwelling on the failure of your friend, ask yourself: Did I respond in a way that was pleasing to God? How could I learn from this situation so that I will be more like Jesus?

_____

_____

_____

_____

WOMEN AND MEN

We expect our women friends to share from the heart, to nurture us with expressed affection, to cherish us. We are disappointed, in fact, when a close woman friend fails to meet this high standard. We aren't surprised at all, however, to discover men who are unable to be this intimate with each other. (There will, of course, be exceptions. There are rare men who are blessed with a gift for intimacy, and a small number of women who are extremely uncomfortable with intimacy.)

Studies indicate that men, like boys, do things together—rotary, softball, hunting—but they do not often relate to each other as confidants.[5] Men tend to be side-by-side, engrossed in an activity, whereas women will be face-to-face. Men may confuse quantity of time spent in the company of other men with intimacy. Ken, a man from Rancho Santa Fe, played golf with the same small group of men for fifteen years. When he gave up golf, he was dismayed to find he seldom saw his companions anymore. "I guess all that we had in common was golf." Reflectively, he added, "Our conversations, as I believe is typical of men, were at the head level, not the heart level."

Most men not only find it difficult to make themselves vulnerable to each other, but they are also often uncomfortable being together unless their attention can be centered on an activity. One pastor told me that in order to have a successful function for men, there must be an activity. Fellowship alone makes them uncomfortable.

Richard Cohen, a columnist for *The Washington Post*, wrote the following sad reflections:

> *My friends have no friends. They are men. They think they have friends, and if you ask them whether they have friends they will say yes, but they don't really. They think, for instance, that I'm their friend, but I'm not. It's OK. They're not my friends either.*
>
> *The reason for that is that we are all men—and men, I have come to believe, cannot or will not have real friends. They have something else—companions, buddies, pals, chums, someone to drink with and someone to wench with and someone to lunch with, but no one when it comes to saying how they feel— especially how they hurt. . . . Women will tell you all the time they don't know the men they live with. They talk of long silences and drifting off and of keeping feelings hidden and never letting on that they are troubled or bothered or whatever.*
>
> *If it's any comfort to women, they should know it's nothing personal. Men treat other men the same way.[6]*

Most men do not have a close male friend. When *friend* was defined as "someone you feel close to, see often, can count on when you need him," four out of five men declared themselves to be friendless. Women are three times more likely than men to have a close confidant.[7] If a man does name a close confidant, he usually names a woman.[8] A young woman commented: "My husband tells me I'm the only friend he needs. I'm flattered, but I can't honestly say the same to him. I need the comfort my women friends give me."

Ladd Wheeler, professor of psychology at the University of Rochester, found that women and men are both less lonely when they spend time with women. The data showed that whenever a woman was involved in interaction, both individuals disclosed more about themselves, and the interaction became distinctly more intimate.[9] When I talk to my closest female friends, I feel my soul being sunned and watered when they ask questions, drawing out the deep waters of my soul, and when they empathize, rejoicing when I rejoice, weeping when I weep.

REFLECTION

For In-depth Groups Only

7. As Dee has explained, most wives who are happily married still need women friends. Studies show that marriages are generally strengthened when a wife has friendships with other women. If you are married, have you found this to be true? If so, why?

_____

_____

_____

8. When might a friendship weaken rather than strengthen a marriage? What would be some warning signs that a friend is detrimental to the sanctity of your marriage?

_____

_____

_____

_____

_____

I can't count the number of times my heart has been gladdened by women: a note expressing her love, a heartfelt hug, an encouraging word, a surprise gift of blueberry muffins, or a green and thriving plant, growing as our friendship grows.

God expects us to use the gifts He has given us! And most women have a gift for intimacy.

Some women have decided that the cost of unwrapping their gift and using it to bless others is too high. They point to the pain they've experienced when a best friend has moved away; or to the fear of being rejected when reaching out; or to the devastation of betrayal.

Other women have exercised their gift faithfully and, along with some pain, have experienced the multiplication of their gift.

SCRIPTURAL REFLECTION

⧗ 9. Read Matthew 25:14-30.

⧗ A. Describe what each of the first two servants did with their "talents" and how the master responded.

Servant 1 _____

_____

_____

Servant 2 _____

_____

_____

⧗ B. What was different about the third servant? What reasons did he give for burying his talent? How did the master respond?

_____

_____

_____

_____

C. What do you know about God that should encourage you to step out in faith and use your gifts diligently?

_____

_____

_____

D. When it comes to intimacy, to nurturing others, how gifted are you on a scale of 1 to 10? (1 = cold fish, 10 = Golden Retriever) Explain your response.

_____

_____

_____

_____

E. What are some reasons that you might have missed opportunities to use your gifts in the past?

_____

_____

_____

_____

F. What are some ways you might use your gift for intimacy that would yield eternal dividends? That could cause it to multiply?

_____

_____

_____

_____

⧖ G. Reflect on what faithful and lazy uses of your gift for intimacy would be. Give some examples.

NOTE: The adjective *faithful* is from a Greek word meaning "trustworthy, can be relied upon." This is in sharp contrast to the adjectives *slothful*, or *lazy*.

FAITHFUL   LAZY

ACTION ASSIGNMENT

⧖ ■ Choose one of the faithful uses and do it before next week. Be ready to share what you did! Right now share your plan with the group.

Because of my husband's medical training and years with the Public Health Service, we have moved eight times, to seven different states. Each time, I am amazed at how quickly my husband adjusts to our new environment. I, on the other hand, am like a full-grown transplanted tree: my roots dangle and branches droop severely, and my family wonders whether I will, indeed, make it. Separating me from the women friends who have nourished me and strengthened me to grow straight and green is a severe trauma. I feel as if I am starving, and I pray God will connect me with new women friends before I wither and die.

REFLECTION

For In-depth Groups Only

10. Have you ever moved? If so, what were some of your feelings?

_____

_____

_____

_____

11. If you experienced pain in moving, what does that teach you about yourself? About women who are new in your community?

_____

_____

_____

_____

_____

I have experienced some beautiful friendships with women, and yet, when I hold them up to the friendships of Scripture, I am humbled.

GOD'S FRIENDSHIP PATTERN

A hole in a cloth seems small until held up to the sun. As rays come streaming through, you realize how great is the hole. In the same way, the inadequacies of the best of our friendships, as women, may seem small—especially when compared to the friendships of men. Yet if we dare to hold our friendships up to the light of the scriptural models of friendship, we realize how far we have to go. I want you to dare.

Insights for unwrapping our gift will be drawn from portraits from three generations:

- Ruth and Naomi
- David and Jonathan
- Mary and Elizabeth

I've included David and Jonathan in a book on the friendships of women for two reasons. First, many have said that Jonathan behaved more like a woman in the way he related to David. That is a high compliment, because Jonathan is one of the most beautiful persons in history! But more importantly, I needed to include David and Jonathan to show you a pattern in God's Word. By juxtaposing these three generations, you will discover truths you may not have seen before. A design unfolds. If you've ever hung wallpaper or worked a weaving loom, you know the delight of seeing a pattern begin to develop. And when the pattern that is emerging is not on your weaving loom, but in the Word of God, you realize that, through repetition, God is endeavoring to impress a friendship principle on our hearts. *God's friendship pattern can unleash and channel a woman's propensity for intimacy and help her to be the redemptive power He planned for her to be.*

Though I've considered myself a good friend, since I've been applying my discoveries from Ruth, Jonathan, and Elizabeth, my friendships have deepened to a richness I had not realized was possible. I've also gained insight into weaknesses I have, as a woman, from the study of Naomi. Insight can be a powerful tool to pull the weeds that are destroying our gift. This book will also deal with weeds of jealousy, betrayal, and lesbianism. (I realize some have picked up this book because they are in the bondage of homosexuality. If you are one of these women, I am confident the story of Rachel will give you hope and insight.)

This, and more. To give you a preview of what is to come, I'm going to give you a glimpse of God's pattern by looking at just one of the threads that weaves its way through the tapestry of these scriptural models of friendship. In each of these three models, our Lord has zoomed His camera in on the meeting and parting of friends. Since these scenes undergird much of this book and were considered worthy to be recorded in Scripture, let us reflect for a moment on their value.

PARTING SCENES AND GREETING SCENES

When I am a detached observer of parting scenes and greeting scenes in airports, I experience a quiet joy. Lovers lingering in bittersweet embraces. Grandparents ecstatic over the first sight of a newborn grandchild. Sisters hugging in reunion with unabashed tears. As I watch, from the safety of my waiting room chair, my heart is warmed.

It is much more exhausting to be an active participant. For it's in these most poignant of moments that latent emotion in a friendship boils to the surface. If we truly have bonded with a friend, then it is a tearing apart. It hurts. But it can also be amazingly sweet. As Romeo said to Juliet, "Parting is such sweet sorrow."[10] There is a bittersweet satisfaction in realizing that it wouldn't hurt so much if we didn't care so much.

I was surprised by the depth of my pain when I put our firstborn on the airplane for college. I was weeping that day with abandon when my dad phoned from California. He was calling to wish me a happy birthday (which it wasn't) and was concerned when he recognized that his daughter had been crying. But once he understood the reason for my sorrow, he laughed! Wisely, he said, "Well, Honey, isn't it wonderful you feel that way? Wouldn't it be sad if you didn't care?"

Each time my husband and I have moved to a new state, there have been tearful parting scenes between my sisters in Christ and myself. And though we, as women, pride ourselves on being able to express our love, there were several times when I truly didn't realize how much my friends cared until the parting.

When we were loading the moving van in Akron, Steve called up the stairs, "Dee, you have a visitor!" I was surprised to find Phyllis, a woman from my Bible study, perched quietly on a big box in the living room. Phyllis had never been to see me before. My surprise grew as she silently held out a beautiful afghan. For months she had been spending evenings crocheting this expression of love. Phyllis, indisputedly the most reserved member of all the women in the study, loved me! Spontaneously, I hugged her. At first her arms hung limply at her sides, but then she returned my embrace. Unwiped tears ran down our cheeks.

Likewise, when we moved from Indianapolis, I called Barb to say good-bye. I admired and loved Barb, but I did not feel assured that I was unique to her, as she is the kind of person who is incredibly warm and caring toward everyone. Because I was unsure of the depth of her feelings, I decided it would be less dramatic to phone than to stop by. To be honest, I didn't want to risk showing that I cared more than she did. But when I called to say good-bye, Barb began stammering expressions of love. "You don't know how much you mean to me," she sobbed. (How right she was—I didn't know!) Despite the pain, I was grateful for the expressions of love that would remain in my memory.

Two of the most poignant passages in all of Scripture are the parting scenes between Ruth and Naomi and David and Jonathan. Since these models have helped me to realize the value of partings, as I hope they will for you, my attitude toward these painful moments has changed. I will not shrink from taking a loved one to the airport. If God permits me the knowledge, I will sit at the bedside of a dying parent or friend. Though the sorrow may be deep, I will not consider it wasted sadness. My presence may give the one I love comfort. Closing expressions of love may give consolation for years to come. The more final the good-bye, the greater the bleeding, but the more cherished the memory.

Even small partings can bring small comforts. I treasure those golden moments as a mother when I tucked a cuddly toddler under her favorite blanket with one last bear hug. Her sweet smile, her arm-spread, "I love you this much!" linger in my memory as her childhood fades away. And I have learned the most meaningful moments of a friend's visit may occur when I take the trouble to walk her to her car. The very act of showing that I care enough to prolong the visit often releases from her a confidence or expression of love that we both treasure. If I'm not willing to create these parting scenes, then they slip between the cracks of time, never to be called to remembrance when remembrance is sorely needed.

PARTING SCENES:
Ruth and Naomi (Ruth 1:9-10); David and Jonathan (1 Sam. 20:41-42)

SCRIPTURAL
REFLECTION

⌛ 12. Read the two parting scenes listed on the above ribbon.

⌛ A. What similarities do you see in these two parting scenes?

_____

_____

_____

⌛ B. Men who are mature spiritually seem to become more comfortable with intimacy. How do you see this in the parting scene between David and Jonathan? In spiritually mature men you know?

_____

_____

⌛ C. Shakespeare said, "Parting is such sweet sorrow." Have you experienced this? If so, explain what Shakespeare means.

_____

_____

_____

⌛ D. How did Jonathan help David find the strength to leave him?

_____

_____

_____

⧗ E. Can you remember a cherished parting scene from your life? Why do you think you remember it?

_____

_____

_____

⧗ F. Despite the pain that parting brings, why is it important to go to the airport, to sit at the bedside of a dying parent, etc.?

_____

_____

_____

⧗ G. Reflect on the value of small partings—walking a friend to a car, sending a child off to school, closing a letter. Give some specific suggestions on how to make these more meaningful.

_____

_____

_____

Greeting scenes can contain the thrill of recognition that God may be involved in bringing you together. Mary recognized that God was giving her an understanding friend in Elizabeth, so she hurried to go see Elizabeth. Likewise, it's fascinating to see how quickly Jonathan bonded to David in their greeting scene. God knew what trials the future held for these men, and so He caused their hearts to be knit together almost instantly.

Being alert to the possibility that God may bring a person across our path will change our attitude toward first meetings. We may capture beautiful friendships that in time past would have slipped away. Growing in appreciation for greeting scenes may also help us to remember those first precious moments. Christina Rossetti wrote, "I wish I could remember that first day/First hour, first moment of your meeting me."

I met Luci Shaw twenty-three years ago when she, as an editor, believed in my ideas and my writing and gave me a chance. Through the years, as I've continued to write Bible study guides for her publishing house, Luci and I have become friends. I have the highest regard for

Luci, not just because she is so gifted as a poet and a writer, but because she is willing to be a real friend and a mentor to those who are just beginning in the publishing world. I interviewed Luci when I stayed at her home, asking her probing questions about her close friendships with authors such as Madeleine L'Engle, Karen Mains, and others. Characteristically, Luci shared openly with me, and I have many of her stories in this book. I was intrigued, for example, by Luci's deep friendship with a woman young enough to be her daughter, fellow poet Margaret D. Smith. This is how Luci described her "greeting scene" with Margaret:

> *The minute we met, we bonded. It was incredible—I've never had such an experience. . . . Somehow she freed me verbally so that I could say things I never even knew I knew. She was a catalyst for me—and I for her. We can talk in a kind of verbal shorthand. We don't have to explain or fill in the gaps.*

GREETING SCENES:
David and Jonathan (1 Sam. 18:1-4); Mary and Elizabeth (Luke 1:39-45)

SCRIPTURAL REFLECTION

13. Read the greeting scene between David and Jonathan, including the preceding context (1 Sam. 17:57–18:4).

   A. Why do you think Jonathan was so drawn to David?

   _____

   _____

   _____

   B. How do you think Jonathan's greeting to David encouraged him?

   _____

   _____

C. If you know the story of David and Jonathan, what reasons can you see for God giving Jonathan to David as a soulmate? (The story can be found in 1 Samuel 18–20; and 23:15-18.)

_____

_____

_____

⌛ 14. Read the greeting scene between Mary and Elizabeth.

⌛ A. Find at least three ways that Elizabeth encouraged Mary with her greeting. How could you do likewise with sisters in Christ?

_____

_____

_____

_____

⌛ B. What are some of the difficulties that lay ahead for Mary? Why might God have given Elizabeth to her as a friend?

_____

_____

_____

_____

⌛ C. Think back to the first time you met a friend who is now very special in your life. Were you aware, in that first meeting, that God might be bringing you together? Does anything else stand out in your memory? If so, why?

_____

_____

_____

_____

⧗ D. If your group is an established group, think back to some of the
positive first impressions you had of members who are still
with you. What were they?

_____

_____

_____

_____

WINDING DOWN

■ As Elizabeth affirmed Mary, close by affirming one another. Have
each person affirm the woman on her right with a sentence. Here
are some examples:

*I'm thankful you came today, Mary. Your warm smile made
me feel welcome.*
*I appreciated what you shared about how we can multiply our
gift for intimacy by mentoring younger women, Ellen. I'm going
to invite a younger woman over for lunch!*

GROUP PRAYER

⧗ ■ Write down an area of concern in your life for which you would
like your sisters in Christ to pray. Make it personal! Requesting
prayer for your Aunt Grace's arthritis is a way of keeping the
others at arm's length. Don't do it unless it's sincerely the deepest
concern of your heart.

_____

_____

_____

_____

Close in prayer. Option 1 is for In-depth Groups; Option 2 is for
Time-conscious Groups.

■ **Option 1: Popcorn Prayer**
Read your prayer request. Then the group will offer short
sentences of prayer for your request. Then the next woman will
read her prayer request, and so on. The following diagram
describes popcorn prayer. It's called popcorn prayer because the
sentences are short "pops"; you aren't sure where they will come
from, and when the popping stops, the next prayer request is read.

POPCORN PRAYER

1. Introduce one person or subject at a time.
2. Prayers should be short "pops" from anyone anywhere in the circle.
3. Continue until "popping" stops.
4. Introduce another person or subject.

⧖ ■ **Option 2: Praying in Twos**

Pair off and read your requests to each other. Pray for each other and then continue praying for each other at home.

The friendship of Luci and Margaret, about which this workbook will share more, models the beauty of intergenerational friendships. Ruth and Naomi and again, Mary and Elizabeth, found a unique strength in becoming good friends with women from another generation. Most women, however, concentrate on peer friendships. It's time we seriously considered intergenerational friendships, for they form another thread in God's friendship pattern.

In addition to looking at scriptural models of friendship and the lives of some well-known Christian women, I've interviewed my friends (and their friends) incessantly. I've asked them the most personal of questions about their friendships, and they've responded beautifully, evidencing their gift for intimacy.

We live in a world that is encouraging women to become more like men. Unless we grow in our appreciation for our gift for intimacy, we may lose it.

It's important, therefore, that we begin by reflecting on the many ways that women are, indeed, friendlier than men.

NEXT WEEK'S ASSIGNMENT

■ When you get home, while your group experience is still fresh, complete the journaling assignment at the end of this chapter.

■ Spend five minutes in silence before God, asking Him if there's a woman or women He'd have you invite to the next meeting. Write down any names He impresses on your heart:

_____

_____

_____

_____

_____

Now call right away and warmly invite her or them—before you lose courage! Solomon warns, in Ecclesiastes 11:4—

Whoever watches the wind will not plant
Whoever looks at the clouds will not reap.

■ Work through the next chapter and the exercises.

PERSONAL JOURNAL

■ If you are doing this study in a small group, when you get home, write down some of your first impressions of new friends, first feelings, first hopes at what God is going to do through this group.

_____

_____

■ What stood out to you in the group discussion? What do you want to remember?

_____

_____

■ How is God leading you to apply what you learned?

_____

_____

Chapter 2
Women Are Friendlier

Quiet your heart before God. Before you begin to read and journal, become aware of God's presence! One way to do this is with the anacronym of ACTS:

- **Adoration:** Read a Psalm or a hymn in praise to God.
- **Confession:** Confess and turn from any known sin.
- **Thanksgiving:** Thank Him for specific blessings.
- **Supplication:** Ask Him for the desires of your heart that you feel are within His will. One would be for you to learn what He longs to teach you in your quiet times. (This might be a good time to divide this chapter into five quiet times for the coming week.)

GROUP PRAYER

- Before you begin to discuss together, quiet your hearts before God. In twos, each say a sentence prayer for the other, keeping it short and simple. If praying out loud is new to you, it can be as simple as: "Thank you, God, for Jean." Then, still in twos, each ask God to be with you in the study. It can be as simple as: "Teach us, God, today."

WARMING UP

Remember! If you are a Time-concious group, discuss only those questions marked ⧗ throughout.

1.⟨ Read Proverbs 20:5—"The purposes of a man's heart are deep waters, but a man of understanding draws them out." Pair off in twos and draw out and record the deep waters of each other's soul by asking as many of the following questions as possible in three minutes. After three minutes, switch roles.

⧗ A. What is something you've been thinking a lot about lately—and why?

_____

_____

⧗ B. Has God been teaching you anything in particular lately? If so, what?

_____

_____

⧗ C. What has been giving you joy lately? Frustration?

_____

_____

⧗ D. Did you do the action assignment of using your gift of intimacy? What did you do?

_____

_____

⧗ 2. Sometimes others can help us discover our own thoughts. Share *one* thing you learned about yourself from the interview.

Both heredity and culture play a part in helping women to be the relational sex. For example, is it heredity or culture that causes women to smile more than men? Heredity seems to be involved, for girl infants smile more than boy infants. Yet culture has an impact as well, for our mass media elevates stern, macho men and warm, smiling women.

REFLECTION

3. What are some other evidences that you can think of that contribute either hereditarily or culturally to the feminine gift for intimacy?

_____

_____

_____

We have found that friendships between women are deeper, more enduring, and more plentiful than those between men.[1]

THE JULY SUN was finally sinking, promising relief from the heat. My husband, our daughter, and I sat motionless on the back porch, listening to the steady hum of cicadas, watching the affectionate antics of our six-month-old springer spaniel puppy. Unaffected by the heat, Effie enthusiastically chased a ball Sally was tossing and carried it back proudly, tail wagging, eyes hopeful for a kind word or loving pat. Reminiscing, I said, "When I was a little girl, I thought dogs were girls and cats were boys, because dogs were so much friendlier."

To the great delight of her dad, Sally responded, "Mom, I'm sure you would say something like that with a guy right here!" We laughed at our daughter's protective reaction, especially because, unknowingly, Sally was proving my point. Studies show that females have greater sensitivity to the feelings of others. This is one of many ways that females tend to be friendlier than males. Women are much freer than men to be intimate with their own sex: women will confide in each other, hug each other, and express their love for each other.

Lillian Rubin interviewed men about their friendships. She asked them why they couldn't put their arms around a man who was crying. One interviewee responded, "Aw, c'mon. I know you're kidding with that one." She assured him she was serious. He squirmed uncomfortably in his seat and said:

> *Men just don't do that, that's all; it's too uncomfortable. . . . I think there must always be some kind of fear about getting close to a man. We used to hug each other when we got together, but even that . . . How can I say it? It was tight and self-conscious. You don't let your body go into the hug and the other guy doesn't either.*[2]

WOMEN ARE LESS FEARFUL THAT THEIR FRIENDSHIPS WILL BE MISUNDERSTOOD

In an article in *Christianity Today*, one author commented:

> *Some Christians consider any close friendship between members of the same sex to be suspect. And there are Christians who are afraid to enter relationships of deep caring and sharing, who carefully avoid words or gestures of affection, and who therefore bind themselves to an emotional poverty.*[3]

Though this problem exists for both men and women, it's much more prevalent with men. When Stuart Miller conducted interviews for his book, *Men and Friendship*, he found he continually had to explain to his male interviewees that his subject was not homosexuality.[4]

Likewise, C.S. Lewis commented that it has "become necessary in our time to rebut the theory that every firm and serious friendship is really homosexual." Men who wish to be close must certainly find this, as Lewis puts it, "a tiresome bit of demolition."[5]

There are strong similarities between the friendships of Ruth with Naomi and David with Jonathan, yet David and Jonathan are more likely to be viewed with suspicion. It is considered natural for Ruth to cling to Naomi, to weep, and to express her commitment of unfailing love in their parting scene, but men especially are intensely uncomfortable when David and Jonathan do the same things in their parting scene. Even Kenneth Taylor, whose Bible paraphrase, *The Living Bible*, is usually candid, dodged when he came to this scene. Taylor changed what the *New International Version* translated:

> *David . . . bowed down before Jonathan three times, with his face to the ground. Then they kissed each other and wept together— but David wept the most* (1 Sam. 20:41, NIV).

to the paraphrase:

> *They sadly shook hands, tears running down their cheeks, until David could weep no more* (1 Sam. 20:41, TLB).

Why are men more troubled by this? One convincing theory (embraced by Harvard's Carol Gilligan and psychotherapist Lillian Rubin) states that since the mother is almost always the primary caregiver in childhood, girls have experienced a deep same-sex friendship in their formative years, whereas boys have not. It feels very natural for us to be close to another woman, but it doesn't feel natural to a man to be close to a man.

If this theory is true, there may be hope that men's friendships will improve as it is becoming more acceptable for fathers to have an active role in parenting. It's heartwarming to hear a testimony like the following from a man in his second marriage.

> *I never read* The Cat in the Hat *the first time around. I never diapered or bathed the babies. I just came home after my wife had them all fed and in their pajamas, and kissed them goodnight. It wasn't macho to really mother them. Now the rules have changed. Real men take care of their kids. I like that.*[6]

Perhaps one day little boys will also grow up to believe that real men can be close to each other.

REFLECTION

■ A close relationship with his father helps a son to have meaningful same-sex friendships as an adult. In *Beside Every Great Dad*, (Nancy

Swihart and Ken Canfield, Tyndale, Wheaton, 1993) the authors explain that, up until the industrial revolution, men were involved in fathering, but then many abdicated their God-given role to their wives. These authors say that many Christian fathers today are returning to their role, often crediting the gentle influence of their wives in helping them to have the confidence to step into those shoes again.

⧗ 4. What are some ways a woman could be an encouragement to her husband in becoming an involved, nurturing father? What are some ways she might unintentionally discourage his involvement?

_____

_____

_____

_____

I'm so thankful that we as women are comfortable with same-sex intimacy. I've never felt the need to reassure a close friend that I'm not a lesbian, nor am I hesitant to put my arms around her when she needs comforting, or to write her an affirming note. I would feel "impoverished" if women were reluctant in expressing intimacy toward me.

REFLECTION

5. Since the original release of *The Friendships of Women*, women from other cultures have written, confirming that American men are particularly troubled by intimacy. Addy Mull, an American living in Africa, wrote:

> *Where I live, the men walk hand in hand. When they greet each other, they kiss. And after a soccer game, they will often agree that both teams won because they feel that competition hinders intimacy.*

A. What are some of the differences you have noticed in this culture between the women and men and their freedom to make themselves vulnerable and to express affection?

_____

_____

_____

B. What evidence do you see from the life of Christ that He was free to make Himself vulnerable and to express affection?

C. Would you feel "impoverished" if you did not feel free to make yourself vulnerable or show affection? Explain.

WOMEN KNOW HOW TO VOLLEY IN CONVERSATION

One woman said, "How come there's no give-and-take in a conversation with a man? Sometimes it's like trying to play tennis with no one in the other court."[7]

Samantha, a bright twelve-year-old who has recently moved across the country from Salt Lake City, amused me when she said,

> *In Maryland, the girls don't like to go outside. Since I like outdoor sports, I have to play with boys. But if I want to have a conversation that's not totally one-sided, I talk to girls—because girls know how to listen and respond. That's an important quality—and boys don't have it.*

There are males who do know how to volley, how to ask questions, and how to respond to feelings. Jonathan was one. My husband is another. But the comment I made to my college roommates about this new man in my life was, "This is the first time I've been able to communicate with a guy the way I can communicate with my girl-friends."

I've been trying to teach our eighteen-year-old son, John, how to draw people out in conversation. John is charming, good-looking, and athletic—and the teenage girls flock around him. But I tease him, noting that it is the girls who do most of the listening. I know this is not unusual in relationships between men and women. Most women will tell you that in their friendships with men, they listen, they draw out with questions, they affirm, and encourage.[8]

I want John to break free of this male mode, to be able, like Christ, to draw others out with questions. I've quoted him the verse: "The purposes of a man's heart are deep waters, but a man of understanding draws them out" (Prov. 20:5). So I engage our son in a game, to which he agrees reluctantly.

"John," I begin, "pretend I'm the new girl at school. Ask me questions that call for more than a one-word answer."

John eyes me with suspicion, but he good-naturedly cooperates. "Hi, good-lookin'!" He puts his arm around me and winks. "What's your name?"

I stiffen. "Alice Smith."

"Where do you live, Alice?"

"902 Elm Street," I reply.

Giving me an exasperated look that implies I'm the problem, John makes one final attempt. "What's your favorite subject?"

"Math."

"Mom! You're just giving me a hard time!"

"Don't give up!" I plead. "With this last question, you're getting somewhere. Now pursue your thought. Ask Alice why she likes math, what it is about math that intrigues her!"

Now John is smiling. "I'm not really sure I care why Alice likes math."

"Aha!" I say, judgmentally.

Although John has labeled my conclusion chauvinistic, I believe the evidence is mounting that women, from infancy on, are better equipped to care about others.

REFLECTION

■ Linguist Deborah Tannen, in *You Just Don't Understand: Men and Women in Conversation* (New York, William Morrow and Company, Inc., 1990), says that men engage in "Report Talk," holding the floor and taking turns monologuing—whereas women engage in "Rapport Talk," drawing one another out. I have found this to be essentially true, although right-brained men are comfortable with verbal intimacy—and likewise, men who are spiritually mature reflect Jesus, who was comfortable with making himself vulnerable and expressing emotion. (Our son John, who is now twenty-six and has made enormous strides in spiritual maturity, is also making enormous strides in drawing others out!) But often, in the early years of marriage, a woman will put unreasonable demands on her husband, expecting him to communicate with her as her women friends do.

6. If a man fails to draw you out in conversation, does it mean he doesn't care? Explain.

_____

_____

7. If a man whom you care about seldom draws you out in conversation, what might you do to enhance the quality of your communication with him?

_____

_____

One woman wrote and said: "My father seldom asks me about my life with probing questions, so I have simply been taking the initiative in telling him what I've been doing, or how God is working in my life. Though he doesn't ask me questions or affirm me, I know he listens because sometimes I hear him telling someone else what I said."

WOMEN'S BRAINS FUNCTION DIFFERENTLY

Doctors are discovering differences between the brain functions of men and women. We may, it seems, think differently than men. (My mother would say, "I could have told them that!")

Our brains have a left and right side, like a walnut. It is almost as if we have two minds, as each hemisphere can operate independently of the other. Each side has its own distinctive strengths. Simplistically put, the left hemisphere is logical and interested in detail; the right hemisphere is creative and interested in the unbounded aspects of the world such as people and emotions. Both men and women tend to be left-brain dominant, but there is increasing scientific evidence that women seem to be less handicapped in the use of the right brain.[9] This is because women seem to think through both hemispheres, whereas men's brains are more lateralized; that is, they think strongly through the left or right side (usually the left).[10]

One theory explaining this difference is related to the communicating link (the *corpus callosum*). Dr. Donald Joy, in an interview with Dr. James Dobson, explained that it seems a male's communicating link is damaged prenatally through a chemical androgen wash. "Males simply cannot talk to themselves back and forth between the hemispheres the way that a woman can."[11] Doctors have also found that when males and females suffer similar injuries to one hemisphere of the brain because of stroke or accident, the males will have a greater loss of function.[12] Because a woman tends to use both hemispheres, one hemisphere can compensate for the other hemisphere's loss.

I am certainly not trying to disparage the male brain! There are some definite advantages when one hemisphere does not hamper the other hemisphere. This may explain the superior mathematical skills of men, as a group, over women, as a group. The right hemisphere is not distracting the logical left hemisphere.

The goal-oriented left hemisphere sets out to solve problems. This can cause frustration between the sexes. Marriage counselor Gary Smalley tells of shopping with his wife. She said she wanted to buy a blouse. So Gary's left brain zeroed in on the problem. ("I wanted to conquer the blouse!") But while they were shopping, his wife didn't really seem that interested in the problem. She was looking at other things and even suggested they sit down and have coffee together! She kept interrupting "the hunt!"[13]

For the small percentage of men who are right-brained (sometimes, but not necessarily, those men who are left-handed; often those who are intensely interested in music, arts, or humanities[14]), they are *very* right-brained: sensitive, in touch with feelings and with people. Later I'll make a case for David and Jonathan being right-brained and therefore equipped to teach even women a few things about friendship.

But most men are handicapped in the use of the right hemisphere and correspondingly, in the perception of emotions and of people, two strengths of the right hemisphere.[15]

One pastor introduced me before I spoke as the woman who said he used half his brain! Let me make it clear that I believe that both men and women are fearfully and wonderfully made! There are strengths in thinking globally, as most women do, and strengths in thinking laterally, as most men do. One strength that left-brained men seem to have is the desire to solve problems. One strength that right-brained men seem to have is to be particularly good marksmen. In Judges 20:16 we are told,

> *Among all these soldiers there were seven hundred chosen men who were left-handed, each of whom could sling a stone at a hair and not miss.*

Far be it for me to disagree with the Creator of the Universe in how He designed us! Scripture makes it clear that both sexes are made in the image of God, and yet they are different: male and female (Gen. 1:27).

REFLECTION

8. If you are married, what ways do you see you and your husband complementing each other?

_____

_____

_____

WOMEN ARE LESS HANDICAPPED IN THE PERCEPTION OF EMOTIONS

The right side of the brain perceives emotions. Therefore, women, who use both hemispheres, are better at getting in touch with feelings. *Parents* magazine cited a study showing that "in the cradle, girl infants are more likely than boy babies to cry (as if in sympathy) when they hear other babies cry."[16] Karen made this comment: "My husband Sid is great, but when we move to a new town, I *crave* a woman friend because a woman can get in touch with my feelings." A man is apt to give you a one-two-three solution to a problem, whereas a woman will empathize.

There is also evidence that the right side of the brain helps in the expression of emotion. Neurologist Elliot Ross of the University of Texas discovered that damage to a particular region of the right hemisphere impairs our ability to express or interpret what we feel, producing what he has labeled *aprodosia*.[17] We've always assumed that the reason men don't cry was cultural, but there may, in fact, be underlying biological factors.

WOMEN ARE LESS HANDICAPPED IN THE PERCEPTION OF PERSONS

Another strength of the right hemisphere is the perception of persons. The Swiss physician Paul Tournier calls this "a sense of the person." Perhaps this is what gave Mary of Bethany the sensitivity to come to Jesus with a jar of expensive perfume and anoint His head, in sympathetic preparation for His burial. The men were shocked at the "waste," but Mary valued the person, and Jesus said, "I tell you the truth, wherever this Gospel is preached throughout the world, what she has done will also be told, in memory of her" (Matt. 26:13).

SCRIPTURAL
REFLECTION

9. Read Matthew 26:6-13.

A. How did the disciples react to Mary's act of anointing Jesus with expensive perfume?

_____

_____

B. How did Jesus respond? Why did He say she did this?

_____

_____

NOTE: In addition to demonstrating Paul Tournier's "woman's sense of the person," Mary also demonstrates spiritual intuition. C.I. Scofield notes: "Mary of Bethany, alone of our Lord's followers, comprehended His thrice-repeated announcement of His coming death and resurrection" (*The Scofield Study Bible: NIV Version*, Oxford Press, New York, 1984, p. 1013)

⌛ C. Mary demonstrated that she was person- rather than material- or task-oriented. List some ways we could follow her example.

_____

_____

_____

ACTION ASSIGNMENT

■ As Mary thought about the needs of Jesus, think about the needs of some of the people in your life. What could you do to minister to one of them? Write down your plan and prepare to be held accountable:

_____

_____

_____

Paul Tournier asks, "Who is it who remembers people's birthdays? Women more than men."[18] Tournier tells of how his wife, Nelly, because of her "sense of person," transformed the medical meetings of which he was in charge:

> *It was the extreme care and interest she showed towards each participant that helped create the personal atmosphere. . . . In any other medical conference only ideas matter, and the delegates are appreciated only in terms of their scientific in-put. But in the Bossey meetings everyone was made welcome and was valued as a person.*[19]

After Nelly's death, her influence continued. The meetings "almost entirely abandoned the old tradition of master lectures, so as to be able to devote time to the personal experiences and problems of the delegates." Nelly's gift for friendship is seeing multiplied results.[20]

The kind of small discussion group that I prefer is one in which each member is made to feel valued. I want the discussion leader to curtail his own tendency to talk and seriously attempt to draw those in the group out. I want him to be alert to each member's facial expression and to occasionally go around the whole group asking for individual feelings or personal applications. I am intensely frustrated by a group—and it happens much more frequently with a man at the helm—that seems to ignore the members and concentrates exclusively on the lesson. I *do* want to study the lesson (and I confess I have observed many women's groups that don't), but I don't want the study of the lesson to supersede the needs of the people. When I am in a group like this I have to repress an urge to stand and to scream: "THESE PEOPLE ARE NOT FEELING VALUED! THEY ARE GOING TO LEAVE THIS ROOM FEELING AS IF THEIR PRESENCE DIDN'T MATTER!"

REFLECTION

10. If you are in a group study, do you feel it is balanced between studying the lesson and valuing people? If not, what could be done?

_____

_____

_____

There are abundant studies which show that a female's sense of the person is evident from a very early age. Preschool boys are more likely to draw objects, and preschool girls, people.[21] Studies at Harvard have found that "girl babies recognize individual human faces and distinguish between voices before male babies of the same age."[22] Another study found that:

> *At four months a boy will react to an inanimate object as readily as to a person. Given the choice between a mother's face and a bright geometric object hanging over the crib, the boy, unlike the girl, will just as frequently babble at the inanimate object as at his mother.*[23]

When our sons were babies, we enjoyed watching them on their backs in their cribs, arms and legs excitedly flailing over a brightly painted mobile. Since it entranced the boys, that mobile gave me free time! When Sally was born, the mobile didn't cast the same spell over her. Then, I was disappointed. Now I understand. Our daughter, like most females, found people more interesting than gadgets.

These studies have helped me to understand why men seem more interested in the activity and women in the person with whom they are enjoying the activity. My friend Jean said, "When my husband goes out to play golf, I'll ask him, 'Who are you golfing with today?'

He'll answer, 'Anyone I can hook up with!' I would never golf that way. I want to choose my companion!"

WOMEN'S INTUITION

The right brain is also the intuitive hemisphere. Dr. Donald Joy compared a woman's mind to a giant computer: she spits out the right answer, but there's no way to check her logic, and even she can't tell you how she got it.[24] Our accuracy in first impressions tends to be higher than those of men. Dr. Dobson says that when he and his wife, Shirley, come home after meeting with people for the first time, Shirley will have correctly assessed personality and character. Dobson says, "Here I've got a Ph.D. in psychology, but it takes me weeks or months of dealing with the people to come to the same conclusion."[25]

Our intuition also gives us speed in perceiving spiritual mysteries. Perhaps that's why God allowed women to be first at the empty tomb. When the women ran to tell the men that Christ had risen, the men "did not believe the women, because their words seemed to them like nonsense" (Luke 24:11). The men had to wait for more facts to satisfy their logical left brains.

Likewise, I believe Mary and Elizabeth intuitively knew the angel was right while their men, Joseph and Zechariah, had to wait for more facts before they could come to the same conclusion. When Gabriel informed Zechariah that his barren wife would be with child, Zechariah, in true left-brain form, responded, "How can I be sure of this?" (Luke 1:18) And Joseph had in mind to divorce Mary quietly (Matt. 1:19).

What comfort, therefore, Mary and Elizabeth gave to each other in their greeting scene! Sensitive to each other's need for encouragement, they affirmed each other's faith. Elizabeth lifts Mary's heart as soon as she sees her young cousin by saying, "Good for you, Mary! You believed!"

AN INTERTWINING OF INTUITION AND HOLY SPIRIT POWER:
Luke 1:34-56; 23:55–24:26

SCRIPTURAL
REFLECTION

⏳ 11. Read Luke 1:13-18 and Luke 1:34-45. Contrast Zechariah's response to Gabriel's news with Mary's response to Gabriel's news.

_____

_____

⏳ 12. Read Luke 1:39-45. List all the ways you can see that these two women were responsive to God, demonstrating trust and obedience.

_____

_____

⏳ 13. What are some truths that God has been impressing on your heart to which you need to respond? (Take time with this question.)

_____

_____

_____

_____

NOTE: Intuition is a gift, but if Scripture disagrees with what you intuitively sense, red flags should go up! One woman said she felt "led" to marry an unbeliever—and yet Scripture is clear that believers are to marry believers (2 Cor. 6:14; 1 Cor. 7:39; Malachi 2:11-12). God never leads against His Word. If we are to use our gift for intuition wisely, we should be meditating on Scripture day and night!

⏳ 14. Read Luke 1:46-56. List all the truths you can find that Mary knew on the basis of her knowledge of Scripture.

_____

_____

15. Read Luke 23:55—24:27

   A. In Luke 23:55, how did the women demonstrate "a sense of the person" and obedience to God?

_____

B. Contrast the reactions of the women in Luke 24 with that of the men.

_____

_____

C. How did Jesus react to the disciples' lack of faith? How did He help them to believe?

_____

_____

D. What can we learn from the example of Jesus here?

_____

_____

As we discover the differences in the brain functions between men and women, we appreciate our need for each other. Gary Smalley commented that one of the reasons God said, "It is not good for the man to be alone" (Gen. 2:18) is that the man needs a woman to help him develop the right side of his brain.[26] My husband, Steve, who has been blessed with a beautifully strong left brain (he's a whiz at math, surgery, and keeping our lives completely organized) tells me I've strengthened his right brain. "I'm appreciating more and more," he told me, "the beauty in life: children, puppies, poetry." How important, therefore, it is for men and women to be friends and also share positions of leadership in the church and in the world. (Is it possible for men and women to be friends and not fall into sexual temptation? Many of the leaders of the evangelical community, particularly in Christian television, have been involved in sexual scandal. I was reassured when at a writer's conference in August 1987, Karen Mains affirmed her belief that it is surely possible for friendship to exist between the sexes without immorality. She and her husband, David, use a mental safety device: they put Christ between themselves and the person to whom they are relating. If we are not friends with members of the opposite sex, then we will fail to help each other become all that God wants us to be.

WOMEN ARE NATURAL NURTURERS
It makes sense to me that the God who created us with the ability to carry babies under our hearts and nurse them tenderly at our breasts would also equip us with a longing and a skill for responding to the

needs of those who are vulnerable.

Most women tend to scatter rose petals on the hard paths of life, whereas men need to be taught to be comforters. When our daughter Sally was little and I left her in Steve's care when I was out of town, she had a complaint to voice upon my return. She snuggled next to me on the sofa and confided intently:

> *Daddy doesn't know how to wake me up. He doesn't turn on the music, or give me a back rub, or even kiss me good morning. He just flicks on the big light and says, "Time to get up!" That's not a very good morning greeting. Will you tell him, for next time?*

(I have. He's repented.)

Recently I stood on our covered porch while mothball-sized hail pelted the ground. It also relentlessly pelted a mother robin who sat stoically on her nest in a nearby plum tree, protecting her scrawny, newly hatched babies from the onslaught. Her instinct was so strong that I found myself thinking of Dr. Seuss's Horton, the elephant who subbed for a lazy Mayzie bird while she flew off to Palm Beach:

> *So Horton kept sitting there, day after day. And soon it was Autumn. The leaves blew away. And then came the Winter . . . the snow and the sleet! And icicles hung from his trunk and his feet. But Horton kept sitting, and said with a sneeze, I'll stay on this egg and I won't let it freeze.*[27]

("Aha!" say those of you who feel I have been guilty of stereotyping men and women. "Horton was a male elephant!" It's true, but Horton was a most exceptional male.)

SCRIPTURAL REFLECTION

16. Read the following passages from Isaiah and write down what you think God implies about mothers.

> *As a mother comforts her child, so will I comfort you* (Isaiah 66:13a).
>
> *Can a mother forget the baby at her breast and have no compassion on the child she has borne? Though she may forget, I will not forget you!* (Isaiah 49:15)

_____

_____

_____

OUR CULTURE DISCOURAGES MALE FRIENDLINESS

On the fertile field of a woman's innate friendliness rolls the snowball of culture. Father robin has no fear that carrying dangling earthworms to his young will tarnish his masculine reputation, but the human male is plagued by such fears.

While little girls are playing with dolls, practicing nurturing, little boys are on teams—competing. Elliot Engel commented that the male twosome seems to be designed "more for combat than for comfort." Whether it's the tennis court or the law court, men are expected to compete. "This almost ensures," Elliot observes, "that our relationship will never develop into intimacy but stay at a superficial guarded level. Vulnerability is not accepted as a healthy component of male relationships."[28]

Culture augments heredity in the areas of smiling and praise. Studies show that even in infancy, girls smile more than boys.[29] As we grow older, we find that it's considered feminine to smile and masculine to be stern and impassive. As Brownies we sang about "the great big Brownie smile," but I doubt that our male counterparts were singing about "the great big Cub Scout smile." In an article in Mademoiselle, Marian Sandmaier pointed out that our world is full of smiling role models for little girls to follow—"from Miss America to Marie Osmond"—and of glowering role models for little boys, "from the lonesome cowboy to the slouching rock star."[30]

After I told my husband that research shows women smile and praise more than men, he had a humorous interaction with a male patient and his family. Steve characterized Mike as the "strong, silent type," sparing with his compliments and smiles. Steve's surgery gave Mike relief from his years of suffering from back pain. It was Mike's wife, however, who caught up with Steve in the hospital corridor to thank him. Smiling warmly, she said, "Doctor, Mike just can't believe his pain is finally gone. He's very grateful, but he's just not the kind who could ever tell you to your face. So I wanted to do it for him."

Later, during Steve's gentle examination, Mike scowled while his wife and mother looked on. Knowing better than to take Mike's countenance personally, Steve couldn't resist teasing his patient with a parting remark. As he turned to walk out the door, Steve said, "Mike, my wife is writing a book on the friendships of women. She has found that all through their lives, women smile more than men." The women burst into gales of laughter and the tiniest flicker of a smile crossed Mike's face.

There are those who are telling us that if we want to succeed in the career world we had better wipe those smiles from our faces. Severity, it seems, increases clout. Frankly, I think it would be better if we could influence men to be friendlier rather than becoming less so ourselves. "A cheerful heart is good medicine," Solomon tells us, "but a crushed spirit dries up the bones" (Prov. 17:22).

Kind words and smiles definitely brighten the world. A woman friend catches my eye in church, and smiles—and I feel cared for, lifted. Our bond has been recognized, affirmed. When I speak, it is women, usually, who are smiling at me, nodding their support, encouraging me, appeasing my fears. I receive notes of encouragement almost every week from women friends, but my husband rarely receives one from another man. The patients who do write to thank him are almost invariably women.

Surly cowboys and hard-boiled detectives are fine for television, but I am not drawn to them as friends. I stay away from them just as I stay away from a cat with an arched back. People—men and women—who have contagious laughs, words of encouragement, and warm and caring smiles are the ones who find themselves magnetically drawing others. I am drawn to them just as I am drawn to a dog whose tail thumps when he sees me.

WOMEN SEE THEMSELVES IN A WEB OF RELATIONSHIPS

Carol Gilligan, associate professor of education at Harvard University, makes the following insightful observation:

> *Since masculinity is defined through separateness while femininity is defined through attachment, male gender identity is threatened by intimacy, while female gender identity is threatened by separation.*[31]

Women see themselves as part of a web of relationships. My husband and I have noticed that when we ask members of a Sunday school class to introduce themselves with a thumbnail sketch, the women will invariably mention their relationships with others, whereas the men will simply talk about themselves.

REFLECTION

■ We studied *The Friendships of Women* in a mixed Sunday School class in my church. The first day, in hopes of demonstrating my point that women define themselves in terms of a web of relationships whereas men define themselves in terms of their jobs, I asked each member to share a few sentences about themselves. I was pleased at how well they were fitting my "stereotype," for every woman was describing her relationships, and every man, his job. But then we got to Ted Sabata, who said: "I'm married to Mary-Jo. We have three children. I play golf with Mike." Then he paused and said, with a smirk. "I've read Dee's book. Men—you have just been set up!"

17. If you were to tell someone a few sentences about yourself in order to help her know you better, what would you say?

_____

_____

_____

_____

Mary is so receptive to Elizabeth's emotion and encouragement that she in turn sings, "My soul doth magnify the Lord, and my spirit hath rejoiced in God my Saviour" (Luke 1:46-47, KJV). Our lack of concern over identity boundaries causes sparks to fly back and forth between us in ever-increasing heat, as iron sharpens iron! (Prov. 27:17)

If our water is sweet, this fluidity means we can have a lovely effect on each other. After her first year in women's Bible study, Beth told her group:

> You've changed me. When I first came here, my heart was hard. I realize that now. But the way you've reached out to me, the sensitivity toward God I've seen in your lives, the tears, the embraces . . . you've made my heart tender. I really didn't think it could happen. I feel like I've regained my innocence.

REFLECTION

⧗ 18. In the above quotation, a woman shares how the sweetness of the women's lives in her Bible study groups made her heart tender. Can you think of ways women who are tender toward the Lord have done that for you? If so, give an example.

_____

_____

_____

Like gently moving streams joining into one river, we round the difficult bends of life together, strengthening each other with a fresh water supply. We are free and flowing and unconcerned with boundaries. This is part of the beauty of the friendships of women, but it is also the danger.

We are afraid to run toward the ocean alone. We feel a sense of panic in solitude. Ironically, it is because we place such a high value on our relationships that we are tempted, sometimes, to be so very cruel.

It is most evident in childhood. Do you remember?

WINDING DOWN

■ If time permits, go around and have women share their answers to the question, "What are some truths that God has been impressing on your heart to which you need to respond?" (p.50) Look back at that and determine if you would be willing to share that with the group. Confession purifies our heart and sweetens the fluidity of our relationships! If you don't want to share, you can pass.

GROUP PRAYER

⌛ ■ Write down an area of concern in your life for which you would like your sisters in Christ to pray. Make it personal!

_____

_____

Close in prayer, either using popcorn prayer (see page 33), or praying in twos.

NEXT WEEK'S ASSIGNMENT

■ When you get home, while the group experience is still fresh, complete the journaling assignment in this chapter.

■ Remember to do your action assignment: meeting another's needs with your "sense of the person" as Mary of Bethany did for Jesus. One way to discover another's needs is by asking the questions you asked of one another at the opening of this chapter.

■ Work through the next chapter and the exercises.

PERSONAL JOURNAL

■ What did God impress on your heart as a result of the group discussion and prayer?

_____

_____

■ How is God leading you to apply what you've learned?

_____

_____

Chapter 3
The Darker Side
of Being Crazy-Glued

PERSONAL PRAYER

Quiet your heart before God. Before you begin to read and journal, become aware of God's presence! Today:

- Read Psalm 103:1-5 and use each verse as a springboard for spontaneous praise to God.

- Confess and turn from sin.

- Now read Psalm 103:9-18. Ask God to help you remember His steadfastness and man's frailty, and to help you trust in Him instead of in people. If you are in a group, pray the same for other group members. (This might be a good time to divide this chapter into five quiet times for the coming week.)

WARMING UP

- In circles of three, share how you used your gift for intimacy in ministering to others. Then reassemble in the larger circle and take nominations for the winner! After having the nominees share with the larger circle what they did, have group members comment on who they thought made the best use of her "talent" and why.

GROUP PRAYER

- Before you begin to discuss together, quiet your hearts before God. Using the popcorn method of prayer, the leader should lift up the two subjects listed below. Women can offer sentence prayers on anything they prefer. When the "popping stops" after the first subject, the leader introduces the second subject. When the popping stops again, she should close with: "We ask these things in the name of Jesus. Amen."

■ Thanks to God
■ Requests for His help in the lesson

This chapter will show that a woman's Achilles' heel is her tendency toward dependency on people rather than on God.

REFLECTION

Remember! If you are a Time-conscious group, discuss only those questions marked ⧖ throughout.

⧖ 1. Explain why a friend may be a friend of character, yet *still* let you down.

_____

_____

NOTE: When I ask this question of myself, I become more forgiving. I know I have failed to write long-distance soulmates as often as I should. There have been times when I have failed to be sensitive to the needs of friends. At times I have failed them in ways that have truly wounded them. I have feet of clay. If I think of myself as a woman of character, and yet I sin, I must realize that the same failings will sometimes be true of the believers in my life, even those who truly love me.

ON A HOT, humid August afternoon, Holly and Kate, two young friends of mine, found refuge in the coolness of Holly's basement. Holly's dark braids were flying as Kate rhythmically turned the jump rope, the other end being tied to the doorknob. "Teddy bear, teddy bear, turn around," they chanted. "Teddy bear, teddy bear, touch the ground . . . "

The phone rang and Holly's mother appeared at the top of the stairs, interrupting the girls mid-rhyme. "Holly, it's Ramona. She'd like to come over. She could meet Kate. Wouldn't that be fun?"

Holly came halfway up the stairs and looked at her mother warily with dark, foreboding eyes. Then, softly, she whispered, "Mother, you know three just doesn't work with girls."

As a friend of Ramona's mother, Holly's mother hedged. "Honey, jump rope would be better with three. You like Kate and Ramona so much—I think they'd like each other."

Reluctantly, Holly gave in. And Kate and Ramona *did* like each other. So much so that when Kate got home she sent Ramona the following letter.

> *Dear Ramona,*
>
> *How are you? I am fine. Would you like to be best friends? I like you better than I like Holly. I do not like Holly at all any more. Let's not like Holly together.*
>
> *Your best friend, Kate*

The following Friday night, when Holly was spending the night at Ramona's, Ramona brought out the traitorous letter. Ramona's mother was alarmed to hear angry words and wails coming from the girls' room. She opened the door to see the offending letter in shreds on the floor and Holly curled up in a fetal position on the bed, sobbing inconsolably.

I suspect that these girls were motivated not by the desire to hurt, but by the desire to secure their own positions. When Holly asked her mother not to allow Ramona to join them in jump rope, she was protecting her relationship with Kate. When Kate wrote Ramona the letter, she was trying to break into the circle. When Ramona revealed Kate's cruel letter, she was trying to show Holly that she was the more worthy friend.

If a girl's needs for intimacy are being met in a friendship or in a close circle of friends, she does not want that threatened by another person. Since the feminine identity is so closely tied to relationships, it is quite natural to want to guard our relationships by making our circle tight—even if the side effect is betrayal.

A male might have trouble empathizing with the girls in the above story. But most of us women understand only too well, for we have experienced this kind of treachery, at least in childhood.

THEY DREW A CIRCLE AND LEFT ME OUT

When Sally was eight, she came home from school one day in tears. She fled up the stairs, slamming her bedroom door behind her. I found her huddled on the floor in the corner, weeping. Hurting because she did, I tried to absorb some of my child's pain by pulling her on my lap and pressing her head close to my breast. I stroked her hair and waited. Eventually, between gasps for breath, she sobbed out her story. Her best friends had formed a club and excluded her.

Taking the role of the pushy mother, I mentioned the problem to Sally's third-grade teacher at parent-teacher conferences that week. She shook her head in frustration. "These clubs of the girls are a continuing problem. They break each other's hearts. Every year I say, 'NO MORE CLUBS!' I threaten them. I punish them. But they continue, secretly."

A few days later the club disbanded. The next week a new secret club formed. It included Sally and excluded a different heartbroken girl. Until little girls can learn to find their security in God alone, exclusive clubs will continue.

REFLECTION

2. Did you have territorial tendencies when you were a child? If so, give an example. Have you witnessed territorial tendencies with girls today? If so, how?

_____

_____

_____

3. Dee mentioned the importance of helping girls to find their security in God. In the following situations, how might you do this?

■ Your daugher has a problem (a lost homework assignment, a difficult task, etc.).

■ Your niece has come to you in tears because her "best" friend has a new "best" friend and is leaving her out.

_____

_____

_____

COLLEGE SORORITIES

The world of college sororities is simply a refinement of the cruelty of elementary school clubs. Their main disgrace is in the way they choose who will become a member. The more prestigious the sorority, the greater their power to exclude. To my shame, I participated in this system, fully, as a young woman at Northwestern University. My only defenses are that I was immature and had not yet trusted Christ as my Lord.

My roommate freshman year was Heather. Someone had matched us up, and assigned us to the only room with a private bath, because they liked our names. (My given name is Meredith.) To our mutual joy, we liked each other immensely and became best friends. Heather, a quiet violin major, was more mature than I, and not enamored with sororities. She tried to point out the value of making friends cautiously (Proverbs 12:26 warns "a righteous man is cautious in friendship") and the danger of throwing in our lot for four years with one group based on a few days of parties. But so strong was my need for connection, so fearful was I of not being identified with a sorority, that I convinced Heather to go through rush and pledge with me.

We chose the sorority I liked best and voted together. Heather's was a "suicide" vote—she requested only that one, and if she didn't get in, she was out. She would then be forced to join the "independents"—a group that made up only 7 percent of the population at N.U. and was, of course, snubbed by the sorority women. The sorority voted to accept me and reject my best friend. I was shocked by our forced separation, for I would eventually have to live apart from Heather in the sorority house. In my naïveté I expected we would both get in: I, because I wanted it so much, and Heather, because she was a lovely brunette with enormous dark eyes, and I knew that beauty was the top requirement. But Heather had told them that she was unsure whether she was going to pledge, and so they coldly decided to reject her before she rejected them.

As a sophomore, I saw the ugly insides of rush. Amidst punch and hors d'oeuvres, we were to chat amiably with the freshmen as they came through the house. After a few minutes of conversation, we were to make mental note of which girls met our high standards. In my sorority, the less attractive members (the ones who were dubbed "surprises" on pledge day) were kept busy in the kitchen. (Can you imagine what being kept behind closed doors would do for your self-esteem?)

I wish I had followed the commendable example of my two older sisters, who had the integrity to deactivate after getting a close look at rush, but my intense need for a feeling of belonging to my feminine friends was stronger than my desire to choose the higher, kinder road. (And sometimes, despite my conversion and additional twenty years, this is still true.)

At night during rush, the cruelty intensified. We discussed the merits and defects of each girl. We knew we had the power to break hearts, and break hearts we did. By keeping a girl out, we were affirming to each other how special and tight was our circle. I was a part of this evil, and along with the shame, took some delight in securing my position as one of the special ones. C.S. Lewis says that just as we find joy in discovering a friend who loves the same beauty—the same poet, truth, or music—so do we delight in sharing a secret evil: "Even now, at whatever age, we all know the perilous charm of a shared hatred or grievance. (It is difficult not to hail as a Friend the only other man in College who really sees the faults of the Sub-Warden.)"[1]

In 1986, Stephanie, a particularly pretty young Christian, was drawn into this kind of back-stabbing scene at her women's college:

> There was so much competition and spitefulness. I got the bid I wanted, but afterwards I wondered if it was really worth it. Girls who had been my friends and didn't get a bid weren't my friends anymore. And a lot of the girls who were chosen acted like the girls on the outside weren't good enough to talk to.

Stephanie told me, with emotion, that she felt her values were being torn apart. It saddens me that so many colleges still introduce freshmen to their world with the cruelty of rush. The nature of sororities seems to bring out the worst in women, for we want so much to be securely connected to others.

REFLECTION

4. Many women have agreed with my opinion of sororities. When I was on Focus on the Family, Dr. Dobson courageously called them "a flesh market." Yet some women wrote, offended, saying that the friends they had made in their sororities were treasured friends, and that I was too harsh. What is your opinion? How do you think Jesus views sororities? Why?

_____

_____

_____

TURNING ON A PEER

Studies show, to our shame, that the feminine sex deserves her reputation for back stabbing. Eva Margolies, in _The Best of Friends, the Worst of Enemies_, observes, "Virtually every research on the subject indicates that while boys can be nasty, they aren't nearly as vicious to one another as girls."[2]

I listened with interest as our daughter and her friend Leisa discussed how quickly the other fifth-grade boys had included a new boy in their recess soccer game. Leisa said, "It's a lot harder to be new if you're a girl. The boys will accept any old boy, but girls are really picky."

A study of first graders by Dr. Norma Feshback corroborates Leisa's observations. She found that boys are much nicer to a newcomer. The initial response of girls to a new member "was more likely to be one of exclusion and rejection."[3]

A girl's intense desire to be close almost automatically makes her crueler. Newcomers threaten her circle of two. Since boys are more likely to play in groups, one more is welcome. Also, a boy's sense of worth is often tied to his activities—does he excel in math, football, soccer? While this is not unimportant to girls, her sense of worth is more apt to be tied to her relationships. Does she have a best friend? Is she one of the popular girls? Girls, more than boys, are threatened by anyone who might change the relationships that give them security and self-esteem. If a girl needs to turn on another in order to secure her own position, she will.

Perhaps one of the reasons Judy Blume's books have become so popular with elementary and adolescent girls is that Blume has effectively portrayed the dark side of little girls. In her book *Blubber*,[4] for example, the vast majority of the book is dedicated to various ways elementary school girls torment a slightly overweight peer whom they nickname Blubber. Amidst giggles and knowing glances, they pass unkind notes around about her; they barricade her way to the bathroom until she repeats, "I am Blubber and I will always be Blubber"; and they throw her sack lunch around the cafeteria. (There is a moralistic twist at the end of the book, but it's too late to redeem the damage to young readers. Little girls don't need inspiration in the area of treachery from an adult author.)

Though we do become kinder in maturity, and certainly in Christ, we still are prone to inflict wounds on others.

SCRIPTURAL REFLECTION

5. As Dee has explained, because little girls find their security in relationships, they are territorial, and often cruel to anyone who threatens their circle of two. Teaching our daughters to be kind, and to respond as Christ would to cruelty, is one of our responsibilities as mothers, or as mentors to young girls. Meditate on the following verses and explain what they say. Then give an example of a situation in which a girl might apply them.

A. "A gentle answer turns away wrath, but a harsh word stirs up anger" (Prov. 15:1).

_____

_____

⧗ B. "Do not be overcome by evil, but overcome evil with good" (Rom. 12:21).

_____

_____

_____

_____

More suggestions to mothers can be found in the sequel to this book, *We Are Sisters* (Victor) and in Dee's Bible study guide, *The Joy of Women's Friendships* (Victor).

GOSSIP

There are two words for *gossip* in the Old Testament Scriptures. The first is the Hebrew word *rakiyl*, and means "traveling" with confidences. Betrayal is involved, for you are sharing a secret that should have remained in your own heart.

Since women are willing to make themselves vulnerable to one another, they have more to spill. One pastor told me, "It's good that women are willing to reveal more of themselves to each other, for without that, you don't have intimacy. But women often fail to be trustworthy with those revelations." Why are we tempted to be faithless? Because of our strong desire for connection. One woman said, "Sometimes I think I'm talking about another person in order to help her, or to pray for her. But perhaps, behind a spiritual cover, I'm simply enjoying the spark of intimacy that gossip provides."

Another woman remarked that she was fairly careful not to break confidences when talking to another woman, but that she felt free to share those same confidences with her husband. "Even though I know that telling him may influence him negatively against that person, I can't seem to help myself. I need to unload to someone, and I think we have that right in marriage."

"Hey, wait a minute," a single woman responded. "It sounds fine to say, 'I would only tell my husband,' but where does that leave me? Don't single persons need to unload too?"

When I'm going through pain in my life inflicted on me by someone, I *do* feel a need to talk it over with my husband or another trusted friend. I have wrestled with this. Is this gossip? The other Hebrew word translated *gossip* has a darker connotation than "traveling." It is *nirgan*, and comes from a Hebrew root word meaning "to roll to pieces." If my sharing is going to roll someone to pieces, then I *am* gossiping. I believe if we examine our hearts and are confident that our motive is to gain wisdom for the situation and not to roll the person to pieces, then there may be some justification in going to a closemouthed spiritual giant. But a higher road would be to wait and see if time will bring healing. I must guard against revenge and my intense desire to verify that I am in the inner circle. One woman understood her own behavior when she said, "I have this desire to confirm in my confidant's mind that she should think more of me than so-and-so, who's been unfair to me."

Karen, a college chemistry teacher, told me that she likes being the only woman in an otherwise all-male department because there's a minimum of infighting and gossip. Her husband's music department is beleaguered by a few gossiping women. Although men do gossip, women gossip more. Until we can learn to find our security in God alone, we will gossip.

SCRIPTURAL REFLECTION

■ Though we shouldn't be astonished when a friend lets us down, for we all have feet of clay, we should endeavor to become like Christ, and rid ourselves of hurtful habits like gossip. What is gossip? Is it talking about people? No—our Lord talked about people. Two Hebrew words which are translated *gossip* help us to understand. In the following proverb, the word translated *gossip* is from the Hebrew word *rakiyl*, and means "traveling with a confidence."

A gossip betrays a confidence;
so avoid a man who talks too much (Prov. 20:20).

6. "Breaking a confidence" constitutes gossip.

⌛ A. How do you feel about someone who betrays your confidence?

_____

_____

_____

⌛ B. If you are doing this study in a group, does your group have a policy about keeping confidences within the group?

_____

_____

_____

_____

⌛ C. What does Solomon link with betraying a confidence in the above proverb? What can you learn from this to protect yourself? What can you learn regarding reducing your own temptation to betray a friend?

_____

_____

_____

7. "Rolling to pieces" constitutes gossip. In the following proverbs, the word translated *gossip* is from the Hebrew word, *nirgan*, and means "to roll someone to pieces."

> *The words of a gossip are like choice morsels, they go down to*
> *a man's inmost parts* (Prov. 18:8; repeated in Prov. 26:22).
> *Without wood a fire goes out; without gossip a quarrel dies*
> *down* (Prov. 26:20).

⌛ A. Why is it tempting to gossip? What damage does it do according to the above proverb? Have you seen this?

_____

_____

_____

B. If you are in a "quarrel" with a friend, when, if ever, is it legitimate to talk about it with a third party?

_____

_____

_____

C. Imagine that a distressed friend comes to you to talk about a quarrel with another friend. You respect both women. Your distressed friend says, "My son went over to Betty's house and she let them watch a PG-13 movie. I am so upset!" What are some ways you think Christ might have you respond?

_____

_____

_____

D. Was the distressed friend gossiping? Why or why not?

_____

_____

⧗ E. What would be some good questions to ask yourself about motivation and effect when you are trying to decide whether or not to say something about someone else?

_____

_____

NOTE: Deborah Tannen, in *You Just Don't Understand: Men and Women in Conversation* (New York, William Morrow and Company, Inc., 1990), has some interesting insights. She says that men often assume talking about people is gossip. However, the topic of conversation isn't what constitutes gossip, but rather the motivation and the effect. I do talk about people with my friends—because I care about people and the events of their lives! Also, a friend can give me insight and empathy into another woman. However, I know that I have a deceitful heart, and that I am capable of justifying gossip. Even if my motivation is pure, my effect can still be harmful. So I must continually examine my effect, as well as my motivation.

F. Do you agree or disagree with the above? Explain.

_____

_____

⧗ G. If you feel a check on your spirit when you are talking, what should you do?

_____

_____

_____

WOMEN'S BIBLE STUDIES

Most women's Bible study groups form beautiful bonds within weeks. Women are sharing vulnerably, weeping, laughing, and encouraging one another, evidencing their gift for intimacy. Each rejoices in the comfortable, womblike warmth of the group.

It takes tremendous maturity to venture outside in order to befriend and invite others in. When your own needs for intimacy are being met, it's easy to slide into complacency about the needs of others.

If a newcomer does come, she senses the group's intimacy and feels like an outsider looking in. The invitations to lunch, the phone calls, and the notes aren't nearly as common as they should be. Too often, the newcomer doesn't come back.

Christian women are also hesitant to divide a Bible study group as their numbers grow. This is a subtle modification of the cruelty of elementary clubs and college sororities. Until women learn to find their security in God alone, Bible studies will be tainted with exclusiveness.

REFLECTION

8. If you are doing this study in a group, how conscientious are you about reaching out, about welcoming newcomers? How could you do better?

_____

_____

_____

RACHEL

Sometimes friends are a surprise gift from God. Rachel, an energetic and witty young woman, has been that for me. I believe that God gave us our friendship, in part, to help me realize that the root problem of lesbians is similar to the root problem that gives straight women a tendency toward cruelty: dependency on a human relationship rather than on God.

I met Rachel at a Right to Life association meeting. Our brief conversation promised that this woman had depth. So I asked her to go out to lunch with me. As we headed toward my favorite restaurant, a cozy place with booths, candles, and the smell of homemade soup, Rachel casually asked me what I was writing presently. When I told her it was a book on the friendships of women, she gasped. I looked at her curiously.

At first, she dodged. "There's a need for that book and I would definitely read it."

I wasn't satisfied. I knew, intuitively, that there was more behind her startled reaction. Beseechingly, my eyes met hers. After a minute she responded. "Just give me a little time to gather my courage, and I'll tell you." She took a deep breath. "I think the Lord must have arranged for us to have this time together, so I'll tell you," she promised. "I will."

After we ordered, Rachel confided how she had been delivered, through Christ, from a lesbian relationship. While not attempting to justify herself, she tried to help me understand why so many women fall into this trap.

"I don't know how it happened," Rachel began, speaking softly and hesitatingly. "I do know that I had a deep need for affirmation. And homosexual relationships between women," she paused, trying to gauge my reaction, "are different in character from homosexual relationships between men. In my opinion, men have such strong physical urges that the priority is often sexual. But with women, there is a nurturing tenderness which can seem deceptively beautiful."

Before I tell Rachel's story, I think it would be helpful to look at a few key insights Christian counselors have gained about homosexuality.

CHRISTIAN COUNSELORS ON HOMOSEXUALITY

Most counselors who have been successful in helping homosexuals gain victory over their lifestyle agree that homosexuality is learned behavior. Author and psychiatrist John White writes, "Homosexuality is something you practice rather than something you are."[5] Jay Adams, a Christian counselor who has had great success in breaking the bondage of homosexuals, says:

> *One is not a homosexual constitutionally any more than one is an adulterer constitutionally. Homosexuality is not considered to be a condition, but an act . . . . To call homosexuality a sickness, for example, does not raise the client's hope. But to call homosexuality sin, as the Bible does, is to offer hope.*[6]

Personally, I think it's possible that in some there may be a contributing genetic tendency toward homosexuality, just as in some there is a contributing genetic tendency toward alcoholism. The fall has made us prone to sin! Yet, in Christ, there is still the power of deliverance from both of these tendencies. God doesn't ask us to abstain from sin unless it is possible to do so.

And the Bible *does* call homosexuality sin (Lev. 18:22; 20:13; Rom. 1:26-27; 1 Cor. 6:9). There are so-called gay churches who, blinded by sin, are attempting to distort the Scriptures and deny their clarity. They say, for example, that the sin of Sodom (Gen. 19:1-5) was not homosexuality but inhospitality, and deliberately ignore the fact that Jude 7 clarifies the fact that Sodom's sin was sexual perversion.[7]

I share this because Rachel has told me that she has met practicing lesbians who profess Christianity and who quote false teachers like these. I have met them also. I have had women come up to me after I have spoken on the friendships of women at retreats and tell me that they do not see a conflict between their practice of lesbianism and Christianity. Satan is a master deceiver. The three lies he tells most frequently to those caught in this lifestyle are "You are not really sinning"; "You can never change"; and "You will not be happy if you leave this lifestyle." If you are in the bondage of lesbianism, I pray Rachel's story and the references in the notes to this chapter will be of real help to you.

SCRIPTURAL REFLECTION

9. What do you learn about how God feels about the practice of homosexuality from the following verses?

> *Do not lie with a man as one lies with a woman; that is detestable* (Lev. 18:22).
> *Do you not know that the wicked will not inherit the kingdom of God? Do not be deceived: Neither the sexually immoral nor idolaters nor adulterers nor male prostitutes nor homosexual offenders nor thieves nor the greedy nor drunkards nor slanderers nor swindlers will inherit the kingdom of God. And that is what some of you were. But you were washed, you were sanctified, you were justified in the name of the Lord Jesus Christ and by the Spirit of our God* (1 Cor. 6:9-11).

NOTE: It is not my wish to take hope from those who are struggling with homosexuality, but to give them the hope that change is possible with God. I have received more mail concerning the following section in this book than any other section—particularly from women who are desperate to escape the bondage of a homosexual relationship. An organization which I highly recommend is Exodus International, a Christian ministry "dedicated to helping men and women overcome homosexual bondage through relationship with the Lord Jesus Christ." They are ready to guide and direct toward help in the form of reading material, retreats, and support in your area. Their address is Exodus International, P.O. Box 2121, San Rafael, CA 94914. Their phone is 415-454-1017.

IT BEGAN AS A BEAUTIFUL FRIENDSHIP

Since homosexuality is learned behavior, it should not surprise us that many male homosexuals are masculine and many female homosexuals are feminine. Often individuals will not take on characteristics of the opposite sex in dress, conversation, or interests until they have chosen a homosexual lifestyle.

Rachel and Laura don't fit the physical stereotype often given to lesbians. Though Rachel is lanky and comfortable in jeans, her gentle manner, blond curls, and porcelain complexion give her a cameo look. Laura is diminutive, dark, and shapely. Her hair cascades down her back in gentle waves. If she were to walk past a city construction site, she would draw wolf whistles.

A traumatic childhood can increase vulnerability to homosexuality. Dr. Jane Flax believes the most common factor leading to lesbianism is growing up with a cold, indifferent mother.[8] (Don't hesitate to express affection to your daughters!)

Maxine Hancock and Karen Mains cite a study in their excellent book *Child Sexual Abuse*,[9] showing a possible link between childhood abuse and lesbianism. In this study, conducted by Karen Meiselman, seven of twenty-three daughters who had experienced incest had "become gay or had significant experiences or conflicts centered on homosexual feelings."[10]

Rachel had been abused sexually, repeatedly and traumatically, by an uncle when she was a child. She said, "He made me do things I wouldn't consider doing in my marriage." It was difficult, therefore, as a young woman, for Rachel to feel an attraction for men. But both Rachel and Laura are convinced that what happened to them could happen to anyone who doesn't have God in first place, as the central focus of her life. Rachel told me of how her friendship with Laura began.

> *It was completely innocent at first. We had that immediate rapport that I believe is a gift from God. Laura is one of the most sensitive people I've ever met. Tenderhearted, she cares deeply about the hurts of others. The unfortunate side-effect of that characteristic is that she's easily bruised. She fed off my strength, my ability to roll with the punches. I fed off her sensitivity. We were a great match. And there was something about Laura that intrigued me, something that made me want to know her better.*

"When did the problem begin?" I asked Rachel. "And why?"

THE SLIPPERY SLIDE FROM SOUL MATES TO DEPENDENCY

> *I had a void in my life. I didn't understand that that void was created in me to be filled with God, so I turned to Laura. We*

began to spend too much time together—taking walks, drinking and partying together, talking into the wee hours of the morning. We began to rely on each other for everything. I see now that's when Satan got a foothold. Everything became a blur as we focused completely on each other: college, our studies, our goals for graduation, fellow students—none of that was important. All that mattered was each other . . . . My love for Laura kept growing. I was shocked to find myself longing to hold her. Just put my arms around her. But I didn't.

In Romans 1:21-25, we are told that the first step leading to homosexuality is worshiping the created thing rather than the Creator. We are wading into quicksand when we begin to look to another person for what God should be in our lives.

In a helpful booklet (available from Exodus International) called *Emotional Dependency: A Threat to Close Friendships,* Lori Thorkelson says, "Whether or not physical involvement exists, sin enters the picture when a friendship becomes a dependent relationship." In a healthy friendship, we desire to see our friend reach her potential—it is a giving friendship in which we build her up, encourage her to reach out to others, and find ways to serve God.

Though most of us may not feel tempted by homosexuality, I believe the evidence is strong that we are tempted by dependency. An emotionally dependent relationship produces bondage. If you have a best friend, do any of your feelings for her sound like the warning signs Thorkelson describes?

• experiences frequent jealousy, possessiveness, and a desire for exclusivism, viewing other people as a threat to the relationship
• prefers to spend time alone with this friend and becomes frustrated when this does not happen
• becomes irrationally angry or depressed when this friend withdraws slightly[11]

REFLECTION ⌛ 10. If the above statements are a description of an unhealthy friendship, how would you describe a healthy friendship?

_____

_____

_____

These signs were present in Rachel and Laura's friendship. The scene was set for a lesbian relationship. Rachel said,

I'll never forget the night. We'd been drinking, playing cards, feeling loose. At one point I looked up at Laura and we exchanged a penetrating look that ripped my heart. I felt the beauty of love and the pain of passion. I knew what was going to happen.

Rachel told me that after the first night she was physically intimate with Laura, she felt "so ashamed."

It was hard to face Laura the next day when we were both sober. We both apologized to the other and attributed it to being drunk out of our gourds. I wanted to believe it would never happen again, but on the other hand, I wanted it to.

So did Laura. John White writes, "Once I experience physical pleasure with a member of my own sex, I am more likely to want to experience it again. The more frequently I experience it, the more fixed the pattern will become."[12]

White also observes that liquor is a fairly common denominator in female homosexuality.[13] Because neither Rachel or Laura could face the stark reality of what they were doing, they used liquor as an excuse. They would party, drink, and become physically intimate.

Finally, however, we didn't need liquor to become intimate. The amazing thing is, I didn't believe we were practicing homosexuality. That, I knew instinctively, would be wrong. "How," I asked myself, "could anything this beautiful be wrong?" Orgasm was not the goal—I never experienced it or wanted to. Without it, our expression of love seemed purer, less selfish. "We aren't homosexuals," I told myself again and again. "We're just very special friends expressing our love."

Rachel's feelings soared from great happiness to soul-wrenching misery. "It wasn't just the fear of being discovered, but the innate knowledge that despite my rationalization, what we were doing was very, very wrong."

I find it interesting that Rachel knew, in her heart, that her behavior was wrong. She hadn't been taught that because she had grown up in a liberal church that didn't use the Bible frequently and taught that our God is a loving God who would never condemn anyone for anything. But God's Spirit was nudging Rachel, whispering danger. There's a solemn warning in the first chapter of Romans to those who are practicing homosexuality and ignoring the still, small voice of the Holy Spirit. In time, God gives them over to a depraved mind so that they actually become confused over what is right and what is wrong (Rom. 1:24-28). Rachel, as she has testified, was beginning to feel some of that confusion, but before God gave her over to a depraved mind, He shouted the truth to Laura.

> *We'd been drinking heavily one night, when suddenly Laura broke down, sobbing uncontrollably. She completely floored me by telling me that our relationship was going to result in eternal suffering in hell. I didn't know what to say. I was stunned.*

What Laura had never told Rachel was that as a junior high student at a youth retreat, she had committed her life to Christ. Rachel believes that it was the light of Christ burning in Laura, however dimly, that first attracted her to her.

> *She was so compassionate and caring. But I didn't know why. I had seen her with her Bible, and I thought it was kind of neat. But she hadn't talked to me about spiritual truths—until that night. Then she poured out her testimony and showed me the Scriptures.*

A KALEIDOSCOPE OF EMOTIONS

> *A kaleidoscope of emotions poured through me—the intense fear of losing Laura, the shame of sin, and the hope of deliverance. I knew she was serious about changing when she told me she had booked a flight to Sarasota over spring break. A strong Christian couple down there had offered to help her. She hoped, she told me weeping, "they will help me straighten out my life, because I can't do it myself."*

Laura went to Sarasota. Most Christian counselors would agree that she took the first two necessary steps for breaking her chains. She admitted that her homosexual lifestyle was sinful, and she sought counseling from mature Christians.

FOR PERSONAL
REFLECTION
ONLY

■ Do you have a sinful habit which has you in bondage? What can you learn from Rachel and Laura about the steps you need to take to break free?

_____

_____

_____

_____

In God's uncanny timing, Rachel had planned to spend her spring break at a journalism seminar in nearby Tampa. When Laura's Christian friends realized Rachel was so close, they invited her down for counsel as well. During that time, Rachel and Laura surrendered their lives fully to Christ: Rachel for the first time, and Laura in recommitment. Rachel said,

> *The day that I dropped to my knees, I promised Jesus that if He would deliver me from the mess I was in, I would turn around and glorify Him. Someday, I vowed, I would help others who were in the same bondage.*

The road to healing for Rachel and Laura was not without pain. They were not instantly delivered from their desire for each other. They stumbled and fell a few times, but there was no joy in the sin anymore.

DELIVERANCE

Counselors advised a time of separation, and they obeyed. Laura moved to another part of the country. Despite the initial pain of obedience, both longed for full deliverance. They longed for normal lives with husbands and children. During that time they kept in touch by letter and phone. Reflecting on those two years of physical separation, Rachel said:

> *There were times when I didn't think I'd get over Laura. There were times I thought I might fall into it with someone else. But, slowly, as I chose to obey, I knew God was doing a work in my heart. In time, the overwhelming feelings I had for Laura, I learned to have in an uplifting way for Christ.*

Both Rachel and Laura are now happily married, serving the Lord, and good friends. Rachel is keeping her promise and working with other women who are in the bondage of lesbianism. She said:

> *If they've lived in this lifestyle a long time, their chains are tight. They also have to deal with tremendous pressure from their partner and from the gay community not to change. That's why a move can be so helpful. I want to give these women hope. Christ can break chains if you are determined to obey. I now know that our friendship became unbalanced when we began to look to each other for the fulfillment of our lives. Every day, I need to choose to keep Christ as the first and foremost focus of my life. I believe any relationship, even that between a husband and a wife, is in the danger zone when they look to each other for the completion they should have in Christ.*

REFLECTION

11. Do you agree with Rachel's statement that "any relationship, even that between a husband and a wife, is in the danger zone when they look to each other for the completion they should have in Christ"? Why or why not?

_____

_____

_____

_____

A. What is the difference between cherishing people and being dependent on them?

_____

_____

_____

_____

B. As you look at your own spiritual life, how are you tracking? Are you making progress? Or are you stagnating, failing to have meaningful quiet times, and failing to respond to the Spirit's prompting? (This question is designed to help you examine whether or not Christ is first in your life. If you are stagnating, ask the group or an individual whom you respect in the group to give you some insight as to how to get out of your rut.)

_____

_____

_____

_____

In her book, *The Long Road To Love*,[14] Darleen Bogle tells of spending seventeen years in the gay culture before deliverance. As she hardened her heart to the Spirit's prompting, she fell into other kinds of sin: occult practices, stealing, and even murder. Her deliverance included deliverance from demon possession. It is a frightening thing to turn your back on God. It is important to respond to His first promptings and not to harden our hearts. So though you may not identify with homosexuality, if you seen in yourself a tendency to lean on another person for your fulfillment in life rather than God, it is important to recognize this as sin and to turn from it.[15]

SCRIPTURAL
REFLECTION

12. Read Romans 1:18-32.

    A. How has God made His divine nature and eternal power clear to people?

_____

_____

_____

    B. What was the first stage of unbelief? (v. 21) What key error did the people make? (v. 25)

_____

_____

_____

    C. Do you have a tendency to worship people instead of God? If so, what warning do you find here?

_____

_____

_____

    D. Three times we are told "God gave them over" (vv. 24, 26, and 28). To what did God give them over in each instance? What other consequences of their behavior do you see in this passage?

_____

_____

_____

⧗ E. What is the last stage of unbelief? (v. 32) Do you see this happening in our society today? If so, how?

_____

_____

_____

_____

⧗ F. What, according to this passage, is the root sin of homosexuality? What, therefore, should a person wanting deliverance do?

_____

_____

_____

_____

NOTE: One woman who has been delivered from a lesbian relationship called me to thank me for Rachel's story and its role in helping her. She told me:

> I always realized that practice of homosexuality was sin, but I didn't know how to be delivered. Your book helped me to see the root problem was dependency—we had transferred our dependency from God to each other. In order to stay delivered, I must keep my first love.

13. Read Jeremiah 17:5-9. How does the prophet contrast the person who trusts in people with the person who trusts in God?

_____

_____

_____

_____

NOTE: A pattern we can see in the lives of godly friends in Scripture is that they *cherished* their friends, but they were *dependent* on God.

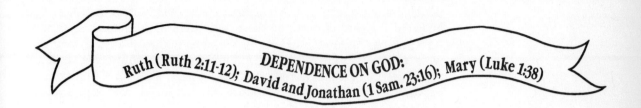

DEPENDENCE ON GOD:
Ruth (Ruth 2:11-12); David and Jonathan (1 Sam. 23:16); Mary (Luke 1:38)

When a woman depends on people for her security rather than God,
she may be more prone to fall into the following pits.

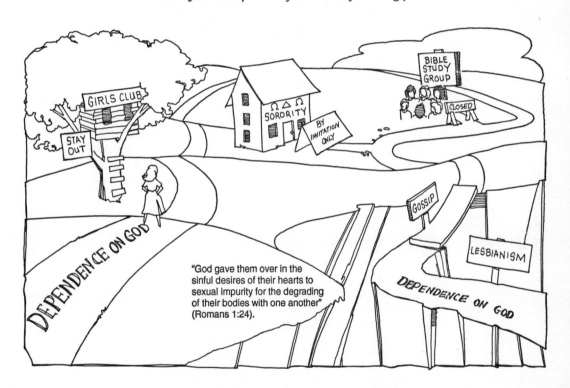

14. If time permits, look up the above passages and share how they
each demonstrate dependence upon God.

WOMEN'S TENDENCY TOWARD DEPENDENCY

Colette Dowling, in her book *The Cinderella Complex*,[17] makes a
convincing case for the theory that women are reared for
dependency. We are more likely than men to fall into dangerously

dependent relationships with either sex. This may stem from insecurity. Ms. Dowling points out that parents protect their daughters more than their sons; expect their daughters to marry and be cared for; and discourage their daughters more than their sons from taking the kinds of risks that lead to maturity. Peg, a young woman whose husband left her, felt great anxiety about being thrust into the role of a single mother. She worried about her ability to handle the checkbook, the insurance, the tax forms, and especially, about establishing a career. Peg told me:

Despite what I've been through, I realize that I'm still raising my daughter with the thought that I want her to marry a man who will protect her. I need to shake myself because that may not happen—it may not even be God's will. To be a good mother to Jamie, I need to help her prepare for a career as well as the possibility of marriage and motherhood. I need to teach her that her security is in God, and not in a relationship with a man. I hope God does bless her with marriage, but I'm doing her a great injustice if I assume that will be her future.

As I've been considering this whole issue of feminine dependency, I have been observing our daughter and her friend Tricia. They are practically joined at the hip. As I am writing this it is summer, and the two have seldom been apart. They zip their sleeping bags together, share their popsicles, and even, when pressed, borrow each other's underwear and toothbrushes. When they are separated, I sense Sally's anxiety. They have told me they will absolutely die if they don't get in the same fifth grade.

Pondering their friendship, I ask, "Do you think you are dependent on each other?"

"What does *dependent* mean?" Tricia asks.

Searching quickly for a simple synonym, I say, "Do you think you need each other?"

In unison they chime, "YES!"

Seeing my perturbed pause, Sally questions, "Is that bad?"

"Well," I respond, "we should be dependent on Jesus."

"Can't I be dependent on Jesus *and* Tricia?" my daughter asks.

I consider this. (I, who recently told my extremely capable tax-form-filler-outer, smoke-alarm-putter-upper, sliver-remover husband that if anything happened to him I hoped a total-care nursing home would accept a forty-two-year-old woman with her three children, contemplate this.) Finally I tell Sally, who is waiting expectantly:

I think we both have some growing up to do. It's important to love our friends, to cherish them, and to be committed to them. Girls and women are good at that—and it's a beautiful side to our friendships. But we need to learn to be dependent, leaning on God, because He's the only one who will never betray us or die or move away.

Sally looks at me quizzically. She cannot imagine any of those things happening to destroy her friendship with Tricia. I too, though no longer a child, am seeing this truth as through a glass darkly. But God has been maturing me through pain in my own friendships and providing more light through my study of Naomi. Look with me now at this woman who is so much like most of us.

WINDING DOWN

■ If time permits, close by having each woman share one thing which she has learned from the discussion of this chapter.

GROUP PRAYER

 ■ Write down an area of concern in your life for which you would like your sisters in Christ to pray. Make it personal! What is it?

_____

_____

_____

Close in prayer, either using popcorn prayer (see page 33), or praying in twos.

NEXT WEEK'S ASSIGNMENT

■ When you get home, while the group experience is still fresh, complete the journaling assignment in this chapter.

■ Work through the next chapter and the exercises.

PERSONAL JOURNAL

■ What did God impress on your heart as a result of the group discussion and prayer?

_____

_____

■ How is God leading you to apply what you've learned?

_____

_____

Chapter 4
Cinderella in the Change of Life

PERSONAL PRAYER

Quiet your heart before God. Before you begin to read and journal, become aware of God's presence! Today:

■ Read 1 Peter 2:9-10 and thank God for some of the ways your life is different because of Him.

■ Be still before the Lord and ask Him how you could better live up to the high calling for your life described in this passage.

■ Ask Him to teach you through the story of Naomi. (This might be a good time to divide this chapter into five quiet times for the coming week.)

GROUP PRAYER

■ Before you begin to discuss together, quiet your hearts before God. Have one woman open in prayer, asking God for His help in understanding and applying the lesson and in the exchange of secret sisters! (Ask someone who is comfortable praying out loud.)

WARMING UP

■ Exchange "secret sisters": Pass a hat and ask women to put their name in. Then pass it again to draw a name out. For the next month, they'll secretly:

• Pray for this woman;
• Send her notes of encouragement;
• Give her small gifts (homemade pie, a book, wildflowers, etc.).

At the end of the month, you will reveal your secret sisters.

How can embracing this fantasy stunt your growth as a single woman? A married woman?

REFLECTION

Remember! If you are a Time-conscious group, discuss only those questions marked ⌛ throughout.

⌛ 1. Have you ever, or are you now, embracing the philosophy that one day Prince Charming will come and make all things right?

_____

_____

⌛ 2. What problems does the above perspective bring to the single woman? To the married woman?

_____

_____

⌛ 3. Read the Book of Ruth. Try to put yourself in the shoes of the women and imagine their feelings. What were some of your first impressions of Naomi and Ruth?

_____

_____

But Naomi said, "Return home, my daughters. Why would you come with me?" (Ruth 1:11)

IT TAKES MATURITY to realize that Cinderella is a fairy tale. Many a woman holds to the hope that someday her prince will come and sweep her onto his white horse, carry her off into the sunset, and make all things right. Like Cinderella, she will never grow old, or fat, or go through menopause.

She imagines life with her husband always at her side, meeting her every desire. She will never be divorced or widowed. And she will never need anyone else in her life—no ugly (or lovely) stepsisters. Prince Charming will certainly be enough.

If you believe that, you are headed for disappointment. If you never marry, you will blame your lack of fulfillment on your single status. If you do marry, your expectations will put undue stress on your marriage, for no man can possibly meet all of a woman's needs for friendship, stability, and spiritual encouragement. That is a fairy tale.

But it's a lovely fairy tale, and a difficult one to release. It's easier to see that Rachel was wrong in making another woman the total focus of her life than to look at Naomi and say she was wrong to make a man the total focus of her life. Yet learning to trust in Christ alone is one of the lessons God longs to impress on all our hearts.

Another lesson we can learn from Naomi's story is that God may choose to meet our needs, not through a man, but through a woman friend. For those of us who have been raised on Cinderella, this may be a new thought.

In the first chapter of Ruth we are allowed to step right in on a heart-wrenching parting scene between Naomi, the Jewish mother-in-law, and Ruth and Orpah, the Gentile daughters-in-law. After a ten-year absence, Naomi is attempting to return to her home in Bethlehem and leave Ruth and Orpah behind in their pagan country of Moab. Naomi has had it with Moab, for while living there, both her husband and her sons died. She is broken and angry with God and will not allow Him to minister to her through Ruth and Orpah. She tells them, "Go back to your mother's home." But they cling to her, weep aloud, and say, "We will go back with you to your people" (Ruth 1:10).

Naomi refuses their pleas. Weeping, Orpah turns around and heads back to Moab. But Ruth is steadfast. She commits her whole life to her mother-in-law and to her mother-in-law's God. She is going with Naomi to Bethlehem. Naomi seems unappreciative: Why?

Let's open God's family album and look at Naomi.

SCRIPTURAL REFLECTION

4. Read Ruth 1:1-11.

⧗ A. List some of the difficulties in Naomi's life.

_____

_____

⌛ B. Despite the fact that Naomi's daughters-in-law didn't share her faith, she seemed to have a good relationship with them. Give evidence for this. What do you learn from this?

_____

_____

_____

⌛ C. What do you think makes a good mother-in-law?

_____

_____

NOTE: I would warn any future mother-in-law that if she wants to continue to see her son after his marriage, she would be wise to love and embrace his wife. So if you have reservations, ask God to help you past them. Your first meeting with your future daughter-in-law is likely to remain etched in her memory—for she is so anxious to know how you feel about her. If she senses lukewarmness, she isn't going to be eager to visit—and believe me, she holds a powerful influence over your son. Reject her and you won't see much of him.

⌛ D. What do you think makes a good daughter-in-law?

_____

_____

⌛ E. How do you think a mother should respond if her child marries an unbeliever? Why?

_____

_____

_____

NOTE: Though we have warned our children from the time they were little not to marry unbelievers, if they do, Naomi has shown us how we must respond. We will love them—hopefully, right into the Kingdom.

⏳ F. If Ruth and Orpah came with Naomi to Bethlehem, where they would be surrounded by believers, there would be a good chance they might be influenced to come into a relationship with the one true God. Yet Naomi tries to send them back to idol-worshiping Moab. What reason does she give? What does this tell you about Naomi?

_____

_____

5. Read Ruth 1:11-13 and 1:20-21.

⏳ A. How does Naomi feel about God? Comment on her reaction.

_____

_____

⏳ B. If you are hurting and angry with God, do you think it is best to hide it? Explain.

_____

_____

_____

Psychiatrists Paul Meier and Frank Minirth stress the importance of allowing ourselves to grieve. They mention that sometimes Christians will not allow themselves to grieve because they think that grieving may hurt their testimony. However, they believe that grieving actually strengthens our testimony—because unbelievers see that we are genuine and honest (Minnirth/Meyer Clinic Radio Broadcast 3/22/94). Notice that Ruth commits herself to Naomi's God during the time when she is listening to Naomi express her anger at God!

6. Learning to trust in Christ alone is one of the lessons God longs to impress on our hearts. If the props were knocked out from under your life—as they were for Job when he lost his loved ones, his wealth, and his health—how do you think you would respond?

Why?

_____

_____

_____

In *Disappointment with God*, Philip Yancy interviews a man whom he calls a modern-day Job. Among other tragedies, Douglas had been hit and disabled by a drunk driver. Yet Douglas said he didn't blame God. He said he didn't confuse the unfairness of life with God—and he believed that God was grieved and angry over his tragedies too. Yancy concludes by looking at the Cross and saying: "At once, the Cross revealed what kind of world we have and what kind of God we have: a World of gross unfairness, a God of sacrificial love" (Philip Yancy, *Disappointment with God*, Zondervan, 1988, p. 186.).

7. Comment on the above.

_____

_____

_____

"GOD, THIS ISN'T FAIR"

An intriguing aspect of the Book of Ruth is the prophetic meaning of the individuals' names. Each eventually rings true.

Naomi's name means "sweet" or "pleasant," but after going through the grief of losing first her husband and then her two sons, she felt her name to be cruelly ironical. I cannot imagine a greater pain than that of the death of your husband and children. I empathize when Naomi cries, "Don't call me Naomi [sweet] . . . . Call me Mara [bitter] because the Almighty has made my life very bitter . . . . Why call me Naomi? The Lord has afflicted me; the Almighty has brought misfortune upon me" (Ruth 1:20-21).

I applaud her honesty, and I cannot be too judgmental of her despair and anger. Expressing her pain not only helped her to grieve, but it let Ruth understand Naomi's deep need for a steadfast friend.

Luci Shaw, my dear friend and favorite of poets, was widowed in midlife. Like Naomi, Luci was in pain. You could see it in her eyes. She described being widowed as "radical surgery—like being cut in half." Luci's reaction to pain was a model to me. She says:

I'm learning to welcome pain, and not to dodge it. It's one of the most valuable of lessons. Pain has a refining work to do in us, if we welcome it. It teaches us what is temporal, what is superficial, and what is abiding and deep. I'm trying to let pain do its work in me.[1]

REFLECTION

For In-depth Groups Only

8. Luci Shaw says that pain can teach us what is temporal, what is superficial, and what is abiding and deep. Similarly, Paul, after describing his persecutions, writes:

These little troubles (which are really so transitory) are winning for us a permanent, glorious and solid reward out of all proportion to our pain. For we are looking all the time not at the visible things but at the invisible. The visible things are transitory: it is the invisible things that are really permanent (2 Cor. 4:17, PH).

A. If the worst that you can imagine happened to you on earth (perhaps the loss of a child, or an injury which resulted in paralysis), how would your thinking be different from that of someone who does not know Christ?

_____

_____

B. Has pain in your life taught you what is transitory and what is permanent and important? If so, give an example and explain.

_____

_____

_____

Luci lived in a wooded suburb of Chicago. We walked together in her front yard and looked at the place where a large oak tree had stood. Her poetic mind, like that of our Lord's, often sees parabolic significance in the earthly, lifting it to the transcendent. A week or so after her husband had died, the tree, ridden with disease, had to be toppled. In her freshly widowed pain, Luci had seen parallels between the screaming power saws and her husband's cancer, between the white-hot fire that burned the debris and stump for two days and his death. Finally, she herself identified with the black-rimmed ashen hole that was left like a wound in the frozen sod. As we stood there, silently, I recalled words she'd written in an article:

I was the frozen sod with the deep wound, and Harold was my tree who was simply . . . gone. Vanished. How unreal it seemed that his roots, that had for over thirty years penetrated deep into my life, that had anchored us, joined us so solidly and securely, were being eroded by the fire of decay. The space above ground that for so long had been filled with his vertical strength and solidity and shape was empty; air had rushed in where, before, the towering trunk had outbranched to leaves.

Now I lie in wait for spring, for the tissue of earth and the skin of sod—the beauty of green instead of the grey ashes of a spent fire—to fill in and heal over the naked scar. And it will. It will.

But the oak tree stands strong and thriving and leafy in my memory, and no one can cut it down.[2]

GRIEVING AS ONE WHO HAS HOPE

Although there are the dissonant sounds of pain in the words of both Luci and Naomi, with Luci there is an underlying steady beat of hope in God's sovereignty and unfailing love. There is no doubt that this is a time of darkness and pain, but Luci is holding firmly to God's unchanging grace and promises. She has planted a sapling where the oak once stood, a symbol of hope, of the resurrection, of her husband's new life.

Luci is also allowing friends, men and women, to fill the lonely corners of her life as a widow. Whereas Naomi wanted to be left alone and seemingly failed to appreciate her women friends, Luci is reaching out, especially, she says, "in this time of adjustment." In support of this conviction, Luci showed me her calendar, dotted with time for friends. "It doesn't take much time to go out for breakfast," she commented. "It doesn't interfere with one's work schedule. I need to make time for that contact. I would feel much more bereft without my friends."

In times of grief, we are apt to hear dark voices—voices that tell us we are no longer people of value, beloved by God. If we withdraw from friends, a common response to depression, then those voices have no competition. We need to be with compassionate women who will come alongside us and show us that we are lovable human beings, precious in God's sight and in their sight. If our friends don't come to be with us, we must take the initiative to ask for their company. Luci does this. She and Karen Mains are good friends. Luci said:

I'll call Karen, and say, "Do you feel like going to a matinee?" and she'll say, "Oh, I've been writing all weekend! Let's go see The Trip to Bountiful." That does wonders for me. It takes my mind off myself and in the company of a friend we can see a meaningful movie.

Research by Daniel Levinson of Yale indicates that difficult times in life, such as midlife or the loss of a mate, are more successfully negotiated by those who have strong same-sex friendships. That is why women seem to cope better than men with the loss of a spouse. Dr. Beth Hess says, "There is a strong hypothesis that friends help women survive. Part of women's ability to sustain themselves in older years depends on their capacity for constructing a network of friends.[4]

Luci Shaw is also close to Madeleine L'Engle, brought together not only by an editorial relationship, but by many other bonds. Luci said, "I feel a sister to Madeleine in so many ways." I wrote to Madeleine L'Engle, asking her to reflect on her friendship with Luci. She responded:

> *As an only child I depend on and rejoice in the sistership of many friends, such as Luci Shaw. The sisterhood of my friends involves an understanding that our Creator is good, and that our lives have meaning; also a loving forbearance of our humanness. Luci and I share much in our love of words as our expression of our love of the Word. And we have shared the illnesses and deaths of our lives' companions, and discovered God's grace and joy in the midst of pain.*

Luci invited Madeleine to come and spend a few days with her in her West Chicago home while they worked together on the editing of Madeleine L'Engle's book *A Stone for a Pillow*. Despite the inevitable conflicts between editor and author, despite the struggles that each were facing in their personal lives, both found great stimulation, camaraderie, and comfort in their multi-leveled relationship. Luci smiled as she remembered how Madeleine had closed a day-long editorial session. "When we were all done, Madeleine said, 'Now we shall rise and sing, "Praise God from Whom All Blessings Flow." ' And we did."

LEARNING TO VALUE WOMEN AS MUCH AS MEN

If Naomi had valued her two daughters-in-law, Ruth and Orpah, this difficult adjustment period could have been softened. Naomi never expected to be left without men. If we, like Naomi, allow our sense of security and self-esteem to be based on Prince Charming's constant presence, then we are headed for trouble. Singles who embrace this fairy tale will miss the happy and fulfilled life God desires for them. Married women who embrace this fairy tale will eventually become bitter, since widowhood, for those wives who don't divorce, is a statistical probability. According to 1983 U.S. census statistics, widows outnumber widowers five to one.[5]

It could be that Naomi's rejection of Ruth and Orpah was not based so much on her feelings for them, but on her feelings about herself. Obviously there was a time when Naomi was lovely and endeared these young women to herself, or she couldn't be eliciting the kind of response we see from them in this opening parting scene. But now, without men in her life, she feels empty and worthless. In fact, that is the very word she uses when she arrives in Bethlehem and her old friends rush out to meet her. She says, "I went away full, but the Lord has brought me back empty" (Ruth 1:21). Empty! How that must have hurt Ruth! The women of Bethlehem could see that Naomi hadn't come back empty. And as the days progressed, they could see what Naomi failed to see: that God had provided her with a real friend in Ruth. For Ruth was helpful and kind and good to her mother-in-law. There's a gentle rebuke at the end of the book when the women of Bethlehem tell Naomi, "Your daughter-in-law . . . loves you and . . . is better to you than seven sons" (Ruth 4:15). In a talk given in June 1986, Pastor John Bronson of Denver commented, "I wonder if Naomi shed a tear and blushed with shame to realize that God's blessing for her had been at her side from the very beginning."

Peg's husband left her for another woman when their daughter was a baby. Peg said:

> *For years I prayed for a father for Jamie. I felt so alone in raising her—I wanted someone with whom I could share not only my parenting problems, but also my joys! Recently it has occurred to me that although God has not given me a man, He has answered my prayer for Jamie, in a sense, in my dear girlfriend. Gay loves Jamie as if she were her own. She's terribly interested in all the little details of her life. And it is Gay to whom I go with my concerns and joys about Jamie.*

God may choose to meet our needs through women, but if we value them less than men, we may not see it. There is still a tendency today to value men over women. And that was even truer in Ruth's day, for every woman belonged to some man as wife, daughter, or slave.[6] When Naomi lost her men, she also lost her social standing. Yet when Ruth lost her man, she did not lose her sense of worth or her hope, because that was in God. Ruth was ahead of her time—and ours!

In an article on the Book of Ruth, Jane Titterington writes,

> *We need to be reminded that our value as human beings is something bestowed on us by God regardless of our marital status. Placing an inordinate value on the man-woman relation-ship tends to produce a rather warped view of humanity. . . . We see men as prey and other women as pawns to be used or rivals to be competed against in this game.[7]*

Although there have been some negative things in the women's movement, one positive effect is that women are beginning to truly value each other. One woman shared:

> *All through college I had friends, mostly in my sorority. Girlfriends were basically to pass the time until I had a real relationship, I thought. . . . It's only now I realize how happy just being with girlfriends made me and how much support they gave me through awful times, like trying to diet off twenty pounds, when they cheered each ounce I lost, or the time two of them stayed up all night with me, helping to type a paper. But there wasn't a time I wouldn't break a date with a friend if I got a chance to go out with a guy. . . . Only recently did I realize how important one special friend was in my life. Her name was Marlene and we roomed together my junior year. It was my happiest year of college, but I never credited Marlene for being the reason. . . . Women friends count. I thank the women's movement for teaching me that.[8]*

Another woman can uniquely empathize with feminine circumstances. (I nearly punched a male doctor who leaned over me when I was in labor and said patronizingly, "Aw, c'mon, it doesn't really hurt that much.") Jane Titterington says, "Just as the hand needs the eye, it also needs the other hand."[9]

SCRIPTURAL REFLECTION

9. Read Ruth 1:11-13. Naomi cannot imagine why her daughters-in-law would want to come with her. Explain why she feels worthless.

_____

_____

10. Read 1 Peter 2:9. On what should our worth be based?

_____

_____

11. How might have Naomi's attitude been different had she based her worth on God's Word instead of society's standards?

_____

_____

NOTE: In many cultures, men seem to have more value than women. In China, for example, where families are limited to one child, many couples give their daughters up for adoption and then try again—for a son! Likewise, in many cultures married persons seem to have more value than single persons. Many singles would tell you that they feel this prejudice even in the church.

12. Read the following passages and contrast these cultural views with Scripture's view of women and singles.

A. Galatians 3:28

_____

_____

B. 1 Corinthians 7:25-35

_____

_____

REFLECTION

13. Do you value women as highly as men? Singles as highly as marrieds? If you said "yes" give evidence from your life. If you said "no," what could you do to change so that your heart and your life are more in keeping with God's view?

_____

_____

_____

14. Do you think you've ever missed God's blessing for you because you failed to appreciate a person He put in your life? If so, how could you reduce your chances of repeating this mistake?

_____

_____

ELIMELECH: PRINCE LESS-THAN-CHARMING?

I believe that having a man was so important to Naomi that she was willing to choose Prince Less-Than-Charming rather than no man at all. Let me build my case.

As the Book of Ruth opens, we are told "in the days when the judges ruled," a famine was in Bethlehem (whose name means "the house of bread"). A famine in the promised land? God had promised His people rain, grain, new wine and oil in exchange for obedience (Deut. 11:13-15). But obedience was lacking and the Jews were living as described in the Book of Judges: "every man did as he saw fit" (Jud. 21:25). The response to the famine that God was looking for from His people was repentance, but Elimelech instead moved his wife Naomi and their two sons to idol-worshiping Moab. A reading of Numbers 25 will show you how depraved were the people of Moab. So a move from Bethlehem to Moab was no ordinary move. Commentator Roy Hession sees it as a departure from the Lord.[10] It was a little like moving from a hard-pressed farm in Iowa to Casino Row in Las Vegas in hopes of striking it rich in the midst of immoral-ity. The real gamble in a move like that is in keeping your teenagers morally pure.

It is possible that Elimelech seemed godly when Naomi married him but later, in adversity, revealed the shallowness of his roots. Or it could be that Naomi chose a poor catch over remaining single.

When I was at Northwestern University, I had a sorority sister whom I will call Jill. Jill was experiencing "senior panic." She had not found a man. To her great relief, during the spring, a man began dating her seriously. The only problem was that she didn't really like him. Nevertheless, they became engaged. I remember the astonish-ment I felt when Jill came back to my room after talking to her fiancé on the phone. She flopped on the bed and moaned, "Oh Dee, I just hate the sound of his voice. It's whiny, nasal, and effeminate." And yet, she married him.

And Naomi married Elimelech. Elimelech died as soon as they got to Moab. It's at least possible that this was God's judgment on Elimelech for taking his family to this detestable land. Certainly his family reaped the bitter fruit of his decision.

THE FRUIT OF UNWISE CHOICES

After their father's death, the two sons married Moabite women, who worshiped idols. Pastor John Bronson comments:

> If we watch television shows that repeatedly lift up the values of the world, what do we expect our children to be like? . . . If we conduct our lives in the privacy of our own homes without reference to God, what do we expect our children to be like? Who did Elimelech and Naomi expect their sons would marry—the rocks and trees?

After Elimelech's death, did Naomi try to persuade her boys not to marry Moabite women who worshiped idols? Or did she believe that it would be better for them to marry unbelievers than to remain single? Marriage was terribly important to Naomi, as we will continue to see. And many Christian women have chosen marriage to an unbeliever over remaining single because, like Naomi, their security is not based upon their relationship to the Lord but upon marriage. One young woman, engaged to an unbeliever, said, "I know Tom isn't a Christian, but I believe God is blessing us. I think Tom will come to Christ." Friends tried to warn her that God's Spirit doesn't go contrary to His Word, but her mind was set. Twenty years later, their home is still divided, their children are divided, and their future looks grim. I know it has been known to work the other way, but it still frightens me to see people fly in the face of God's clear command not to be unequally yoked.

Steve and I have tried diligently to impress our children with the importance of marrying believers, if they marry. We were pleased to see that point had been staked down when a visitor for dinner asked our then five-year-old son, J.R., what his parents had taught him. Quickly he responded, "I must never marry somebody who doesn't love Jesus and I must never ride a motorcycle." (Steve has spent many hospital nights, often in vain, trying to rescue injured motorcyclists.) We laughed at hearing those two warnings placed side by side, but we actually have been most serious in our hope that J.R. will never endanger his life by doing either of those two things.

I believe Naomi's sons, Mahlon and Kilion, endangered their lives by marrying unbelieving women. The Targum, an ancient commentary written a short time before the Christian era, says that these brothers had their "days cut off because they transgressed the decree of the Lord"[11] in marrying foreign women who worshiped idols. (See Deuteronomy 7:3-4 and Ezra 9:10-14.) This should sober us if we have a tendency to take God's commands lightly. The meaning of each of the son's names reveals that God knew their destiny: *Mahlon* means "infirmity" and *Kilion* means "finished."

REFLECTION

15. Why might a Christian woman marry an unbeliever or a weak believer?

_____

_____

16. Sometimes God will give me an opportunity to dissuade a friend away from an unwise choice, such as divorce, or abortion, or marriage to an unbeliever. If I give them Scriptures, or tell them that their choice is wrong, I seem to meet with increased resistance. However, if I gently share with them what I think their lives will be like if they make that choice, sometimes I have gained a listening ear. If you were to attempt to tell a young person why

she shouldn't marry (or perhaps date) an unbeliever, what would you tell her?

_____

_____

⧗ 17. If you are single and have determined in your heart that, if you marry, it will only be to a strong believer, what steps could you take to make sure you hold to that high standard?

_____

_____

MENOPAUSE

I believe another factor magnified Naomi's sense of worthlessness. My calculations put her in the change of life. (She would have been close to forty when both sons were of marrying age, and close to fifty after they had been married ten years.) Menopause usually occurs between forty-five and fifty-five years of age.

Not only her age but her words give support to the theory that Naomi was menopausal. She tells Ruth and Orpah, in effect, that she is an "empty bag" with very little hope for conceiving more children. "I am too old! It's too late for me!"

This must have been particularly devastating to Naomi, whose only natural children had died. But Naomi wouldn't allow her women friends to comfort her. Instead she tried to send them away. "What I need," she must have thought, "is men—a husband and sons—not women!"

Menopause also, doctors tell us, can make your emotions run rampant. The symptoms can be similar to those of premenstrual syndrome. In Hans Christian Andersen's fairy tale "The Snow Queen," there is a "horrid mirror in which all good and great things were magnified and every flaw became very apparent."[12] That is often how I feel during premenstrual days. I sympathize with Naomi.

Dr. James Dobson describes how menopause changed his mother from a joyful, peaceful woman to a woman who was extremely irritable and depressed for weeks at a time. Six physicians told her the problem was psychological. Yet when she began receiving estrogen treatments, her condition changed. We need help from the medical community, and we need understanding from each other. We must believe the best about each other and realize that a friend's irritability may be a reaction to the chemistry in her body. One of the menopausal symptoms Dr. Dobson lists is "extremely low self-esteem, bringing feelings of utter worthlessness and disinterest in living."[13] This is how Naomi sounds when she calls herself "empty" and "without hope."

How much insight did Ruth and Orpah have into Naomi's behavior? It's intriguing to see how much they loved her in the face of her unloveliness. There must have been a time when Naomi was like her name, sweet and pleasant, loving Ruth and Orpah as if they were her own. They are determined to go with her to Bethlehem: willing to leave their own homes, people, and country just to be with Naomi! They do not intend to part from Naomi. It is Naomi who creates the parting scene.

REFLECTION

For In-Depth Groups Only
18. Understanding ourselves and our friends.

A. Do you become irritable on the days before your menstrual period? If so, have you found some ways to cope with this?

_____

_____

B. Have you ever told a friend or family member to give you extra understanding because of PMS? If so, has it been helpful? Explain.

_____

_____

C. Have you ever had a friend or family member tell you that they think your attitude is due to PMS? If so, was that helpful? Explain.

_____

_____

_____

NOTE: When giving a retreat on the friendships of women, I spoke on Naomi and mentioned that she might have been menopausal, which could have augmented her grief. Afterwards a woman came up to me who had lost her only two sons in a motorcycle accident. She said "I don't think you understand what it's like to lose your children. Naomi wasn't desperate because of menopause." Sobered, I decided I'd been insensitive, seemingly making light of Naomi's grief.

I know it makes me angry when someone infers that my irritability is due to PMS. Even if they are partially right, I feel as if they're dismissing my pain.

    D. What responses do you find helpful when you are feeling irritable? Why?

_____

_____

THE PARTING SCENE
Firmly she turns to Ruth and Orpah and says:

> *Go back, each of you, to your mother's home. May the Lord show kindness to you, as you have shown to your dead and to me. May the Lord grant that each of you will find rest in the home of another husband* (Ruth 1:8-9).

Her words must have felt like sword thrusts to her daughters-in-law. If Naomi didn't know how much they loved her before, you would think she would see it now. Ruth and Orpah were experiencing intense emotional pain. Those of us who have moved or watched a best friend move to another city or state can empathize with these women. At least we can comfort each other with promises to write, call, or visit. In 1100 B.C. there would be little hope of that. There were no trains, planes, or post offices. This was a permanent good-bye.

Orpah and Ruth cling to Naomi. She kisses them and they weep aloud, persisting: "We will go back with you to your people" (Ruth 1:10).

But again, Naomi repeats her argument, this time elaborating. The highest priority in life to Naomi is marriage, and she thinks that their chances of remarriage are going to be better in Moab than in Bethlehem. She's probably right, but what Naomi has lost sight of is that their chances of remaining in idol worship are also better in Moab than in Bethlehem. Depressed and within herself, confused by the Cinderella Syndrome, Naomi does not have an eternal view of the situation. So she sends them back.

ORPAH, THE WOMAN WHO GOES BACK
Naomi had the opportunity to make an eternal difference in Orpah's life, but because of bitterness, she blew it.

Oprah Winfrey, the television talk-show hostess, was named after

Orpah, though her parents misspelled the name. They must have simply liked the name, for why would you name a daughter after the woman who goes back? Though Orpah was a kind woman, she was unsteady, and a weaker woman, spiritually, than Ruth. Her name is close to the Hebrew word *oreph* which means "the back of the neck," "stiff-necked," or "double-minded." It would be unmerciful, however, to be too critical of Orpah. She is freshly widowed and the woman whom she loves most seems determined to leave her behind. Pastor John Bronson says that when Naomi persisted with, "GO BACK!" Orpah may have thought, "Yeah, maybe I will."

When we are being hurt or rejected, it is difficult to see beyond our own pain to the pain of the person inflicting the injury. Orpah's reaction was natural.

Ruth's reaction was supernatural.

REFLECTION

19. Symbolically, Orpah's choice is an age-old one: between following the Lord or staying in the land of idol worship. Joshua put it like this:

> *Now fear the Lord and serve Him with all faithfulness. Throw away the gods your forefathers worshiped beyond the River and in Egypt, and serve the Lord. But if serving the Lord seems undesirable to you, then choose for yourselves this day whom you will serve, whether the gods your forefathers served beyond the River, or the gods of the Amorites, in whose land you are living. But as for me and my household, we will serve the Lord* (Joshua 24:15).

A. What are some of the reasons serving the Lord might seem undesirable to people in general? To Orpah? To you?

_____

_____

B. Why do you think people choose to serve the Lord? If you have, why did you?

_____

_____

_____

WINDING DOWN

■ If time permits, close by having each woman share one thing which she has learned from the discussion of this chapter.

GROUP PRAYER

■ Write down an area of concern in your life for which you would like your sisters in Christ to pray. Make it personal! What is it?

_____

_____

Pray, using popcorn prayer or by pairing off.

NEXT WEEK'S ASSIGNMENT

■ When you get home, while the group experience is still fresh, complete the journaling assignment in this chapter.

■ Write a note to your secret sister or make a surprise delivery of food or a small gift. (Get an accomplice to deliver it!)

■ Work through the next chapter and the exercises.

PERSONAL JOURNAL

■ What did God impress on your heart as a result of the group discussion and prayer?

_____

_____

■ How is God leading you to apply what you've learned?

_____

_____

Chapter 5
Binding Up the Brokenhearted

PERSONAL PRAYER

Quiet your heart before God. Before you begin to read and journal, become aware of God's presence!

- Sing a song about God's mercy toward us, such as "Great Is Thy Faithfulness" or "Thy Lovingkindness."

- Intercede on behalf of a brokenhearted person in your life.

- Ask God to teach you something from this study. (This might be a good time to divide this chapter into five quiet times for the coming week.)

GROUP PRAYER

- Before you begin to discuss together, quiet your hearts before God. Using popcorn prayer, ask several to share sentence prayers for your time together sharing the lesson.

WARMING UP

Remember! If you are a Time-concious group, discuss only those questions marked ⧗ throughout.

1. Did your secret sister do anything for you last week that you would like to share?

_____

_____

2. Can you think of a time when you were hurting and a friend comforted you? Briefly describe your hurt and precisely what the friend did that was helpful.

_____

_____

Entreat me not to leave thee, or to return from following after thee: for whither thou goest, I will go; and where thou lodgest, I will lodge: thy people shall be my people, and thy God my God. Where thou diest, will I die, and there will I be buried: the Lord do so to me, and more also, if ought but death part thee and me (Ruth 1:16-17, KJV).

I GLADLY CLAIM Ruth as a member of my sex. When Naomi was rejecting her, Ruth faced her squarely and said the words quoted above, which have touched the souls of Christians and non-Christians alike. She makes six promises, and then to convince Naomi she is serious, she calls God's wrath upon her if she doesn't keep them. The loveliness and the gravity of these vows take my breath away. Vows made not, as the composers of wedding music would have us believe, by a bride to her groom, but by one woman to another. What a model of feminine friendship! Ruth shows us the height of which we, as believing women, are capable, for God uses Ruth like a good medicine to restore an ailing Naomi.

In response to these vows, Naomi does not throw her arms around Ruth and weep tears of gratitude. Instead, as we have already seen, Naomi is silent. What is she thinking? We find out when she and Ruth arrive in Bethlehem and friends rush out, asking, "Can this be Naomi?" (It's only been ten years, but bitterness has changed her appearance dramatically.)

"Don't call me Naomi. . . . Call me Mara, because the Almighty has made my life very bitter. I went away full, but the Lord has brought me back empty" (Ruth 1:20-21). (*Empty!* And Ruth is right at her side.)

If I had been Ruth, I would have been tempted to forget about my promises and turn around and go back to Moab where I might be more appreciated. But Ruth overlooks Naomi's words and gives her unfailing love, like that of the Lord.

Do you see the fierce tension between Ruth and Naomi? John Bronson described it beautifully in one sermon I heard:

Naomi says: "Go back!"
Ruth says: "I will come."
Naomi says: "I have no hope!"
Ruth says: "My destiny is joined to yours."
Naomi says: "I am not pleasant. I am bitter."
Ruth says: "I choose you, Naomi."

Then, at the very time that Naomi is testifying against her God, Ruth commits herself to that God. Bronson continued:

> *Naomi says: "My God has witnessed against me and His hand has gone out against me."*
> *Ruth says: "My God is your God."*

How was Ruth able to overcome Naomi's rejection and stay at her side? And how did Ruth know Naomi's God was trustworthy when Naomi was testifying against Him?

I believe we witness here an intertwining of a woman's gift of intuition with Holy Spirit power.

RUTH'S INTUITION AND THE HOLY SPIRIT'S POWER

Had Ruth been thinking only with her left brain, she might have come to the seemingly logical conclusion that Naomi didn't need her or want her. Had Ruth more androgen hormones, she might have responded to Naomi's attack with attack. But Ruth reads between the lines, somehow coming to the correct conclusion that she should not leave Naomi. She stays calm and steadfast in her purpose. How fitting that *Ruth* means "a woman friend"!

SCRIPTURAL
REFLECTION

⧗ 3. Read Ruth 1:11-22.

⧗ A. Try to put yourself in the shoes of each of the following women: Naomi, Orpah, and Ruth. What do you think each was feeling? Why is there so much emotion in each case?

_____

_____

_____

⧗ B. List the promises that Ruth makes to Naomi in verses 16-17. Why do you think Ruth is making promises of such magnitude?

_____

_____

_____

_____

⌛ C. Describe Naomi's response to Ruth's commitment. Why do you think she doesn't throw her arms around Ruth and say, "Thank God for a friend like you in my time of need"?

_____

_____

⌛ D. Think about a time when you went out of your way to extend kindness to someone and he or she didn't seem to appreciate it. What were some of your feelings?

_____

_____

⌛ E. Why do you think Ruth was able to continue to be loving and kind to Naomi after receiving so little affirmation?

_____

_____

⌛ F. Broken-hearted people are often like wounded animals, thrashing out at anyone who comes near. Those who are hurt, hurt others. Have you ever hurt someone, not because you were angry with that person, but because you were wounded yourself? What can you learn from this about binding up the brokenhearted?

_____

_____

Ruth also seemed to know intuitively, despite her mother-in-law's negative testimony, that the God of Israel was trustworthy. And God responded to Ruth's mustard seed of faith by flooding her with Holy Spirit power.

Paul was able to say, "Follow my example, as I follow the example of Christ" (1 Cor. 11:1). Ruth could legitimately say the same to women who wish to use their gift for friendship to bless the world in a redemptive way. Let's consider how we can bind up the brokenhearted by following in Ruth's steps.

FRIENDS IN GRIEF NEED EMPATHY

Author Paula D'Arcy began keeping a diary during her pregnancy. She wrote "letters" to her baby, telling the child about all the wonderful feelings she was having in anticipating the birth. When Sarah was born, Paula continued her diary, recording the joy she and her husband, Roy, found in their daughter. When Sarah was two, the family was coming home from a holiday and was hit head-on by a drunk driver. Roy and Sarah died in the hospital. The following letter from Paula's diary was written about a month after the tragedy.

September, 1975

Dear Sarah: I can't be polite to one more visitor. No one would like me if they knew what I really was thinking when they say how lucky I am that I wasn't badly injured. That I lived. The person I used to be would have understood their intentions. . . .
But today I can't pass off the words. This new person doesn't have energy left to do anything but stay alive and not scream. I don't want to hear anyone else's awkward attempts. They make me angrier than I already am.[1]

Paul exhorts us to "carry each other's burdens" (Gal. 6:2). The word he uses for burdens refers to the temporary "overburden" that a sister may be carrying, as distinct from the "everyday load" he refers to in Galatians 6:5. When we are temporarily overburdened due to the stress of death, divorce, illness, and so on, we definitely need the supportive help of our sisters. We need someone to come alongside and help shoulder the overburden.

The best way to do that is by empathizing, weeping with those who weep. Your quiet and listening presence will help absorb some of the pain and relieve some of the burden. If we attempt to deny the burden by pointing out blessings, we add to the pain. Solomon clarifies this with similes: "Like one who takes away a garment on a cold day, or like vinegar poured on soda, is one who sings songs to a heavy heart" (Prov. 25:20). Too much cheerfulness or the offering of solutions intensifies grief.

Women are usually better at empathizing than men. Women's feeling-oriented right brains overcome the left-brain response of coming up with solutions. "It's OK to hurt; it's OK to grieve," the right brain says.

During a discussion in our Sunday School class on marriage, wife after wife lamented that men's natural response to problems seemed to be to jump in and find solutions rather than provide comfort: "I don't want to hear how I could avoid this kind of pain in the future. I want to hear that he cares I'm hurting!" "I don't want any solutions. No advice. I want him to hold me tenderly and be quiet!"

I told the class that as a newlywed I had to teach Steve to put his arms around me and say simply, "Poor Dee Dee!" At this they laughed uproariously, and now the men tell us that when their wives are upset, they do exactly as I suggested. One man went so far as to say that he doesn't even say, "Poor Marsi!" to his wife, using her name, but "Poor Dee Dee!"

A study of 15,000 women by *Family Circle* in 1986 found that 69% of women would rather talk to their best friends when they're feeling unhappy than to their spouses.[2] An interesting study on listening skills found that women are much more empathetic listeners. The sympathetic responses like "umhmmm," and "go on" were recorded, and women far outdistanced men.[3] Most people who have been through a crisis find it therapeutic to go over and over the details. They need a listening, caring presence.

Elaina's husband left her and their daughter to pursue a gay lifestyle. Reflectively, Elaina said:

> *After my divorce, I really felt like I'd been given a bum rap. If I hadn't had my women friends to pour out my heart to, I'd have killed myself. I was so caught up in my misery, I never asked them one question about themselves. I know I wasn't fun as a friend then—but they stood by me. I was a real drain, but they saw me through the long haul.*

SCRIPTURAL REFLECTION

4. Scripture talks about two different kinds of loads. One is an "everyday" load (Greek word: *phortion*) as mentioned in Galatians 6:5: "Each one should carry his own load." One example of an everyday load would be the responsibility of putting your dirty clothes in the hamper.

   A. Give some other examples of everyday loads.

   _____

   B. Another kind of load is actually an "abundance, or an over-burden" (Greek word: *baros*) referred to in Galatians 6:2: "Carry each other's burdens." One example of an overburden would be the stress a single parent feels in raising a child alone. Give some other examples of overburdens.

   _____

   _____

   C. How can understanding the difference between these two loads give you discernment as to when it is wise to help someone and when it is unwise?

   _____

_____

_____

D. Proverbs 25:20 compares singing songs to a heavy heart to taking a friend's coat on a cold day. Give some examples of singing songs to a heavy heart.

_____

_____

_____

E. Why does this increase pain?

_____

_____

_____

Often, people who are left-brained want to "fix the problem." Therefore, they offer solutions. This is how God has wired many men and some women. This is good in some situations, and disastrous in others. On the other hand, people who are right-brained or think globally tend to be more empathetic. This is good in some situations, and disastrous in others.

SCRIPTURAL REFLECTION

5. Solomon tells us there "is a time to tear and a time to mend, a time to be silent and a time to speak" (Ecc. 3:7).

A. When is it the time to be silent, to cry with a friend? When isn't it? Why?

_____

_____

B. When is it the time to offer solutions or constructive criticisms? When isn't it? Why?

_____

_____

DON'T CRITICIZE THE PERSON IN DESPAIR

Not only did Naomi fail to appreciate Ruth, she neglected her. It was dangerous for a foreign woman to glean in the fields, and Naomi should have steered Ruth toward the safer field of their near kinsman, Boaz. But Naomi was so overburdened, so immobilized by depression, that she wasn't thinking of Ruth's needs.

Yet during this whole time, not one critical word flows from Ruth's mouth. Not one. Wisely she realizes there is a time to speak and a time to be silent, and high-tide grief is often the time to be silent. Ruth simply comes alongside Naomi and quietly shoulders part of her burden. Naomi didn't need more judgment, but instead desperately needed to experience the goodness of the Lord, and Ruth made that possible through her obedience and trust in Him.

BE PATIENT

How long do we carry an overburden for another? As long as necessary. Emily, whose teenage daughter drowned three years ago, said:

> I'm better now—I'm not thinking of Amy every waking moment. There are even days when I don't cry. But I still need a lot of support. Sometimes my mother will say, "It's time now to get past this." I can't take that. I understand she says that because it hurts her to see me hurting. But I still need Mom to simply open her arms and hold me.

I asked author Joe Bayly, who was acquainted with grief through the loss of three children, about a young friend of mine who had been widowed two years previous: "Is it time to tell her to stop grieving?" Eyes full of compassion, he shook his head. "Give her the time she needs."

One of the reasons I am eager for a person to get past her grief is that I am weary of helping her carry her burden. Perhaps that is why Paul tells us a few sentences after telling us to bear one another's burdens, "Let us not become weary in doing good, for at the proper time we will reap a harvest if we do not give up" (Gal. 6:9).

We should stay alongside until we see restoration. The first glimmer of restoration occurs in Naomi when Ruth returns from the field of Boaz, arms overflowing with grain. Naomi brightens and asks, "Where did you glean today? Where did you work? Blessed be the man who took notice of you!" (Ruth 2:19)

When Ruth tells Naomi that she'd been in the field of Boaz, Naomi realizes for the first time in a long time that her God has not forgotten her. According to levirate law, Boaz has a responsibility toward them. In order to carry on the name of a married man who died childless, this law called for a near kinsman to marry the widow and raise up a child in his late kinsman's name. Naomi realizes that God was involved in leading Ruth to the field of Boaz. With tears in her eyes, Naomi gives God the glory: "The Lord has not stopped showing His kindness to the living and the dead." She adds, "That man is our close relative; he is one of our kinsman-redeemers" (Ruth 2:20).

SCRIPTURAL REFLECTION

6. Read Ruth 2:1-16.

   A. What are some ways you see Ruth being a steadfast friend to Naomi?

   _____

   _____

   B. What are some ways you see God blessing Ruth?

   _____

   _____

   C. What kind of impression is Ruth making in Bethlehem?

   _____

   _____

7. Read Deuteronomy 25:5-6. Describe the law in this passage and how it might relate to Naomi and Ruth.

   _____

   _____

   _____

8. Read Ruth 2:17-23.

   A. Describe Naomi's response to God's blessing upon Ruth.

   _____

   _____

   _____

B. What change do you see occurring in Naomi? Why do you think it is happening?

_____

_____

⧗ C. What can you learn from Ruth about binding up the broken-hearted which you could apply to your own life?

_____

_____

HURTING PEOPLE MAY NOT ASK FOR HELP

Most of us are extremely reluctant to ask for help. And when we're injured (emotionally or physically), we tend to send people away when we need them the most! Like a man hanging to the edge of a precipice by his fingernails, we refuse the outstretched hand and say, "That's OK—I think I can make it."

Lynn waited all night for news of her boyfriend, Craig, who was the pilot of a missing emergency medical helicopter. When search teams found the wreckage and Lynn's worst fears were confirmed, she headed to the telephone and called her best friend, Susy. "Do you want me to come?" Susy asked. Lynn said,

> *I told her, "It's not necessary—I'll be OK." Susy lived so far away; I didn't want to inconvenience her. I didn't realize how desperately I would need her when the shock wore off. Thank God she came.*
>
> *. . . I also told my friend Deb to go on home after the helicopter was reported missing. She had worked a long shift and I hated to make her stay—I knew it could be a long, long time. But she stayed all night. She was with me in the morning, when they told me they found the bodies. She cried with me and held me. I'll never forget that.*

I asked Lynn what she thought a person should do if a good friend tells her not to come during a time like this.

Lynn said, "If she's a good friend—GO!"

If we are the ones who are hurting, we should remember that those who truly love us *want* to help bear our burdens. Though it's hard to admit we need help, we need to learn to do it. Luci Shaw told me about a week in the year following her husband's death when she was very ill with the flu:

I was all alone in the house that week—my temperature soared to 103 degrees and I was drifting in and out of reality. I was so weak that I was really afraid of walking downstairs to get a ginger ale. I thought, "If I fall and break my leg, then I'll really be in trouble."

Luci finally decided to call her good friend Karen Mains (author and cohost of the Chapel of the Air radio broadcast) from her bedside phone and ask her to stop at a store and bring her something to drink. "I knew she was busy, *loaded*—she had five broadcasts to do that week! But I also knew that there was a supermarket near where she worked and my home was near hers, so it wouldn't take too much of her time."

Luci called and Karen wasn't there. Luci dared to persist by leaving a message explaining her predicament. She smiled as she remembered Karen's response:

She breezed in and took over. She gave me popsicles and Gatorade, took my temperature, and gave me a cool rubdown. And you know, it made her feel contented and happy that a friend would feel free to call her. When friends are close we don't need to fear to ask for help. If we could just realize that!

We need to overcome our reluctance in asking people to help us bear our temporary overburdens. And we need to be discerning, like Ruth, and realize that a friend may really need us despite her protestations otherwise.

Sometimes a friend in need doesn't ask for support because severe depression has immobilized her. Chris, mother of three, has battled with clinical depression for years. "I can't relate to people during those times because I don't even understand what is going on in my own head. But friends sustain me through cards, letters, and flowers—letting me know that they care about me when I don't care about myself."

THE MULTIPLIED BURDEN OF GRIEF AND SHAME

When a woman loses a husband to death, the Christian community is better at coming alongside than when she loses a husband to divorce. Likewise, if a woman has a child who is desperately ill, her friends are there; but if she has a child who is involved with drinking or drugs, there really isn't the same support. We're hesitant to bring up the subject for fear of making our friend feel worse, but ironically, our silence may be misinterpreted as an accusation. We need to learn to say enough to show empathy and an open door if the person would like to talk or pray with us. There isn't one of us who couldn't be in their shoes, and we need to let them know that.

Sharon, a godly woman whose son has just been given a prison sentence, hugged me hard when I said, "I hear you're going through a rough time."

She said, "Oh, Dee, most people don't say anything."

When Adele's husband, who had been a pastor of a conservative church, became involved with another woman, Adele said that their Christian friends seemed to disappear from their lives. Adele said:

> *I needed my friends so badly when Jim moved out, but they weren't really there. I wasn't able to ask them to come and spend time with me, for it's extremely difficult for a hurting person to verbalize a need for help. After the divorce was final, people would tell me, "When I knew there was a problem, I wanted to come to see you, but I didn't know what to say. So I didn't come." And my heart cried out within me, "Oh, if only you had just come!"*

When her husband left her, Adele's value as a person had been attacked. I asked Adele what kinds of things she would have asked for, had she been able—and she gave me a list! So that we can better reach out to our friends, this deserves posting on the refrigerator.

- *Contact the person often. Call. If you don't know what to say, ask, "How is your day going?" Write a note showing you care. Stop by. (I felt so isolated. I kept the cards people sent on my piano. Looking at them strengthened me to face the day.)*

- *Invite them to share a normal activity with you: a walk, a sporting event, an errand, a meal.*

- *Sit with them in church. They feel unworthy to join you. Don't let them sit there alone.*

- *Touch them, hug them. (I am hungry for touch. I miss the physical touch of one who cares.)*

- *Identify with their feelings. Don't be afraid to mention the other party by name. (A friend of mine saw me cutting the lawn and asked, "Did Jim used to cut the lawn?" Just mentioning him made me feel freer to talk to her.)*

- *Pray with them. And daily pray for them! Put their name on your mirror so you don't forget!*

FOR PERSONAL REFLECTION ONLY

■ Is there someone in your life who is going through high-tide grief?

_____

_____

■ Is there someone in your life who is carrying the multiplied burden of shame and grief?

_____

_____

ACTION ASSIGNMENT

■ Ask the Lord to show you to whom you should minister and what you should do. It can be simple—as the above list demonstrates. Then do something today! Be ready to share with the group what you did. (It might not be appropriate, however, to share names.) Record your plan and results below.

Plan:

_____

_____

Results:

_____

_____

A TIME TO SPEAK

Solomon tells us there is a time to be silent and a time to speak (Ecc. 3:7). All through this chapter I've been encouraging you to exercise your feminine gift for empathy, and I've stressed that the person in grief doesn't need solutions or confrontation, but your empathizing presence.

But there are times when we must speak up. If we make the mistake of quietly empathizing when we should be alerting our friend to danger, we may actually be holding her hand as she walks toward the cliff. I was convicted by an observation Christian counselor Jay Adams makes in *Competent to Counsel*. He says that too often when a friend makes a comment like, "I guess I haven't been much of a mother or a wife," we respond by minimizing her confession. We'll say, "Don't talk like that Susie; you know you haven't been that bad." I've done this—even if I know Susie is a terrible wife or mother! This is a destructive use of my feminine gift for empathy.

Adams says it would be much more productive to say, "Well now, that's a serious matter before God; how have you failed as a wife?"[4]

Likewise, I'm sure Satan is pleased when we fail to speak up and expose his deception when we suspect a friend is considering divorce, an abortion, an affair, or marriage to an unbeliever.

Galatians 6:1 tells us, "Brothers, if someone is caught in a sin, you who are spiritual should restore him gently." How can you confront gently? By helping her discover how this sin will hurt her. Christian psychiatrist Louis McBurney finds that when dealing with those considering divorce, taking "a hard-line, frontal assault with Scripture verses flying only increases defensiveness and resistance."[5] He has better results when he examines the world's view that divorce is a "quick relief." Gently he shows them that "after the initial relief, most people face a period of grief for a year or more."[6] Only a small percentage of individuals, ten years later, are glad they divorced. Sometimes caring questions can help the person begin to think more realistically about the effect of her choice: "If you go ahead with this divorce, what do you think your life will be like financially? If you have this abortion, what kind of thoughts do you think you will have about this baby in years to come? If you marry Joe (an unbeliever), will you go to church alone?" Gently steer her toward a realistic view of the long-term consequences of her choice.[7]

If you are close to the person and have all the facts (unfortunately, it is often acquaintances who confront and close friends who stay mum), then God may very well be calling you to go, in a spirit of gentleness, and help your friend see what could be the consequences of her sin.

We should confront when we think it might save our friend from disaster. But sometimes it's too late for confrontation. The damage has been done: the marriage vows have been spoken; the divorce is final; the abortion has been committed; the money has been gambled away in the commodities. In a play entitled *A Raisin in the Sun*, there's a scene I'll never forget. Walter has lost all of the family's savings, savings that were going to make this black family's dream come true. Now this dream has dried up like "a raisin in the sun." Beneatha is so disgusted with her brother that she says, "There ain't nuthin left to love."

In a climactic, emotion-filled moment, Mama puts her hands on her daughter's shoulders, looks her directly in the eyes, and says:

> *"Child, when do you think is the time to love somebody the most; when they done good and made things easy for everybody? Well, then, you ain't through learning—because that ain't the time at*

all. It's when he's at his lowest and can't believe in hisself 'cause the world done whipped him so."[8]

REFLECTION

9. Can you think of a time in your life when you let someone down and yet received forgiveness and love in return? If so, share something about it.

_____

_____

_____

FOR PERSONAL REFLECTION ONLY

■ Is there someone in your life who is letting you down? How do you think God would have you respond to him or her? Why?

_____

_____

_____

Ruth is a model to me, not just in the way she restored Naomi, but in another important way. This characteristic of Ruth, which I deal with in the next chapter, will show you how to make a friend and develop friendships of depth.

Walter Wangerin, author of *The Book of the Dun Cow*, told Margaret Smith, "You like to jump into a friendship and not start at the beginning but in the middle." She said, "That's exactly right!" And I agree. Who wants to go through the boring preliminaries? If I can avoid them, I will! And Ruth is showing me how.

WINDING DOWN

■ If time permits, close by having each woman share one thing which she has learned from the discussion of this chapter.

GROUP PRAYER

■ Write down an area of concern in your life for which you would like your sisters in Christ to pray. Make it personal! What is it?

_____

_____

_____

Pray, using popcorn prayer or praying in twos.

NEXT WEEK'S ASSIGNMENT

■ When you get home, while the group experience is still fresh, complete the journaling assignment in this chapter.

■ Pray for your secret sister!

■ Work through the next chapter and the exercises.

PERSONAL JOURNAL

■ What did God impress on your heart as a result of the group discussion and prayer?

_____

_____

■ How is God leading you to apply what you've learned?

_____

_____

Chapter 6
The Risk of Love

PERSONAL PRAYER

Quiet your heart before God. Before you begin to read and journal, become aware of God's presence! Use the anacronym of ACTS:

- **Adoration:** Praise the Lord for taking the risk of love toward you. Sing a praise song about His love.
- **Confession:** Confess and turn from anything that He brings to mind which is not pleasing to Him.
- **Thanksgiving:** Thank Him for some recent blessings in your life.
- **Supplication:** Ask Him for the desires of your heart that you feel are within His will. Ask God to teach you something from this study. (This might be a good time to divide this chapter into five quiet times for the coming week.)

GROUP PRAYER

- Before you begin to discuss together, quiet your hearts before God. Ask one woman who is comfortable praying out loud to open in prayer and ask God to teach you from this lesson.

WARMING UP

Remember! If you are a Time-concious group, discuss only those questions marked ⧖ throughout.
1. Write down what you'd be willing to share from each of the following rooms of your life.

⧖ A. Some of the things that are going on in the "front hall" of my

SHAME IN
THE PAST

SELFISH-
NESS

G
R
E
E
D

*Bonding and growth can take place if we will allow a trusted friend
past the "front hall" of our life and all the way back
to the secrets we keep in our "closets."*

life which I'd readily share with almost anyone are:

_____

⧗ B. Some of the things that are going on in the "living room" of my
life which I would be willing to ask prayer for from sisters in
Christ are:

_____

_____

⧗ C. Something that is going on in the "closet" of my life which I
would share only with someone I trust enormously is:

_____

_____

NOTE: You will not be asked to share your final answer in the group—but you will be encouraged to consider sharing it with a trusted friend sometime!)

2. Describe a risk you've taken in friendship which you are glad you took.

_____

_____

_____

_____

_____

The risk of love
is that of being unreturned.

For if I love too deep,
too hard, too long
and you love me little
or you love
me not at all
then is my treasure given,
gone,
flown away lonely.

But if you give me back
passion for my passion,
return my burning,
add your own
dark fire to flame my heart
then is love perfect
hot, round, augmented,
whole, endless, infinite,
and it is fear
that flies.

Luci Shaw[1]

INTIMACY IS RISKY. No doubt about it. If I reach out to a woman to whom I am drawn, she may reject me. If I tell a woman that I love her, that I cherish her as a friend, she may respond little (or not at all). If I open my soul to another, trusting her with my dark side of failure, she may draw back in shocked silence (or she may tell others). If I, out of the overflow of my heart, promise another unfailing love until the day I die, then I have bound myself before God (and I bring upon myself His wrath if I break my vow). Risky. Risky. Risky.

Then why do it? Why set ourselves up for hurt? Why not play it safe, as most men do? Because daring to take risks, as Ruth did, ignites the flame for bonding. In Sunday School many of us were told, "Dare to be a Daniel!" Perhaps we should be telling girls, "Risk being a Ruth!"

REFLECTION

⧗ 3. How do you feel when a friend makes herself vulnerable to you?

_____

_____

_____

4. Do you hold friends at arm's length? Or do you make yourself vulnerable? Why do you think you are the way you are?

_____

_____

RISK REACHING OUT

There was a time when a newcomer to the neighborhood was heralded as a joyous event. Those nearby embraced them with visits, gifts of food, and genuine interest. Not so today.

In Vance Packard's book, *A Nation of Strangers,* a woman from Darien, Connecticut describes what most of us as transplants have experienced: "No one on the lane of some twenty-two families phoned or called to welcome us to the community. We have been here a year and have only a nodding acquaintance with the neighbors—and not all of them."[2]

Kathleen said, "The first two months after moving from Texas, my phone bill to friends back home was astronomical. I figured I'd write it off as a medical deduction!"

I identify with Kathleen. In 1970 when we moved from Seattle to a suburb of Portland, Oregon, I too felt the anxiety of being separated from my women friends. It didn't help that it rained, steadily, for the first three weeks. (I was beginning to have great empathy for Noah!) No cheery neighbor braved the rain with a plateful of chocolate chip cookies. The gloom outside my window augmented the gloom in my spirit. If I wanted a friend, I was going to have to take the initiative.

I began to plead unrelentingly with the Lord for a local sister in

Christ who could be my friend. (And I have found that when my prayers are in earnest, then I am much more alert for the Lord's response.)

Knowing that group Bible study is usually a good source for friends, I decided to try Bible Study Fellowship, a national interdenominational organization. Portland's group happened to be meeting in a large church in our suburb.

On Tuesday morning I drove up to the church in a downpour. I was astounded by the number of cars. Every space in the huge parking lot was taken, as were any available spaces on the streets near the church. I parked three blocks away and ran sloshing through the puddles, trying to hurry yet avoid the earthworms that had crawled out for air.

I walked through the double doors to hear the singing already in progress, acutely aware that I was late. The sanctuary was packed to overflowing with women. Somehow the camaraderie of the crowd made me feel lonelier than ever.

I was going to slip into one of the chairs set up at the back for latecomers when a beautiful woman in the center section, front pew, caught my eye. She had the clean look that blonds without bangs have, her long, platinum hair pulled back in a neat, thick braid. *Why do I feel so drawn to her?* I wondered. *Is it simply because she is so attractive? Or is it possible that the Holy Spirit is drawing my attention to her? Is she the friend for whom I've been praying?*

If God was leading me, I was going to have to walk in my wet and bedraggled state in front of everyone in order to sit next to her. All the way down the aisle. Risky. Maybe crazy. But so intense was my need for a friend that I did it.

She looked up from her hymnal, startled by my presence.

(She looked so sophisticated—so dry!) But she smiled reassuringly, moved over to give me room, and shared her hymnal. I felt hopeful until the singing and the lecture ended and she left, without a word, to go to her small group. I stayed with a handful of newcomers to get my instructions. We filled out some forms and then were dismissed early, being told we would be assigned to regular small groups the next week. No one spoke to me personally. I went home, feeling lonelier than before I came.

I did risk going back however. I didn't see the tall, cool blond until we divided into our small groups. I was assigned to room 101, the room for those whose last names began with letters *Br* through *Ca*. When I walked in, I was surprised to see her, seated at a round table with nine other women. (I wondered, *Providence or coincidence?*) Her name was Pam Carlson. When she saw me, her face didn't register recognition. (I do look different, however, when I'm not dripping wet.)

Reserved, Pam spoke only once during the whole hour, but then with an earnestness and insightfulness that stilled the room. She was an intent listener, leaning forward in her chair, looking directly into the eyes of whomever was speaking. At one point, when a description of the crucifixion was read from Scripture, her eyes filled with tears. I felt coldhearted in comparison. Pam hadn't lost her first love. Again, I felt drawn to her. Again, I determined to risk reaching out to her.

After the study, Pam swept up her books and darted out the door. Determined, I charged after her. I fell into step with her in the church parking lot. I told her I appreciated the comment she'd made. (I was hoping she'd realize this was an overture of friendship.) But instead our conversation took a nosedive as she said, "Thank you! See you next week!" and ran toward her car, leaving me standing alone, slightly embarrassed.

I chastised myself: *You're behaving foolishly. God is not leading and Pam is not interested in being your friend.* I decided to abandon my wild goose chase while I still had dignity. (Had I been familiar with Ruth's persistence in the face of rejection, I might have been stronger.) But just as I was about to give up, God intervened.

Steve and I had tried four different churches during our first month in Oregon. None of them seemed right for us. That Sunday we decided to visit a small church in the country. When we walked in the door, Pam saw me before I saw her. She and her husband were the official greeters. "Dee!" she called out to me. I turned, surprised that anyone would know my name. When I saw her I had the sensation you have when you realize the pieces are fitting together and you *know* God is answering prayer. Encouraged, I asked Pam if she could come over for coffee the next day. She smiled warmly and said, "I'd love to!"

With kindred spirits, with a friendship given to you by God, it *is* possible to jump in at the "middle of a friendship." You can begin with personal issues right away. Before I had even poured coffee for Pam, she asked me, "How did you come to Christ?" She was an active listener, prodding me with questions. Then she told me her story.

On a lark, Pam had gone with some women from work to a Billy Graham crusade. On the way home, her friends were laughing, ridiculing Dr. Graham. Pam alone was silent, thinking seriously about the reality of Jesus Christ. The Holy Spirit was at work. Compelled, Pam went back the next night and gave her life to Christ. Her sincerity was evidenced by the fact that she and her husband were taking in troubled teenage foster boys, eager to share the overflow of love they'd both found in Christ. I was impressed and encouraged by her lifestyle of obedience.

Pam risked opening herself up to me, telling me of her struggle to live simply. "I *love* nice things—and they have a giant grip on my mind and heart." We talked about how we thought a Christian *should* live, if she's not being squeezed into the world's mold. Then Pam broke the intensity of our discussion and sent us into gales of laughter by commenting, "I'm so glad I got my antiques before I was saved!"

Pam and I were finishing the other's sentences, eager to press on to the height of our thoughts. Author Randolph Bourne said, "One comes from friends . . . with a high sense of elation and the brimming adequacy of life . . . the keen thoughts, the trains of arguments, the pregnant thoughts that spring so spontaneously to mind."[3]

God knew how Pam and I would mesh, how we could sharpen each other, and He had given us the gift of friendship. We both thrilled in discovering it.

Since my experience with Pam early on in my Christian walk, I have been more willing to risk reaching out to someone to whom I am drawn. Even if she is not initially responsive, if I think the Lord may be leading, I will risk again.

REFLECTION

5. Risks

   A. In Luci Shaw's poem "The Risk of Love" on page 121, what are the dangers of taking risks? The possible gains?

_____

_____

   B. Dee described the risks she took in reaching out to a friend after she had moved to Oregon. What were some of those risks?

_____

_____

   C. Why do you think Pam was not initially responsive to Dee? How might you discern when to persist in reaching out to someone and when to give up?

_____

_____

_____

One way to take risks is by taking the initiative in talking to someone, or inviting them over. Another way to take risks is by being alert to a person's needs and finding ways to minister to her, whether it is a kind word or a kind deed. Boaz did both of these things when he met Ruth. And Ruth says, "Thou hast spoken friendly unto thy handmaid." The word "friendly" comes from the Hebrew word meaning the inner person, the inner set of emotions. In other words, Boaz spoke and ministered to Ruth's deepest needs.

SCRIPTURAL REFLECTION

⏳ 6. Read Ruth 2:11-16. List all the ways Boaz risked being kind or "friendly" to Ruth.

_____

_____

⏳ 7. What are some ways people have risked ministering to your inner self, your deepest needs, with kind words or deeds? How did it make you feel about that person?

_____

_____

ON-THE-SPOT ACTION ASSIGNMENT

For In-depth Groups Only

■ Take some risks and speak to one another's inner person, saying some things you've thought but have never articulated. This exercise might go something like this:

Leader: Let's minister to Sue's inner person.

Amy: Sue, I want you to know how much you are missed when you can't be here. When I come and realize you aren't coming, I think: "I miss Sue!"

Beth: I feel that way too. It's like there's a big hole when you're gone.

Anne: And we want you to know we know this is a stressful time because of your dad's illness—and we remember to pray for him when you aren't here.

Group: Yes!

Jo: On a lighter note, something I've never risked telling you, Sue, is that I think you have gorgeous skin!

Group: Laughter. Agreement.

Pause

Leader: Let's minister to Amy's inner person.

START IN THE MIDDLE

There's an art to skipping the superficial and beginning a friendship in the middle, and it's tied to asking questions. Pam and I asked each other how we had come to Christ. Ruth asks, upon first meeting Boaz, "Why have I found such favor in your eyes that you notice me—a foreigner?" (Ruth 2:10) She's really asking him why he is drawn to her—an amazingly open and searching question—and Boaz, in responding, intimately affirms her.

I've found that with a new acquaintance or an old friend our conversation goes much deeper, faster, if I ask, "What concerns have been on your heart lately?" Or, "What have you been thinking about lately?" rather than, "How are you?" With a friend who is a believer, we'll often share our heart concerns and then pray together. And praying with a friend bonds you faster than anything I know.

One author suggests some wonderful questions to ask people about their vocations: "Tell me what it takes to do a job like yours with excellence. What are the great challenges a person faces? Where do you confront ethical and moral questions?"[4]

Karen and David Mains have introduced "The God Hunt" through their Chapel of the Air radio broadcast, and thousands are joining in. They suggest keeping a daily journal in which you record a sentence (just a sentence) describing how you've seen God in your life that day. It could be an obvious answer to prayer or timing that seems too perfect to be coincidence. By keeping a notebook and mentally walking through your day, you are going to "spy" God where you might have missed Him. Not only is this a tremendous encouragement spiritually, but it's a wonderful conversation starter with believing friends. You will bond together and sharpen each other in the Lord as you share the ways you've spied God in your life. Even if they are not familiar with the God hunt, you can ask them to share a time when they were very aware of God's presence, help, or timing. It works every time.

ON-THE-SPOT ACTION ASSIGNMENT	8. Go around, giving women the freedom to pass, and have each finish this sentence: "One way I have seen God working in my life recently is:_____ _____ _____."
ACTION ASSIGNMENT	■ Write down some probing questions you can ask at the next meal you will be sharing with family or friends. What will you ask? _____ _____ _____ _____

- After the meal, record any positive results. Share them with the group.

_____

_____

- Memorize Proverbs 20:5. Kay Arthur says that she memorizes a verse by saying it three times in the morning, three times at noon, and three times at night.

RISK MAKING YOURSELF VULNERABLE

When a friend does probe beneath the surface, make yourself vulnerable. My bonding with Pam was hastened by our willingness to strip away pretense. Ruth told her mother-in-law "everything" about her night with Boaz (Ruth 3:16). C.S. Lewis wrote, "Eros will have naked bodies; Friendship naked personalities."[5]

Women seem more willing to make themselves vulnerable than men. One semester my husband and I decided to abandon our team teaching of adult Sunday School and each lead a class with members of our own sex. Our reasoning was that people might feel freer to make themselves vulnerable when the opposite sex was absent. "It will be great," I assured my hesitant husband.

And my class *was* great. In three weeks the women were sharing openly, weeping, and hugging.

Steve's class, however, bombed. The men stayed on the surface, unwilling to talk about personal struggles or feelings. Steve no longer wants to teach a class that is exclusively male because, he has concluded, "a class needs women. Women are almost always the ones to risk saying what is really on their hearts. Once they begin, they act as a catalyst and there is genuine sharing from both sexes."

NOTE: Since the original release of *The Friendships of Women*, I have seen some encouraging changes among Christian men in America. Groups such as "Promise-Keepers" are encouraging men to risk making themselves vulnerable to one another, to pray together, and to hold one another accountable.

Our lack of inhibition in making ourselves vulnerable is one of the main reasons, I am convinced, that women have real friends. Ruth and Naomi might have stayed on an "in-law" basis had Ruth held Naomi at arm's length when asked about her night with Boaz. But instead, Ruth told her mother-in-law everything! Vulnerability hastens bonding. Charlotte explained it like this: "When a woman friend confides in me, I feel honored, esteemed that she would trust me so."

Jim, an executive from Milwaukee, told me that he thinks it is easier for women to make themselves vulnerable to each other because there will be reciprocation. Who wants to disrobe before someone who gawks judgmentally and refuses to disrobe himself?

Though we are better than men in being open, we're still too cautious with trusted friends. We have some stripping to do. Authors Ann and Jan Kiemel would tell you that though they were twins, and sisters in Christ as well, it took them many years to appreciate the value of making themselves vulnerable to each other. Ann admits that she had the mistaken idea that people wouldn't like her if she told them bad things about herself. Ann writes: "Jan started to be honest and vulnerable before I did. . . . As I watched her, I began to see that being vulnerable actually draws people to us, because the world is full of people . . . that are bleeding and hurting."[6]

Sometimes we are hesitant to risk vulnerability because we fear our listener might not keep our confidence. This can be a healthy fear. Ruth was open with Naomi because she trusted her. Solomon warns us: "A gossip betrays a confidence; so avoid a man who talks too much" (Prov. 20:19). A man or a woman who talks too much is less likely to be able to keep a rein on confidences. Author Gail MacDonald says, "I usually find if a person easily talks about other people in a negative way, I can assume she's going to do the same thing about me."[7] There are women, however, who can be trusted.

Vulnerability not only hastens bonding, it can embolden a hurting person to open a festering wound that needs to be opened. A godly woman told me, "Sometimes, when I am aware that it would be helpful to a friend to open up to me about a problem, but sense hesitancy, I'll lead the way by making myself vulnerable. I'll share where I am hurting or failing." This kind of risk-taking springs from a heart that is seeking the other's best, that is desiring to live a life pleasing to God.

REFLECTION

9. Facilitating Trust.

   A. Do people hear you talking negatively about other people?

   _____

   _____

   B. Are you trustworthy with confidences?

   _____

   _____

C. Might God use you to facilitate openness in a small group or with a friend by asking you to be the first to make yourself vulnerable? What might you be willing to share?

_____

_____

_____

D. Read James 5:16. What does God tell us to do in this verse? Why?

_____

_____

_____

_____

RISK FOLLOWING GOD'S LEADING

The most striking example of Ruth's risk taking occurs when Naomi proposes a daring plan to her daughter-in-law. First, Naomi tells Ruth to wash, perfume herself, and dress in her best clothes. (That's the easy part.) Then she is to take note of where Boaz sleeps—guarding the grain, on the threshing room floor. Under the cover of the black Bethlehem sky, unstained by modern city lights, Naomi tells Ruth to slip out, tiptoe up to the sleeping Boaz, uncover his feet, and lie down! Ruth's response? "I will do whatever you say" (Ruth 3:5).

I understood this strange plan better when I read that it was a custom for women in the East to approach their marriage bed from the bottom, lifting the covers and creeping up next to their husbands. This was a sign of modesty and submission.[8] (I am passing on this. It would jumble the cords of our electric blanket.) In light of this custom, Naomi's instructions to Ruth to lie at the bottom carried the symbolism of a request for marriage. But this was certainly a perilous plan. From his peaceful sleep on the threshing floor, Boaz *was* startled to sense the presence of another person. (The Hebrew indicates that he "quaked with terror.") I know how terrifying it can be to have someone suddenly appear at your bed in the middle of the night when your sleep is deepest. Early in our marriage, before Steve learned to identify himself clearly when coming into the bedroom after a late emergency call, I would startle from sleep and sit straight up, shrieking. It was not the greeting for which my husband was hoping!

If I were guarding precious grain from thieves, I expect I would have even less restraint. By doing what Naomi requested, Ruth was risking bodily harm, rape, and rejection. And yet Ruth was willing to risk her life in order to follow what she perceived as God's leading.

Boaz doesn't harm or reject her. Though startled, he looks before he leaps and asks, "Who are you?"

"I am your servant Ruth," she said. "Spread the corner of your garment over me, since you are a kinsman-redeemer" (Ruth 3:9). This was Ruth's way of saying, "Take me as your bride." In Eastern marriage ceremonies, it was a custom for a groom to throw the corner of his skirt over the bride as a sign of taking her under his protection. Boaz responds to Ruth's request with an echo of her own words to Naomi in Ruth 3:5, saying, "I will do for you all you ask" (Ruth 3:11).

There is, however, a problem. There's a nearer kinsman than Boaz! And Boaz, being a righteous man, believes they need to offer Ruth to him first. (Can you imagine Ruth's thoughts?) There's a lesson in this for young lovers, though. If God is in it, a relationship won't have to be forced. The nearer kinsman refused Ruth, and I'm sure Boaz thought, *Praise the Lord!*

And so, we have a wedding. At the festivities, the elders offer a lovely prayer for fertility and a famous name in Bethlehem. God answers this prayer by "enabling Ruth to conceive" and she gives birth to Obed, who becomes the grandfather of David, King of Israel. So Ruth, a Gentile of Moabite background, has her name listed in the genealogy of Jesus! (Matt. 1:5) God had said that no Moabite would enter the assembly of the Lord even down to the tenth generation (Deut. 23:3), but our Lord no longer sees Ruth as a Moabite. She is a new creation; her past has been wiped away.

Author and speaker Win Couchman asked me, "Don't you think Ruth has a merry spirit?" How true! Never does she protest, "Oh, not that—think of the possible consequences!" In leaving Moab, in following Naomi's plan, in allowing Boaz to offer her to an unknown nearer kinsman, she trusts God. Because she is persuaded that God is faithful, she risks everything over and over again. Consistent with her spirit, in the closing verses of the book, we see that Ruth has given her firstborn son, Obed, to Naomi! Ruth is not dependent on a man, a friend, or a child, but leans completely on God, and He is faithful, blessing her with His power and presence and with earthly friendships.

Ruth's model shows me that it is possible to have a very close friendship, even a best friend, and still be dependent on God. Perhaps Ruth passed this truth on to Obed, and he to Jesse, and he to David. For like his great-grandmother, David shows us how to be knit to a friend and yet be dependent on God alone.

RISK TAKING:
Ruth 1:16-17; 2:2; 3:5-6; 3:12-14; 3:16

SCRIPTURAL
REFLECTION

10. Read Ruth 3. (In your group, read aloud Ruth 3:9-12 and 16-18.)

⌛ A. Describe all the risks you find Ruth taking in this chapter. Describe also how Ruth is a model to us in each case.

_____

_____

_____

B. Boaz tells Ruth he has a responsibility to offer her to the nearer kinsman first, and she apparently does not object. What does this tell you about both Boaz and Ruth? What lesson is here for young lovers?

_____

_____

_____

_____

C. Likewise, there may be a time in your life when you have done everything you can to hold a soulmate friendship together, and yet it seems to be ending. What lesson might you learn from Ruth and Boaz for that circumstance?

_____

_____

_____

⧗ D. What do you learn from Ruth about being a good daughter-in-
law? If you are a daughter-in-law, do you see any application
for your life?

_____

_____

_____

11. Read Ruth 4.

A. What did the people of Bethlehem pray for Ruth and Boaz at
their wedding?

_____

B. How did God answer that prayer? What was remarkable about
this?

_____

C. Give an example from your life of when someone interceded
for you in prayer and you saw God answer.

_____

D. What gentle rebuke do the women of Bethlehem give to Naomi
in verse 15?

_____

⧗ E. What stands out to you about Ruth? Is there an application for
your life?

_____

_____

_____

C.I. Scofield comments: "Behind the story of Ruth's fidelity there
are clear implications of our Lord's redeeming work. Boaz, the
kinsman-redeemer, points to Christ. Ruth portrays those who enter
into a new life through trust in Him" (C.I. Scofield, *The New Scofield
Study Bible*, Oxford University Press, 1967, p. 274).

12. In the following passages from Ruth, explain either how Boaz points to Christ or how Ruth portrays those who receive new life through Him.

A. 1:16-17

_____

B. 2:5

_____

C. 2:8-9

_____

D. 2:10

_____

E. 2:12

_____

F. 2:13

_____

G. 2:14-16

_____

H. 2:18

_____

I. 2:22

_____

J. 3:1-9

_____

K. 4:9-10

_____

_____

13. Read 1 Peter 1:18-19. How did Christ pay to redeem us?

_____

_____

14. Read Romans 10:9-13. What is our responsibility for that redemption to be effective?

_____

_____

⧗ 15. Have you trusted in the shed blood of Christ for your salvation? If so, share, in a sentence, how it happened, and two ways He has changed your life.

_____

_____

WINDING DOWN

■ If time permits, close by having each woman share one thing which she has learned from the discussion of this chapter.

GROUP PRAYER

⧗ ■ Write down an area of concern in your life for which you would like your sisters in Christ to pray. Take a risk and share an area where you repeatedly fail, or an anxiety you carry! What is it?

_____

_____

Pray in twos or use popcorn prayer.

NEXT WEEK'S ASSIGNMENT

■ When you get home, while the group experience is still fresh, complete the journaling assignment in this chapter.

■ As God leads, choose to take one of the following risks:

    A. Confess a sin that causes you to stumble with a trusted friend and ask her to pray for you.

    B. Ask an adult or a child if you could share with her how Christ has redeemed you and changed your life.

■ Complete the next chapter and exercises.

PERSONAL JOURNAL

■ What did God impress on your heart as a result of the group discussion and prayer?

_____

_____

■ How is God leading you to apply what you've learned?

_____

_____

Chapter 7
Best Friends

PERSONAL PRAYER

Quiet your heart before God. Before you begin to read and journal, become aware of God's presence! In the next two lessons, you will be studying the friendship of David and Jonathan. David wrote many of the psalms which are prayers.

- Read slowly through Psalm 19. Put some of the phrases into your own words and make this your personal prayer to God. Then ask God to teach you from this study. (This might be a good time to divide this chapter into five quiet times for the coming week.)

GROUP PRAYER

- Before you begin to discuss together, quiet your hearts before God. In 1 Samuel 23:16 we are told that Jonathan helped David find strength in God. Follow their example and pair off. Each woman should say a sentence prayer, asking God to teach and be with her and her partner in the group.

While a best friend is not knit with you in body, she is knit with your soul. ("... The soul of Jonathan was knit with the soul of David, and Jonathan loved him as his own soul" 1 Sam. 18:1, KJV.) This word knit shows why, as Lillian Rubin says, a best friend has the power to help or to hurt that no one but a mate or lover can match.

WARMING UP

Remember! If you are a Time-concious group, discuss only those questions marked ⧗ throughout.

⧗ 1. Share a time when a best friend was able to give you deeply needed support.

137

_____

_____

_____

When you have a falling out with a best friend, or when a best friend moves away or dies, the pain can be intense, because you are knit—and in the separation, you inevitably leave a part of your soul, much the way you might leave part of your hand if it froze to an icy pipe.

REFLECTION

2. If you have experienced soulmate pain, describe your feelings.

_____

_____

_____

I've dreamed of meeting her all my life . . . a bosom friend—an intimate friend, you know—a really kindred spirit to whom I can confide my inmost soul.
                              Anne of Green Gables[1]

EACH TIME WE have moved, I have been restless until I have found a woman who can be the kind of friend that Anne of Green Gables has described. Though my husband is my dearest friend, I need a special woman friend to whom I can confide my inmost soul. Best friend-ships reflect, most clearly, the gold in the friendships of women—but also the dross. I would give my very life for a best friend, but I have also become as petulant as a jilted lover when a soul mate has withdrawn for a season. Lillian Rubin says, "Best friends have the power to help and to hurt in ways that no one but a mate or a lover can match."[2]

Naomi has shown me *why* I am so vulnerable. Like Naomi, I have a tendency to depend on my human relationships rather than God. I have set myself up for pain, for even the dearest friend may betray me or move away or die. Naomi has shown me my folly, but David and Jonathan have modeled for me just *how* to prune away this ugly weed of dependency.

David and Jonathan were knit together, but it was in a threefold cord with God. We're told that Jonathan helped David find strength in God (1 Sam. 23:16). Gail MacDonald says we need to ask, "Do you drive your friend to God or to you? Are your friends dependent on you or are they drawn to God?"

SCRIPTURAL REFLECTION

■ While a person can find friends by being friendly, soulmates are special gifts from God. God may give you a soulmate for strength for a difficult journey ahead, or to create a powerful ministry team, or simply as a way of showing you His unfailing love. Some people, however, seem unable to enter into deep relationships. This may very well be because they do not have a strong relationship with God. It has been my experience that God has not trusted me with a soulmate relationship if my relationship with Him is suffering. Gary Inrez, in his book *Quality Friendships* (Moody Press, 1981), says, "There is a direct link between the ability to stand alone by faith in God and the ability to enter into deep relationships." David and Jonathan model this for us. Some people plunge into deep relationships in an unhealthy way, depending on the person instead of on God. David and Jonathan model a healthy soulmate friendship for us because their dependence was on God. They helped each other find strength in God (1 Sam. 23:16). When Jonathan was killed in battle, though David's pain was intense, he was not abandoned, for his strength was in God.

3. Find evidence in the following passages for Jonathan or David's ability to stand alone by faith in God.

   A. 1 Samuel 14:6_____

   _____

   B. Psalm 27:1, 10-14_____

   _____

   C. 1 Samuel 17:37, 45-47_____

   _____

⧗ 4. In the above passages, what did Jonathan and David know about God that helped each to trust God in difficult situations?

   _____

   _____

   _____

   _____

5. Can you give evidence from your own life demonstrating an ability to stand alone by faith in God? If so, what?

_____

_____

⧗ 6. Is there a situation in your life right now in which your faith is being tested? If so, what is it and what do you know about God which could help you trust in Him alone?

_____

_____

ACTION ASSIGNMENT

■ Read 1 Samuel 17–20 in its entirety. Bracket in red any passages which involve or strongly impact the friendship of David and Jonathan. Record any new observations.

DREAM DREAMS FOR YOUR BEST FRIENDS
One of the ways we can drive a friend to God as David and Jonathan did is by dreaming dreams for her—dreams that will help her grow toward her potential in Christ.

My friend Pat encouraged me to send a Bible study I'd written for a small group of women to a publisher. When I resisted, she pushed! Her persistence was the beginning of my writing career. Do you see talents and gifts in your friend? Do you dream dreams for her of how she could more fully use them?

Listen to what Jonathan dreams for David: "Don't be afraid. . . . My father Saul will not lay a hand on you. You will be king over Israel, and I will be second to you" (1 Sam. 23:17).

ON-THE-SPOT ACTION ASSIGNMENT

For In-depth Groups Only
■ Bill Hybels, Pastor of Willow Creek Church, has recommended a checklist for dreaming dreams:

• Does this dream fit with Scripture?
• Does it correspond to the person's giftedness?
• Does it make you a servant or a star? (If a star, he recommends caution!)

■ Keeping these tests in mind, spend a minute dreaming dreams for one another. For example:

Leader: What dreams might you see as possible for Amy?

Beth: Amy is so gifted with children - and they love her.
Jo: Maybe you'll have five kids and homeschool them into
         spiritual giants!
Lauri: Or have a backyard Bible Club with thirty kids!
Beth: You have such a strong walk for being so young, Amy.
         I see you mentoring teenage girls.
Pause
Leader: What dreams might you see as possible for Beth?

MAKE SACRIFICES TO HELP HER
REALIZE HER POTENTIAL
Amy said, "Katherine and I led a women's Bible study together. Katherine is extremely gifted—and much more experienced than I. Yet she stepped aside and gave me the reins, because she wanted to encourage the gift she saw in me."

In Jonathan and David's greeting scene we're told, "Jonathan took off the robe he was wearing and gave it to David, along with his tunic and even his sword, his bow and his belt" (1 Sam. 18:4). Jonathan, though he was next in line for the throne, believed David was the man in God's plan to be king of Israel. His gifts were symbolic of this; he was saying, "Let me make it clear, friend. All that I have is yours— even my right to the throne."

One sacrifice we each need to make for a best friend is space— space that gives her time for ministry. My friend Shell and I hold each other accountable for spending time with the lost and lonely, even though we often would prefer to spend that time with each other. We are committed to help each other live obediently.

PRAY TOGETHER
My dear friend Jean told me, "Sometimes I have wanted to pray with a friend when we've talked about a problem, but I don't always like to be the one to take the initiative. And yet I would appreciate it so much if they would suggest it." I see an analogy between making love with your husband and praying with a best friend. Both can be deeply spiritual experiences, bonding you in a threefold cord with God. And I understand Jean's wish that I share in taking the initiative to pray, just as I understand the desire of husbands for their wives to occasionally initiate lovemaking. I also realize that both lovemaking and prayer can be mishandled. They can be approached perfunctorily, outside of an atmosphere of deep caring or expectancy of God's involvement: the form without the power. In Akron I had a friend named Carole who used to breathe deeply before we would pray together, and I knew she was stilling her heart before the Creator of the universe. She drove my thoughts to Him. Likewise, my friend Jean enters into prayer with so much caring for me that I feel

deeply moved—toward her and toward God. She also has an attitude of expectancy, evidenced by the fact that she inquires a few days later, "How has God been answering our prayer?"

SCRIPTURAL REFLECTION

7. Read the following individual passages again. Jot down what you learn. Then write down anything it teaches you about soulmate friendships.

A. 1 Samuel 17:20-28

What is happening?_____

_____

What relevance could this have to David and Jonathan's friendship?_____

_____

B. 1 Samuel 17:48-58

What is happening?_____

_____

What relevance could this have to David and Jonathan's friendship?_____

_____

C. 1 Samuel 18:1-4

What is happening?_____

_____

_____

What friendship principle(s) do you see?_____

_____

_____

_____

D. 1 Samuel 19:1-5

What is happening?_____

_____

What friendship principle(s) do you see?_____

_____

E. 1 Samuel 20:1-4

What is happening?_____

_____

What friendship principle(s) do you see?

_____

_____

"Whatever you ask me to do, I will do for you."
Ruth 3:5; 1 Sam. 20:4

F. What significance do you see in the fact that both Ruth and Jonathan responded with "Whatever you ask me to do, I will do for you" when their best friends asked something difficult of them?

_____

_____

G. 1 Samuel 20:12-16

What is happening?

_____

_____

What friendship principle(s) do you see?

_____

_____

H. 1 Samuel 20:41-41

What is happening?

_____

_____

What friendship principle(s) do you see?

_____

_____

I. 1 Samuel 23:15-18

What is happening?

_____

_____

What friendship principle(s) do you see?

_____

_____

⧖ 8. Which of the above principles is God leading you to apply to your life right now? What will you do?

_____

_____

_____

_____

WHAT IS A BEST FRIEND?

When I talked to women and asked them if they had a best friend, some would say, "I have two best friends," or "I have three best friends." When I objected, saying that seemed to contradict the word *best*, they persisted. I came to realize that while *best friend* often does mean the friend you love the most, it can also mean a friend with whom you have a deep rapport and would consider a soul mate, a kindred spirit. There is a special bond that sets friends like these apart from the rest, and though they are very rare, you may be blessed with more than one. In fact, considering the feminine tendency toward dependency, it would be healthy to seek more than one soul mate and to give our closest friends freedom to do the same.

Since I have developed two "best" friendships in my town, I've found that I'm less demanding of each of these women and that having more than one special friend has been a fatal chop to the grasping weed that has choked the life out of best friendships in my past. How we need to loosen our hold on our best friends! We need to encourage them not only to run to God but also to develop friendships with others. Ann, a woman from Milwaukee, said, "Sally and I are best friends, but that doesn't mean we're always together. We may not even sit together in a meeting. We each try to be open to other people whom the Lord may put across our paths."

Aristotle expressed the concept of soul mates when he said, "Friendship is a single soul living in two bodies." Bets said of her friendship with Beth:

> There is not another person in the world who knows the things about me that Beth knows. She knows me inside and out. It's something spiritual, something in our souls—we are to each other like second selves. And it's funny, but my daughter, as a little girl, recognized our bond. Beth had been in Texas for three years, and during that time Adrienne was born. When Beth returned, she walked in the room and saw Adrienne for the first time. Beth closed her eyes and uttered a low, "Oh!" and somehow Adrienne seemed to know that she had a second mother in Beth, and loved her immediately.

Studies show that men, in sharp contrast to women, are not likely to be able to name a best friend. In her research, Lillian Rubin found that men shrugged off her questions about best friends: "Best friends are for kids." One man, piqued, said, "Only a woman would have so damn many questions about friends and make it so important."[3]

How interesting, therefore, that the very best friends in Scripture are two men! I suspect that David and Jonathan were rare right-brained males. Let me build my case.

Both were extremely accurate marksmen (David with his slingshot,

Jonathan with his bow) and this, scientists now suspect, is one indication of a dominant right hemisphere.[4] (There's an interesting passage in Judges 20:16 that tells of "seven hundred chosen men who were left-handed, each of whom could sling a stone at a hair and not miss.") David was a poet, a psalmist, a harpist—all gifts that we would attribute to the creative right hemisphere. And, as we will see, Jonathan was certainly able to express his feelings, which is also a strength of the right hemisphere.

KNIT TOGETHER IN SOUL, NOT IN BODY

Their friendship is unusual, surpassing even the friendships of most women. People have accused David and Jonathan of being homosexual. But if that were so, then the Lord, who clearly defines homosexuality as sin, couldn't have said what He did about David: "For David had done what was right in the eyes of the Lord and had not failed to keep any of the Lord's commands all the days of his life—except in the case of Uriah the Hittite" (1 Kings 15:5). I believe that the reason many men are uncomfortable with David and Jonathan is that they have never experienced this kind of friendship, except perhaps with a woman with whom they are also sexually one.

In an article in *Christianity Today*,[5] the point is made that many men cannot grasp the difference between a one-flesh relationship and a one-soul relationship, but there is a great difference. In a one-soul relationship there is a union of minds, hearts, and spirits, but not a union of bodies. The *King James Version* eloquently translates the "one in spirit" concept. It says the soul of Jonathan was *knit* with the *soul* of David (1 Sam. 18:1).

This Hebrew word translated "knit" is the very same word that is used to describe the intense love that Jacob had for his youngest son, Benjamin (Gen. 44:30). We are told that if any mischief came upon Benjamin, it would send Jacob to the grave in sorrow because his soul was knit with the soul of Benjamin. If we have been blessed with a good relationship with our parents or our children, we understand this. We feel their pain or joy as if it were our own. We are knit together, but not sexually.

In order to be knit to a friend with whom you do not share the same blood, you need to find a "second self." Cicero wrote, "What is in fact sweeter than to have him with whom you dare to speak as with yourself?" In David, Jonathan found a "second self," a right-brained male who hungered after God's heart. It is a high compliment to each of the men that each desired the other for a best friend, a soulmate. A person's choice of a soulmate speaks volumes about her character.

REFLECTION

■ Since the original release of *The Friendships of Women*, I was challenged concerning my definition of a soulmate as a "second self." While speaking in Dallas, my sister, who was at the retreat, said, "Where in Scripture does it say that a soulmate must be a second self? My soulmate and I are very different, but we balance one another." I have come to see the truth of my sister's words, for though I think a soulmate is often "a second self," *she doesn't have to be.* One of my soulmates, for example, is much stricter with her children than I am. We now lovingly call each other "Law" and "Grace" and believe that one of the reasons God led us together was to bring us each more toward the center.

⧗ 9. A scriptural definition of a soulmate can be found in 1 Samuel 18:1. What two qualities exist in a soulmate friendship according to this verse?

_____

_____

_____

_____

THE GREETING SCENE

After listening to David for just a short time, Jonathan recognizes a kindred spirit. Amazingly, he then commits his life to David. I am reminded of the commitment Ruth made to Naomi. The distinguishing difference is that Ruth and Naomi had known each other for ten years, but David and Jonathan had just met.

> *After David had finished talking with Saul, Jonathan became one in spirit with David, and he loved him as himself. From that day Saul kept David with him and did not let him return to his father's house. And Jonathan made a covenant with David because he loved him as himself* (1 Sam. 18:1-3).

Although Jonathan's choice of David as a best friend seems almost abrupt, it was a very wise choice. We will be blessed if we seek best friends with David's qualities.

BEING DRAWN TO SAINTS AND POETS

What drew Jonathan to David? As Jonathan listened to David converse with his father, he must have recognized the poet, the psalmist, in David. And as this right-brained male recognized a kindred spirit, his soul was knit with the soul of David.

I played the role of Emily in our high school's presentation of *Our Town*. One scene lingers in my memory. After Emily has died, she is allowed to watch her loved ones on earth. She is poignantly aware that they are scurrying about, taking life for granted, just as she did. With tears in her eyes, Emily watches her Mama, and remembers the little things, like "sunflowers, coffee, new-ironed dresses and hot baths." She cries, "Oh, earth, you're too wonderful for anybody to realize you." Then she turns and asks the stage manager, "Do any human beings ever realize life while they live it?—every, every minute?"

And he answers, "No. The saints and poets, maybe—they do, some."[6]

Poets and saints see things other people miss. Luci Shaw takes a fast mile walk along country roads every morning, and when she comes home, she often sits down and writes the metaphors that God has helped her to see. Luci is alert for "pictures in her head." She believes God has opened her inner eyes, that He speaks through her imagination.

When I am with Luci I find that I start seeing things that I couldn't before. Her vision flows into me a little, and it's as though Jesus has put His healing hands on my sightless eyes and helped me to see a little better.

Genuine poets are rare. But if we look carefully, most of us can find people who have poets' imaginations, who stretch us because their thoughts and their lifestyles have not been squeezed into the world's mold. We can also find "saints" who are so abiding in Christ and His Word that they see life differently than most Christians. Marla said of her soul mate: "I think she's my best friend because she stimulates me to think." A best friendship with a thinking person can be a catalyst in your life, helping you to reach beyond that which you've known before.

BEING DRAWN TO GIANT SLAYERS

There's another important clue illuminating the instant bonding between Jonathan and David. It appears two verses before this famous greeting scene. "As soon as David returned from killing the Philistine, Abner took him and brought him before Saul, with David still holding the Philistine's head" (1 Sam. 17:57). Picture this: David is holding the bloody and glassy-eyed head of Goliath when Jonathan first meets him. A gory but significant detail. It helps me to understand Jonathan's bonding to David, for I too am drawn to those who slay giants who defy God.

Kathy said, "I am drawn to a person whom I would like to be

like—I see that she has some quality that I would like to have." I believe we are drawn to giant slayers because they do what we long to do but sometimes are afraid to do.

My young friend Phyllis is a giant slayer. As David was angry about Goliath, Phyllis is angry about the giant pornography. She speaks to women, showing them how pornography has contributed, significantly, to violent sexual crimes against women and children. Recently Phyllis was grocery shopping with her children and noticed that her store had begun carrying *Playboy* magazine and X-rated videos. She asked, politely, if she might see the store's manager. When he came out, she warmly extended her hand and introduced herself and her three wide-eyed children. "What may I do for you, Ma'am?" he asked.

"I have liked shopping here," Phyllis began. "I appreciate your cleanliness, your good service, and your fair prices—but I've noticed that you are now carrying pornographic magazines and X-rated videos. Do you think this kind of material is appropriate in your family-centered store?"

The manager removed all of the unsavory material from his store. And I am drawn to Phyllis as she stands there holding a giant's head.

Giant slayers seem to have better spiritual vision than other Christians. Perhaps this is because obedience, which is the essence of giant slaying, breeds deeper vision. It makes sense that God would trust those who obey with more of His wisdom. Why waste it on those who aren't going to apply it?

REFLECTION

10. Radical obedience leads to greater wisdom, deeper vision. This happened with Ruth, David, and Mary. What would radical obedience mean in your life?

_____

_____

_____

BECOMING ALERT TO FRIENDS WHO WILL HELP US GROW

A best friendship begins, often, with the same sort of feelings that lovers feel when meeting. We notice something and are pulled. It may be giant slaying, it may be poetic vision, or it may be something ineffable, but we are drawn.

We would be wise to consider what attracts us to a woman. When we are pulled to that which is lovely and Christlike, when we notice someone who is living a radically obedient life, then those are the best impulses to act on. This is when it is definitely worth taking a risk in reaching out to someone. For we will become like our closest friends. One of the costliest mistakes we can make is to have a weak Christian for a *best* friend. Paul has some grave warnings in 1 Corinthians 5:11 about choosing a close friend who calls himself a brother (or a sister) and yet is sexually immoral, or greedy, an idolater or a slanderer. Does your best friend feel she was born to shop? Does she cut others down with gossip? Soon you will be like her. She won't drive you to God; she will drive you to sin.

This does not mean we should not befriend non-Christians, and Paul makes this clear in the same passage (1 Cor. 5:9-10). Indeed, we have a responsibility to move beyond our Christian cloister and truly love the lost into the kingdom. (Research shows that most adults who came to Christ did so through the influence of a genuine friend. It also shows, sadly, that most Christians are not truly befriending non-Christians.[7]) By stating that our best friends should be strong Christians, I am in no way negating our responsibility to become genuine friends with non-Christians.

CAN WE MAKE IT HAPPEN?

I've not had a best friend, a soul mate, in each of the eight states in which I have lived. But since studying David and Jonathan, I have experienced more success in making it happen.

I ask the Lord to make me alert to "poets," to signs that a mind has resisted the world's mold: perhaps she doesn't own a television, or is home schooling her children, or haunts the library, or asks probing, caring questions revealing an unselfish and healthy curiosity.

I look for giant slayers on the front lines: I notice the woman who is willing to take charge of Vacation Bible School or has adopted a retarded child. I would expect to find a few giant slayers at my local Right to Life group, PTA, or even the Women's Christian Temperance Union (they do more than just fight substance abuse). I know this: giant slayers won't be sitting back with fear or apathy as giants defame God's name.

FOR PERSONAL
REFLECTION
ONLY

■ As you are still before the Lord, whom does He impress on your heart as friends who have unusual spiritual strength, who have eternal vision, or the faith to take on giants? If you feel drawn to them, list them.

_____

_____

_____

REFLECTION

11. Last week you were asked to share your faith or confess your sins to another. If you can share something which will be helpful to the others about that assignment, do so.

_____

_____

⏳ 12. What stood out to you from the text of this chapter? Why?

_____

_____

Ruth and Jonathan sharpened their friends, driving them to trust in God. Both also chose their soul mates wisely, determining in their hearts to cement a friendship with a person they deeply admired. Their repeated risks eventually resulted in a best friendship that glorified God.

Yet most of us are aware that many friends who were once very dear to us have now faded from our lives. In a day of impermanence and easy good-byes, is it possible to keep a best friend? I am eager to show you another thread from God's friendship pattern—a thread that will give strength and endurance to your friendships.

WINDING DOWN

■ If time permits, close by having each woman share one thing which she has learned from the discussion.

GROUP PRAYER

⏳ ■ Early in this lesson, you reflected a situation in your life right now in which you felt you were being tested. This would be a good area to share for group prayer. Write it down again and how you would like your sisters in Christ to pray for you.

_____

_____

_____

Pray, using popcorn prayer or praying in twos.

NEXT WEEK'S ASSIGNMENT

■ When you get home, while the group experience is still fresh, complete the journaling assignment in this chapter.

■ This is your last week as a secret sister. Write a note to your secret sister telling her some things you admire about her. Then give her one clue as to your identity! (Your group might want to have a meal together as a group for the revealing of secret sisters next week.)

■ Complete the new chapter and exercises.

PERSONAL JOURNAL

■ What did God impress on your heart as a result of the group discussion and prayer?

_____

_____

■ How is God leading you to apply what you've learned?

_____

_____

Chapter 8
Promise Me
Unfailing Love

PERSONAL PRAYER

Quiet your heart before God. Before you begin to read and journal, become aware of God's presence!

■ Read the following:

"It is because of the Lord's mercies that we are not consumed, because His compassions fail not. They are new every monring; great is Thy faithfulness" (Lamentations 3:22-23, KJV).

■ Thank God for some specific ways He has been faithful to you.

■ Confess any known sin and thank Him for a fresh slate each monging. Ask Him to be with you as you study. (This might be a good time to divide this chapter into five quiet times for the coming week.)

GROUP PRAYER

■ Before you begin to discuss together, quiet your hearts before God. In 1 Samuel 23:16, we are told that Jonathan helped David find strength in God. Follow their example and pair off. Each woman should say a sentence prayer asking God to be with her and her partner during their group time together.

WARMING UP

Remember! If you are a Time-concious group, discuss only those questions marked ⌛ throughout.

1. Have each woman share something about her secret sister—and then have her guess who she is. Then Read Lamentations 3:22-23 aloud.

A. What is one way God has shown you unfailing love in the last year?

_____

_____

B. What is one way a friend has shown you unfailing love in the last year?

_____

_____

I can name the day, the hour, that my friendship with Kristen ended.

Linda, a woman from Nebraska

WHEN I WAS ten, I locked my sister's boyfriend in the fruit cellar for an hour. I thought it a tremendous joke as I watched her steam increase over his tardiness. But though she may have wanted to, Sally didn't disown me. She's my sister, and blood ties rarely end.

My adolescent passage was torment for the family confined to my shelter. Mother said it was like living with someone who was going through three nonstop years of premenstrual tension: if she raised an eyebrow, it could release hysteria from me. But she held on and waited for this time to pass. She's my mother, and blood ties rarely end.

My sisters and I live in three different states: Texas, Utah, and Nebraska. We have not been geographically close since we left our childhood home. But we see each other at least annually, and we stay in touch by letter and phone. We are not going to allow the mobility of our lives to keep us from being close. We are sisters, and blood ties rarely end.

BLOOD IS THICKER THAN WATER

Writer Lesley Dormen said that her family isn't going to cross her off their Christmas card list if she is impatient or crabby. She elaborates:

If my mother and I exchange hurtful words, the incident has the power to pierce both of us to the heart. But I know with absolute certainty that neither my mother nor my brother will ever abandon me. We're bound to each other for good. We're family. . . . If I have a falling-out with a friend, I can't just assume that the breach will heal itself. A small fissure in a friendship has a way of leading to permanent rupture unless both parties take special care to mend it.[1]

Wistfully, Karen said, "Even though I may care very deeply for a friend, and she for me—after a move, the friendship is pretty much in the past. I'm not a very good correspondent."

Family ties seem to be stronger than friendship ties. In the case of best friends, this realization can breed anxiety. Lillian Rubin says, "There is a particular urgency between best friends that seems to seek constant reassurance . . . perhaps because of the experience of all the friends who have passed through our lives and are long gone."[2]

REFLECTION

For In-depth Groups Only

2. Is blood truly thicker than water in your life?

A. Has it been your experience that your relationship with your family members is stronger and longer than your relationship with friends?

_____

_____

B. If you said yes, why do you think that is?

_____

_____

C. Do you agree with Lillian Rubin's quotation that "there is a particular urgency between best friends that seems to seek constant reassurance . . . perhaps because of the experience of all the friends who have passed through our lives and are long gone"? If so, what could you learn from this?

_____

_____

_____

For believers, there is an idea for overcoming this problem that most of us have not considered, though Ruth, Jonathan, and Jesus model it for us. There is a way to make best friends become like family, yet without the disadvantages of family. For there are ways that friends are sweeter than family.

FRIENDS CAN BE SWEETER THAN FAMILY

There are barriers to be overcome in sibling relationships. Mom really might have liked her better. Or we may have been frequently compared to a prettier, smarter, more popular sister. My sisters were both high school homecoming queens, and I wasn't. Sally was only a sophomore when she was crowned queen, and my parents were so proud. I remember their glowing faces at the crowning! Three years later, their second daughter, Bonnie, was homecoming queen. I, the third daughter, never even made the court.

My parents tried to make me feel valuable ("You're the best water skier!") and were the epitome of fairness (Dad still makes sure he writes an equal number of times to each of us). But still, I felt I did not measure up to my popular sisters. And though no one may be at fault, memories like this can make it difficult to rejoice with an adult sister when she is promoted to an executive position or to weep with her when she gains ten pounds. Kathleen, a striking brunette, told me intently:

> *I have two sisters who are very, very precious to me. But friends are different because you don't take a friend back to childhood with all of those old sibling rivalries that, no matter how old you are, are still there when you get to be a grown-up. There's an advantage to that because sometimes, when you are having a problem, your family will kind of sit back and empathize and help you on the outside, but inside they're thinking,* GOOD!

There are barriers of birth order to be overcome as well. Tammy, the oldest in a family of four, said of her sisters, "I don't see them as my friends. I see them as people I'm responsible for."[3] Middle sisters often feel resentful of both the older and younger sisters as they had to compete for the attention over the firstborn and the baby. Younger sisters complain that they are never taken seriously. Katie said, "I wish my sister would stop treating me like a little sister. She sees my Christian beliefs as just another phase I'm going through—something that will pass in time."[4]

Maturity and Christ's love *can* break down these barriers. My sisters are now two of my very best friends. It isn't just that they're turning gray before me; I love them deeply. When they hurt, I hurt. When they are full of joy, I am full of joy. But coming to this point took time and prayer. It isn't that way with friends. You start fresh. No memories of childhood quarrels. No parental favoritism. No sibling rivalry.

NOTE: (In *We Are Sisters,* the sequel to this book, I look at the relationship between sisters more closely.)

HESED COMBINES THE BEST OF BOTH WORLDS

Just as it is possible to overcome the past and become real friends with your siblings, it is possible to make best friends as permanent as family. This can happen by applying the Hebrew concept of *hesed* or "unfailing love."

Solomon says that we each yearn for *hesed*: "What a man desires is unfailing love" (Prov. 19:22). The phrase "unfailing love" is the translation of the Hebrew word *hesed* and expresses one of the most beautiful concepts in Scripture. It is also a thread that weaves its way through the generations of friendship we are examining. It's crucial, and if you only apply one pattern from these models, I pray it will be *hesed*.

There are two main thoughts intertwined in this complex Hebrew word. The first is that of mercy or kindness. The second is faithfulness. We want God's mercy, and we want it to keep on coming! The whole idea is perhaps expressed best in Lamentations 3:22-23: "Because of the Lord's great love we are not consumed for His compassions never fail. They are new every morning; great is Your faithfulness."

In their parting scene, Naomi prayed the Lord would show Ruth and Orpah *hesed* (translated "kindness" in most translations in Ruth 1:8). And when Ruth comes home from the field of Boaz with her arms full of grain, Naomi recognizes the answer to her prayer. She exclaims, "The Lord has not stopped showing His kindness [*hesed*] to the living and the dead (Ruth 2:20).

Hesed is what we yearn for from the Lord and from one another. We want our friends to be kind to us, and to never abandon us. We want the kindness of friends intertwined with the permanence of family.

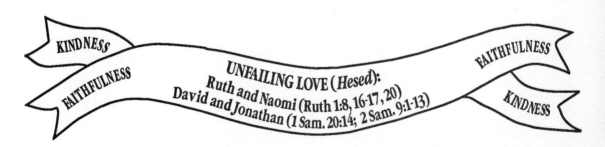

KINDNESS
FAITHFULNESS
UNFAILING LOVE (*Hesed*):
Ruth and Naomi (Ruth 1:8, 16-17, 20)
David and Jonathan (1 Sam. 20:14; 2 Sam. 9:1-13)
FAITHFULNESS
KINDNESS

A VOW OF *HESED*

Chris, a woman in her late thirties, said, "I told my friend that I had always wanted a sister, and it was a little late for my mother to adopt. She laughed and said, 'If it will make you feel any better, I'll adopt you. I'll be your sister.' " In making our friends like family, we are saying, "I may let you down, I may move away—but please, don't let that end our bond. Let's be as permanent as family." This unfailing love is *hesed*. Christ embodies *hesed*, and as we embody Christ, our best friendships should never end.

Jonathan promised *hesed* to David in their greeting scene, and then later requested it of David when he said, "Show me unfailing kindness [*hesed*] like that of the Lord as long as I live" (1 Sam. 20:14). And David made a covenant with Jonathan, promising him unfailing love. This passage becomes even more moving when you realize that it was the custom when a new king came to power for the old king's family to be murdered. Though Jonathan was next in line for the throne, he felt that David was God's man. In supporting David, he was endangering not only his own life, but the lives of his future children. So he asks David for an oath of unfailing love, "so that I may not be killed." And he adds, "And do not ever cut off your kindness from my family" (1 Sam. 20:15).

This promise of unfailing love made David and Jonathan like brothers. In fact, *The Living Bible* has David saying to Jonathan, "Do this for me as my sworn brother" (1 Sam. 20:8).

When I juxtapose the promise that Ruth made to Naomi in Ruth 1:16-17 ("Whither thou goest . . . ") with the covenant of David and Jonathan, I cannot help but wonder if this pattern is a possibility for us. If a wedding vow given sincerely can undergird a marriage in loveless times, could not a friendship vow do the same to maintain a treasured friendship?

My dear friend Shell and I taught the story of David and Jonathan to teenagers one summer during Vacation Bible School. Moved by their model, Shell wrote me a note. She told me that she loved me and respected me, and then she quoted Jonathan: "Whatever you want me to do, I'll do for you" (1 Sam. 20:4). Then she promised me unfailing love.

Shell, like Jonathan, is a person of high moral character, so this promise meant a great deal to me. I knew these were not words glibly written. This was not an empty promise. I, in turn, felt led to promise Shell unfailing love. And we have become like sisters.

SCRIPTURAL REFLECTION

Time-conscious groups ask two or three to share the verse that most impressed them.

3. The Hebrew word *hesed* is used in the following passages and may be translated "kindness, unfailing kindness, mercy, or great love." Describe the context in each case and also what you learn about *hesed* from the context:

   A. Ruth 1:8

B. Ruth 1:20

C. 1 Samuel 20:14

D. 2 Samuel 9:1

E. Proverbs 19:22a

F. Proverbs 20:6

G. Lamentations 3:22-23

⧗ 4. Based on what you've learned, define *hesed*.

5. If you were to give someone *hesed*, describe how you would behave in the following circumstances:

A. She moves 2,000 miles away.

_____

_____

B. You're trying to get ready for a dinner party you're having that night and she calls you, needing a shoulder to cry on.

_____

_____

C. She hurts your feelings and doesn't seem repentant.

_____

_____

NOTE: Scripture seems clear that the one who should go to the other is not necessarily the one who is wrong (for both probably feel the other is wrong), but the one who is stronger spiritually. Insofar as it lies within us, we are told to be at peace with all (Romans 12:18). Confess any sin to her that you are aware of in your life. And show her unfailing love through a gift of cookies, a note telling her what you value in her, or a smile. Love, we are told, covers a multitude of sins (1 Peter 4:8).

ACTION ASSIGNMENT

■ The tests mentioned in the above question are distance, stress, and the feeling you've been betrayed. Do you have a friend who has passed all these tests with you? If so, write her a note and thank her!

GOD TESTS PROMISES

After Ruth made her famous commitment to Naomi, Naomi tells the women of Bethlehem that she has come back "empty." How difficult it must have been for Ruth to experience that lack of appreciation! But Ruth doesn't renege on her promise.

After Jonathan makes a covenant with David, Jonathan's father begins throwing spears at David. How difficult it must have been for Jonathan to have his father *hate* his covenant friend. But Jonathan doesn't renege. At great peril to his own life, he remains faithful to David.

After Shell and I promised each other unfailing love, we were tested. About a year later, Shell came to me, asking me for advice concerning a personal area of her life. Loving the role of sage, I plowed in without really listening to Shell, without prayer, and without thinking about what a sensitive area she was exposing to me. And I wounded her deeply.

Shell's initial reaction was to withdraw. (Who doesn't withdraw her hand from a hot stove?) She was calling less, coming over less, cooling. When I asked her what was wrong, she was noncommittal. (Later she explained that she believed that as long as she was experiencing pain, it was the time to be silent, for you can't take back words spoken in anger. I've come to appreciate her restraint.)

My friend Ann told me, "I am more upset over a disagreement with a friend than I am with family because I know my relatives will always be there for me. But unkind words between friends may signal the cooling or even the end of a friendship." As I saw Shell backing away, this was exactly how I felt. The warmth in our friendship was gone; we barely saw each other for a whole summer. I remember thinking, *We're best friends and we've promised each other unfailing love! How can this be happening?*

One autumn morning I awoke with a terrible head cold. During my quiet time, I told the Lord how unlovely and friendless I felt and asked Him for some evidence of His unfailing love. And on that very day Shell whizzed in with dinner, acting as if nothing had ever happened. Later, she told me, "God simply wouldn't let me forget that I had promised you unfailing love. So even though I didn't feel loving yet, I knew I needed to obey and trust that my feelings would follow."

SCRIPTURAL
REFLECTION

6. How was Ruth tested after she made her promise to Naomi? (Ruth 1:19–2:2) Did she pass or fail? Explain.

_____

_____

7. How was Jonathan tested after he made his promise to David? (1 Samuel 18:3; 19:1-5) Did he pass or fail? Explain.

_____

_____

8. Have you promised unfailing love to anyone? If so, has your promise been tested? If yes, what did you learn?

_____

_____

⌛ 9. Shell said that when she didn't feel loving toward Dee, she obediently acted loving, and trusted her feelings would follow. How is this an example of 1 John 2:5-6? Have you experienced the truth of this verse? Explain.

_____

_____

⌛ 10. Is there someone to whom you need to show unfailing love even though you don't feel like it? If so, what will you do?

_____

_____

BASING RELATIONSHIPS ON COMMITMENT

When Steve and I were starry-eyed newlyweds, we were convinced that our marriage would remain strong on love alone. I'm a hopeless romantic (my dad's fault) and so is Steve. Perhaps that is why we were attracted to Dan and Lorinda, a handsome couple who lived in a historic Seattle home on top of Queen Anne Hill. Dan and Lorinda entertained often—gatherings with music, candlelight, laughter, and abundant flowers from their lush garden. One evening after dinner, as we were lingering over coffee and fresh raspberry pie, Dan began talking about the glue of his marriage. He surprised us by saying that his marriage to Lorinda was going to last because of commitment, not love. (*How unromantic!* we thought.) He said his feelings for Lorinda might rise and fall (*Lovely Lorinda?* we questioned) but that his commitment to her would be steadfast.

As the years passed, we've come to see the wisdom of Dan's words. And just as marriages need to be based on commitment rather than feelings, so do cherished friendships. Sooner or later, we will all reveal our feet of clay.

And women, probably more than men, tend to have their feelings hurt. Our hides are tender, and the very fact that we are closer and value friendship so makes us correspondingly more vulnerable.

Mary told me about how her best friendship ended:

> I was pregnant and I wasn't ready to tell anyone—not even Annie. She suspected and asked me, and I lied. It was wrong; I'm

sorry I did it—but I did. She felt so betrayed when she found out the truth that she never really could find it in her heart to forgive me. We tried to mend things, but it was never the same. And then, when she moved away, she didn't write. Ever. And when she came back to visit, she didn't come to see me. I felt rejected. We were so close—and we were sisters in Christ! I wish she would forgive me.

If Annie's friendship with Mary had been based on commitment rather than feelings, I believe the friendship would have been salvaged. There still would have been a period when Annie would have not felt the same love for Mary that she had once, but I believe God would have restored those feelings, as He did in my friendship with Shell, had Annie obediently showed unfailing love to Mary.

When the church at Ephesus was not feeling the same love for Christ that they had once, Jesus told them to do three things: Remember the height from which you have fallen; repent; and do the things you did at first (Rev. 2:5). This is what Shell did when she brought dinner over. And this is what I did when I felt betrayed that Shell was withdrawing from me. I continued to call her and meet her needs with kindness.

Author Ann Kiemel warns aspiring writers that God may take them through the fire to teach them more. That has certainly been true with this book. I went through a period when two other close friends in addition to Shell seemed to be angry with me. I asked my husband, "How can I write about the friendships of women when I'm losing all of mine?" But now, months later, I can see that God allowed me to go through pain in my friendships to see whether I would apply the principles I've been writing about. I can tell you honestly that I have, that I've followed Ruth's example and given unfailing love when I've felt rejected. God has restored friendships, blessed me with new friendships, and helped me grow through criticism.

WHEN AN ANGRY FRIEND DOESN'T RESPOND
After trying repeatedly to restore one friendship with words of apology, gifts, and notes, I realized that every attempt I'd made had intensified my friend's anger. I went to my sister Sally for advice. She suspected it was an attack from Satan. I was so drained of energy and concentration from my futile attempts at trying to restore this broken relationship that I listened carefully when my sister said:

Lay it down before the Lord, Dee. You've done what you can to be at peace with her. When she comes to mind, you can pray for her and for healing, but lay it down and trust God's sovereignty.

In most cases, unfailing love, given sincerely, will restore a broken relationship—but if it doesn't, then my sister's advice is wise. If you've tried to restore the friendship with the same gentleness and skill that a cardiovascular surgeon uses when performing open heart surgery, and you intuitively sense that the "patient" (your friendship) is getting worse, then stop! Don't plunge the knife in out of frustration or anger, but stop the surgery, sew it up, and take your hands off. Leave your friend prayerfully in God's hands and trust His sovereignty. Joseph had to do this when his brothers hated him, and eventually God brought good out of a very painful situation (Gen. 37; 39–45). God restored my friendship just before the final editing of this book, but not before He brought some good things out of the pain.

In some cases, restoration may not take place—for Jesus said that allegiance to Him may turn an unbeliever against a believer (Matt. 10:34-36)—but even in this, if we continually respond to evil with unfailing love, God will be glorified and we will be refined, like gold over the fire.

REFLECTION

■ The feeling you've been betrayed is the hardest test. It's difficult to show a friend unfailing love when it seems as if she doesn't care for you. Instead of stoking the fire, you feel like laying the poker down—and the fire dies.

⌛ 11. Sometimes people hurt your feelings, not because they don't care for you, but because they are hurting themselves. How was this true in the case of Naomi?

_____

_____

⌛ 12. Why is it important to remember that people who are hurt tend to hurt people? Has this thought ever been helpful to you?

_____

_____

⌛ 13. It's easy to get into a downward spiral in a relationship when your feelings have been hurt. Yet God can use you to turn the spiral around. Read the rebuke Jesus gave the church in Ephesus in Revelation 2:4-5. What was it and what three things did He tell them to do to reverse the spiral?

_____

⧗ 14. How could you apply these to a marital relationship or a soulmate friendship that has lost its fervor?

_____

_____

⧗ 15. If you've forgiven your friend from your heart, stoked the fire with genuine acts of kindness, and she still doesn't respond, what do you think God would have you do? Why?

_____

_____

UNFAILING LOVE IS COSTLY

If you choose to give someone unfailing love, be prepared to pay a price. There are going to be times when it seems easier to say good-bye—because you've been genuinely hurt, or because the friend is needing so much help, or because it simply takes discipline to keep up a long-distance friendship. But this is where Christians should be different than those who do not have the model and the strength of Christ.

Jonathan asked David to show him "unfailing love like that of the Lord." And what is that like? It is love given at great personal cost. As Christ gave His life for us when we were betraying Him, so should we continue on loving even when we are feeling betrayed.

Betrayal, according to a test administered by *Psychology Today*[5] to 40,000 friends, is the main reason close friendships end. Sooner or later one friend is going to reveal her feet of clay and commit an act of mild or severe betrayal.

Marriage counselor Karen Huston told me that most intimate relationships, such as marriage and best friendships, have a natural rhythm of intense closeness and drifting apart. Since both of these conditions have a degree of inherent discomfort, we vacillate between the two: we're close, and then we feel the need for space; we're apart, and then we miss each other. If we interpret the natural drifting apart period as betrayal (which it isn't), then out of hurt or anger we may become the betrayer. In *The Best of Friends, The Worst of Enemies*,[6] author Eva Margolies tells of how hurt Cara was when she wasn't seeing as much of her best friend, Irene. Rather than continuing to give Irene unfailing love, Cara found an opportunity, when Irene's father died, to hurt Irene as she had been hurt. Cara decided, despite a tearful call from Irene, to skip the funeral. Irene was deeply wounded at a vulnerable time in her life—her "acquaintances" all came to the funeral, but her best friend was missing. Eventually, because of a confrontation from Irene, Cara and Irene were able to work out their differences. But so often in a situation like this, we simply let a cherished friendship die.

The most difficult time to give a friend unfailing love is when we're feeling as though they no longer care deeply for us. Our carnal nature desires to inflict pain, not extend kindness! And yet, when we give unfailing love to a person who doesn't seem to deserve it, that is when we are most like Christ.

The value of a promise is that it is a reminder of our need to remain faithful, no matter the cost. We may have to hold each other accountable to our vows. I find it interesting that David and Jonathan continually reaffirmed their vow of unfailing love.

Both men had high prices to pay to keep their vow. But they did it. At great peril to his own life, Jonathan demonstrated unfailing love by discovering his father's plan to murder David and warned his friend. Weeping because of the pain of parting, Jonathan nevertheless insisted that David flee for his life.

THE PARTING SCENE

In this most poignant of parting scenes, David is facedown before Jonathan, weeping with abandon. It is Jonathan who helps David to gain control by saying: "Go in peace, for we have sworn friendship with each other in the name of the Lord, saying, `The Lord is witness between you and me, and between your descendants and my descendants forever' " (1 Sam. 20:42).

This scene reminds me of one Kathleen described concerning her move from Texas. As she and her best friend were having a good cry, Kathleen sobbed, "What will I do without you?"

Kathleen's friend gained control of herself and said, "You'll be fine." Kathleen said:

> I wanted to say, "How can you say that? I won't be fine! I'll be miserable!" But that was truly the best thing she could have said to me. If she had allowed herself to continue to be as morose and depressed as I was, then she couldn't have helped me. Instead she gave me strength. She was really truly being my friend.

And Jonathan was truly being David's friend, giving him strength and control with a reminder of their promise of unfailing love. I believe that the model of Ruth and of Jonathan should at least make us prayerfully consider the possibility of making a promise of unfailing love to a kindred spirit. Yet it is important to realize the seriousness of vows before God.

DO NOT BE HASTY TO MAKE PROMISES

It is a terrible thing to break a vow. Though the world seems apathetic to this sin and breaks wedding vows regularly, we as Christians should be different. Solomon warns:

> *Do not be quick with your mouth, do not be hasty in your heart to utter anything before God. God is in heaven and you are on earth, so let your words be few. . . . When you make a vow to God, do not delay in fulfilling it. He has no pleasure in fools; fulfill your vow. It is better not to make a vow than to make a vow and not fulfill it. Do not let your mouth lead you into sin. And do not protest to the temple messenger, "My vow was a mistake." Why should God be angry at what you say and destroy the work of your hands?* (Ecc. 5:2, 4-6)

One night at supper I was sharing my discovery that God will "destroy the work of your hands" if you break a promise to Him. Our twenty-one-year-old son grew unusually quiet. He had promised God he would share the Gospel with an elderly friend in a nursing home and hadn't. A healthy fear of the Lord caused him to fulfill his promise that very night.

A broken promise not only draws the wrath of God, it hurts people deeply, because promises give hope and broken promises crush hope. Proverbs 13:12 says, "Hope deferred makes the heart sick." A child who has been anticipating a circus trip feels sick when the promise maker fails to come through. And as adults we aren't too different. Broken promises break hearts. It is better not to vow than to vow and not follow through.

IMPLICIT BONDS

Since we are to regard vows with the utmost solemnity, we would be wise to make them sparingly or not at all. In *King Lear*, Cordelia will not promise her father unfailing love as her sisters do, because she says there is an unspoken bond between them. And interestingly, only Cordelia remains true to her father. Shakespeare is teaching us that not only are vows only as good as the character of the person making them, but there are implicit bonds that should remain strong without vows.

Bets and Beth, best friends, have not spoken vows to each other, but each is aware of an implicit bond. Bets said, "I know, I am absolutely convinced, that if I *ever* need Beth, she'll be there for me. We don't need to promise it." And Beth agrees: "I am in this friendship for the long haul—no matter what."

Twelve years ago Lee and I bonded when the Lord used me as a vessel to bring Lee to Christ. Though we've been separated geographically for ten years, we've nurtured our friendship through letters.

Recently I called Lee at her Ohio home when I was going to be speaking at a women's retreat in Buffalo, New York. "Do you think you could come and join me for the weekend?"

"I'll be there—with bells on!" she responded, warming my heart with her enthusiasm. Later she discovered that her husband's birthday fell on the weekend. But he, knowing what our friendship meant to both of us, told her she absolutely had to go! (Thank you, Vince!)

We spent a wonderful weekend, laughing, crying, praying—reaffirming our bond. Lee listened to me speak and heard me suggest to my listeners the possibility of making a vow of unfailing love to a soul mate. That night Lee told me, earnestly, "I can't make a promise, because I'm so afraid I would break it." I respect Lee's hesitancy, for it springs out of a healthy fear of the Lord. I am also confident of our implicit bond and our unspoken commitment to nurture it. As Lee and I rode in the airport bus to catch our separate planes, we felt the bittersweet pain of parting. Lee caught my hands in hers and said, "We are knit together, my friend. As Jonathan was knit to David, so I am knit to you."

Each of us needs to assess our implicit bonds. There are those who are going to feel rightfully let down if we fail them, even though no blood ties exist and no promises have been made. Leisa said, "I know I've got to get over it, but I was absolutely shocked when my best friend since kindergarten didn't come to my wedding." There was an implicit bond there that was not honored.

There may very well be a time under heaven to close the door on friendships, especially the loose ties. Each of us can maintain only a limited number of close ties. But I believe we too easily are closing doors on the "real connections," and falling into the world's mold of impermanence and easy good-byes when we fail to be true to the people whose souls have been knit with ours.

The model we have in the New Testament is continued prayer, letter writing, and if possible, occasional visits to those who have been our cherished friends. It really doesn't take that long to sit down and write a few letters to dear friends, or to remember their birthdays with the help of a perennial birthday calendar. When Jan moved from Scottsbluff, Nebraska halfway across the state to Kearney, she pined for Nancy, the soul mate she'd left behind. I had lunch with Jan recently and she showed me a picture of Nancy and her husband, hanging, like the picture of a treasured family member, on Jan's wall. She also showed me the figures of two little straw girls hugging each other that Nancy had recently sent to her. "Not a week goes by when we don't write or call. This is a permanent friendship."

For friends nearby, bonds can be maintained with lunch dates, phone calls, and short notes of love. Unfailing love means anticipating a friend's needs, following up on her concerns. My friend Carol will make a brief phone call to check on me. My neighbor Jo told me that she lay awake one night thinking of a title for this book, a concern she knew had been on my heart. Charlotte put it like this: "They're paying attention."

We need to assess our real connections and then remain true. Ruth, a fifty-eight-year-old nurse said, "A good, warm friendship, like a good, warm fire, needs continual stoking."[7]

SCRIPTURAL REFLECTION

⌛ 16. Find as many reasons as you can in Ecclesiastes 5:2-7 for approaching vows very cautiously.

_____

_____

Cordelia told her father, in Shakespeare's *King Lear*, that she would not vow unfailing love to him because there was already an implicit vow. In addition to immediate family members, it's good to reflect on those with whom you may have "an implicit vow." Because I have moved so many times, I have friends in many places who are dear to me. Yet I cannot show them all unfailing love—there is simply not enough time during my fleeting days on earth. Therefore, about five years ago I asked the Lord to show me to whom I should be true. Some of the questions I asked myself were:

- Is there an "implicit vow" or an actual vow?

- Has she shown a desire to be true to me?

- How are You leading, Lord?

God then impressed on my heart the names of four long-distance friends to whom I am endeavoring to show unfailing love. This exercise has not only freed me from the guilt of failing to be true to the 300 people on my Christmas card list, but it has helped me to be a better friend to these four women. Last summer I surprised my friend Lee by flying to her daughter's wedding. She said, "I wept when I opened your RSVP—and my heart is still warmed by the thought of you coming." I'm so glad I went—it's a precious memory—and I'm not sure I would have had I not been still before the Lord and asked Him "To whom do You want me to show unfailing love?"

FOR PERSONAL REFLECTION ONLY

■ To whom is God calling you to show unfailing love?

_____

_____

We would also be wise to expect close friends to occasionally fail us. We are sinners, and despite the best of intentions, we are going to let each other down. Genuine friends are like roses—breathtakingly lovely and worth the pain of an occasional surprising jab from a hidden thorn.

There are people, however, who look like roses, but aren't roses at all. They are alligators. Can you tell the difference between a rose and an alligator?

WINDING DOWN

■ If time permits, close by having each woman share one thing which she has learned from the discussion.

GROUP PRAYER

■ Write down an area of concern in your life for which you would like your sisters in Christ to pray. What is it?

_____

_____

Pray, using popcorn prayer or praying in twos.

NEXT WEEK'S ASSIGNMENT

■ When you get home, while the group experience is still fresh, complete the journaling assignment in this chapter.

■ Complete the new chapter and exercises.

PERSONAL JOURNAL

■ What did God impress on your heart as a result of the group discussion and prayer?

_____

_____

■ How is God leading you to apply what you've learned?

_____

_____

Chapter 9
Roses and Alligators

PERSONAL PRAYER

Quiet your heart before God. Before you begin to read and journal, become aware of God's presence! Use the anacronym of ACTS:

- **Adoration:** Read Psalm 18:1-3, which David wrote after God delivered him from the hand of Saul. Praise God for being your stronghold, refuge, and deliverer.
- **Confession:** Confess any known sin in your life and turn from it. Are there "thorns" which grieve others?
- **Thanksgiving:** Thank God for three ways He has intervened in your life.
- **Supplication:** Ask Him for wisdom with this lesson. (This might be a good time to divide this chapter into five quiet times for the coming week.)

GROUP PRAYER

- Before you begin to discuss together, quiet your hearts before God. Whoever is leading the discussion should ask for the Lord's help for herself and for all the women as they share and interact.

WARMING UP

Remember! If you are a Time-concious group, discuss only those questions marked ⧗ throughout.
⧗ 1. What is the difference between an alligator and a rose?

The two ways to handling conflict with a rose are:
1. Overlooking it in love –
"Love covers over a multitude of sins"
(1 Peter 4:8). Ruth's example with Naomi.
2. Confronting in love –
"Speaking the truth in love" (Eph. 4:15).
David's example with Jonathan (1Sam. 20:1-4).

The only way to handle conflict with
an alligator is forgiveness and flight.
"Do not make friends with a hot-tempered man,
do not associate with one easily angered"
(Prov. 22:24). David's example with Saul.

⌛ A. What are the two ways of handling conflict with a rose? Give examples of each from your own life.

_____

_____

⌛ B. How should you handle conflict with an alligator? Give an example.

_____

_____

⌛ 2. What is something that people tend to misunderstand about you?

_____

_____

_____

Kristen Ingram recalls the following conversation with her grandson Andrew when he was almost three.

"Gra'mother?"
"Yes, Andrew?"
"Gra'mother, a dog is a friend!"
"Yes," I said, "A dog is a friend."
There was a period of silence, and then . . .
"Gra'mother?"
"Yes, Andrew?"
"A cat is a friend!" he said.
"Yes, Andrew," I agreed, "A cat is a friend."
There was a much longer silence, and then . . .
"Gra'mother!"
"Yes, Andrew?"
"Gra'mother, I don't think an alligator is a friend," he said with
sad certainty.[1]

MOST WOMEN ARE like roses. As roses vary from quiet pink to sunny yellow to razzmatazz red, so do women. And when you draw near to a woman, she will often quite willingly open to you petal after petal of fragrant loveliness.

But lurking beneath the glossy, green leaves of roses are surprisingly nasty thorns. After experiencing a few jabs into your soft, tender flesh, you handle roses with more respect. A dedicated rose gardener, one who believes that the glory of the rose more than compensates for the occasional wounds it inflicts, learns to bear the pain and to handle roses in such a way that she is seldom jabbed.

DON'T BE SHOCKED BY BETRAYAL

When a friend lets us down, we show that our theology is off base when we're overcome with shock. The Bible teaches that we're all going to let each other down. Even the most beautiful rose has thorns. Pastor Greg Scharf of Fargo, North Dakota says, "When someone fails you, don't be stunned! It's more appropriate to think, *Hmmmm! That confirms what Scripture teaches—that we're all sinners, that there's none that is righteous, no, not one.*" Hopefully you've realized the folly of putting your trust in people. It's a hard lesson to learn. Charlie Brown has to relearn it every fall when Lucy convinces him to trust her and let her hold the football for him. Every fall Charlie Brown falls flat on his back.

We need to mature to the point where we realize that while it is important to love and cherish our friends, our dependence should be in God alone—for only He is without sin, and only He will never let us down.

It does hurt to be jabbed by a thorn, especially if we have tried to show that friend unfailing love and it seems unappreciated. But we need to learn to be as tolerant of others' failings as we are of our own. It's also vital to our spiritual health to forgive those jabs. We're to be tenderhearted and compassionate toward others, just as in Christ, God has been tenderhearted and forgiving toward us (Eph. 4:32). It also helps to realize that when a person does let us down, it is usually not intentional.

DON'T TAKE OFFENSES PERSONALLY

When a rose gardener is jabbed by a thorn, she realizes the rose had no personal animosity toward her but was simply born with thorns. We'd be wise to see people that way.

Polly's friend Kim was incensed when Polly forgot to stop by after work as planned so that Kim could fit a dress she was making for Polly. On the phone, despite Polly's sincere apology, her friend said, "Obviously you don't respect the fact that my time is valuable!" Polly said:

> *It wasn't that at all. I respect Kim immensely and I could kick myself that I forgot. It was especially bad because I kept her waiting for thirty minutes at a restaurant just last month. But neither incident was a result of my feelings for her. Both were due to the fact that I'm juggling too many balls in my life and sometimes I drop one. Maybe you've got to be a single mother to understand that, but I still think she should have accepted my apology before she brought me to tears. She said, "Promise that it won't happen again." I couldn't even do that—because although you can be sure I'm going to try, I know I'm not perfect.*

As women, we are quicker than men to assume that an injury is the result of a person's feelings toward us. One husband despaired:

> *Susie has been in a blue funk all week, simply because I mentioned the top of the refrigerator was dusty. She's too short to see the dust, so I pointed it out, but I certainly regret it! How do I make her realize that my comment had nothing to do with my feelings about her or about her worthiness as a homemaker?*

Perhaps our sensitivity shows how little confidence we have in ourselves. Perhaps it is a negative side effect of our global brain functions. A man can zero in on a problem, but a woman has trouble separating a problem from her feelings. We could thicken our skin if we would realize that most hurts are not a reflection of the perpetrator's dislike for us, but rather a reflection of a hardship in the person's life or a character flaw, or even a reflection of respect based on the assessment that we can handle criticism given in love.

Since I have grasped this principle, I'm more tolerant of friends who keep me waiting. I used to assume that their lack of punctuality was directly related to their feelings for me. While I was waiting, I stewed about that. Now I realize that people who are habitually late would keep the pope waiting!

SCRIPTURAL REFLECTION

3. People hurt other people for many reasons: because they are human and have a sinful nature; because they are hurting themselves; or because they are trying to help you through constructive criticism. Jeremiah 17:9 says: "The heart is deceitful above all things and beyond cure. Who can understand it?" Romans 3:23 says: "All have sinned and fall short of the glory of God."

⧖ A. What doctrinal truths do the above verses teach?

_____

_____

_____

⧖ B. Why is it then, that we are often shocked when others let us down?

_____

_____

_____

⧖ C. Often people who are hurting hurt other people. How was it true with Naomi? Has this been true in your life? If so, give an example.

_____

_____

_____

_____

Sometimes we take it personally when a friend lets us down. I was hurt when a close friend never wrote me after I moved away. When I confronted her (on the telephone), she said, "Dee—I don't write my own mother!" That helped me to see that her failure to write was due to a lack of discipline rather than a lack of caring for me.

⧗ D. Is there someone in your life who hurts you because she is tense, or abrupt, or sarcastic? Would it help you if you knew she was that way with other people as well? Why or why not?

_____

_____

COVER AN OFFENSE WITH LOVE

The most important time to appreciate the beauty of a rose is immediately after being stuck by a thorn. Writer Gini Kopecky said that she has a friend who thinks nothing of canceling long-term plans with her if something more attractive comes up. "It really insulted and infuriated me at first. So much so that at one point I seriously contemplated breaking off the friendship." But the more Gini thought about it, the more she realized that she didn't want to end the friendship.

> *There were too many things about this woman that I valued— her incredible energy, her sense of humor, her amazing kindness. I remember once she gave a party and right in the middle of it I got dizzy and almost fainted. And she was right there. She took me across the hall into a neighbor's empty apartment and sat with me until I had recovered. I'll never forget that.*
> *Now, I simply don't make long-term plans with this friend. I know what I can expect from our friendship, and I know what I can't. It's worth it to me not to demand from her what I know she can't give.*[2]

Gini reflected on the things that she appreciated about her friend, and also reminded herself of a past evidence of her love. This is what 1 Peter 4:8 means when it says, "Love covers over a multitude of sins." Gini also wisely took a good look at the thorn (the canceling of long-term plans) and determined how to avoid being jabbed in the future. I've done this with a friend who cannot keep confidences. She's a dear friend and would do almost anything for me except keep my secrets. Because I treasure her and don't want to write her off as a friend, I am simply cautious about sharing any confidences with her that I wouldn't want spilled.

FOR PERSONAL REFLECTION ONLY

■ Do you have a close friend who frequently lets you down in a particular way? If so, list the things that you value about her.

_____

■ Perhaps you have confronted your friend about this thorn and yet it remains. Is there any way you could avoid being jabbed by it or minimize your pain when you are? What is it?

_____

_____

■ Do you have thorns which friends or family have overlooked in love? What are they? How do you feel about their forbearance?

_____

_____

_____

If I decide that I cannot cover a particular offense with love because the offense is too dismaying, then I have another scriptural alternative.

CONFRONT WITH LOVE

Confrontation is tricky. It's painful and has ended many a friendship. We all have logs in our own eyes, so it seems a bit presumptuous to go after the speck in our sister's eye. Charlotte said, "I don't think we can go willy-nilly telling our friends that they would be all right if they would just take a little tuck here and a little tuck there!" I agree.

Yet Solomon tells us, "Better is open rebuke than hidden love" (Prov. 27:5) and "Faithful are the wounds of a friend" (Prov. 27:6). So there is a time for confrontation, but it should pass a few tests.

First, pray about it and ask, "How likely is it that confrontation is going to change the person's behavior?" Our motive for confrontation should be changed behavior rather than the release of our anger. If the person is unlikely to respond, why do it?

Next, be sure your anger is healed. God tells us, "Man's anger does not bring about the righteous life that God desires" (James 1:20). When your anger is healed, ask the Lord to help you plan your words. Retreat speaker Clarice Rose says, "Tell your friend what you are feeling and then what you want to happen between you." Otherwise, confrontation is likely to be misinterpreted as a personal attack rather than an effort to improve the relationship. Billie prayed about confronting her friend Rhonda for a long time and then prepared carefully. Billie tells the story:

Rhonda led me to the Lord and I owed her my life! I also cherished her as a friend. She's terribly funny, yet serious about her walk with Christ. I truly loved her. But she was smothering me. If I wasn't with her, I felt like I had to give her an accounting. If I didn't have time to be with her, I could hear this hurt sound in her voice. I really didn't want to flee the friendship, but it couldn't go on like this.

After praying about it, literally for weeks, I went to her and shared my feelings. I told her that I felt I was too dependent on her and that the Lord was showing me it was time to develop other friendships. I also told her how much she meant to me and that I didn't want to lose her. To prove it, I asked her if we could have a standing, monthly lunch-date to catch up on each other's lives and to pray together. It worked. We're still good friends and I'm much happier with the friendship.

Luci Shaw told me that confrontation is difficult for her because she is afraid that if she is outspoken and critical, she may lose the love and approval of the people who matter to her. But still, Luci is learning to speak truth in love. Recently, she mustered the courage to confront a treasured friend about a broken promise. "I felt, for the sake of our friendship, that I had to. She broke down and we cried together. She felt that she had failed me, but we were closer after that because I had been honest. As hard as it was for both of us, it was worth it."

In both of the above incidents, the women confronted in order to save the friendship. Our motivation for confrontation should always spring from a desire to improve the relationship or seek the other person's best.

If we confront just to release anger, we destroy rather than build up. I met Brooke, a career woman who could have passed for a *Vogue* model, on a flight to San Francisco. At first I felt intimidated by her sophisticated physical appearance and by the discovery that she had built up a thriving investment business in downtown Cleveland. But Brooke helped me over my sense of inferiority with warm and caring questions. Soon we were talking about the friendships of women and I was surprised to see tears in the eyes of this woman I'd judged as being invincible. Brooke's pain came from a confrontation that she had received from Ellen, a close friend since kindergarten, whose life had taken a different path from hers. "She has a lovely family—I adore her children. Perhaps all the more since I don't have a family of my own." Brooke told me the story:

It was the afternoon after Ellen had picked me up at my office. She'd never been there before and it happened to be that crazy day when the stock market fell so many points. I had to handle a few long-distance calls and give several orders to employees before I could leave. Watching me, Ellen seemed impatient, strained . . . and her mood continued through lunch. I didn't know what was wrong, but later she called me and said, "I never want to see you in your place of work again. You can come to my home, or we can meet to shop. But I never want to see you there again."

I asked Brooke if she had probed Ellen for an explanation. She answered:

A little, but frankly, I was afraid to. I'd already been dealt a staggering blow, and I wasn't sure I could take more. This incident has diminished both of us. Our friendship will suffer, for now I feel that when I'm with her I'm going to have to be a different person. My career is 95 percent of who I am, and she doesn't want to see that part of me.

Ellen didn't confront a specific behavior, but attacked the person and her whole identity. (Perhaps that's why confronting a friend about her children's behavior or her child-raising methods usually backfires. She feels, whether she should or not, attacked in her whole identity.) If we're not specific and don't tell our friend what we hope to see changed, we're being unkind, and our motive is probably impure.

Most of us can tell whether we are being confronted in order to help, in a spirit of genuine love and good will, or whether the confrontation is intended to hurt and destroy.

REFLECTION

4. Confrontation Principles

⧗ A. What are some pure motives for confrontation?

_____

_____

_____

⧗ B. What are some impure motives for confrontation?

_____

_____

_____

⌛ C. If you are considering confrontation, what are some good questions to ask yourself?

_____

_____

⌛ D. Considering how difficult it is to hear criticism, what are some ways you might increase the receptivity of the listener?

_____

_____

REFLECTION

For In-depth Groups Only

5. Confrontation in Practice. Imagine that you feel led to speak the truth in love in the following circumstances. Write down how you might approach her. After a woman shares, have the group critique her approach, remembering to speak the truth in love!

A. A friend asks you if she can borrow your copyrighted cassettes to make copies for herself. You know this is against the law, and you don't feel like you can lend her your cassettes for that purpose. On the other hand, you don't want to hurt her or end the friendship by making a big issue of this.

_____

_____

B. A friend seems jealous of the time you spend with your husband and is very critical of him. You love her and don't want to lose her friendship, but you want her to be supportive of your marriage.

_____

_____

GROW AT THE HANDS OF YOUR CRITICS

Whether the person's motive for confronting us is good or evil, we'd be wise to learn a lesson from Dawson Trotman, the founder of the Navigators. No matter how unfair the criticism might seem to be, he would prayerfully spread it before the Lord in his prayer closet and say, "Lord, please show me the kernel of truth hidden in this criticism."[3] One of the ways we can measure our maturity is by how we respond to confrontation. Solomon says:

> *Do not rebuke a mocker or he will hate you; rebuke a wise man and he will love you. Instruct a wise man and he will be wiser still; teach a righteous man and he will add to his learning* (Prov. 9:8-9).

SCRIPTURAL REFLECTION

6. Read Proverbs 9:7-9.

⧗ A. What do you learn about receiving criticism from the above proverbs?

_____

_____

⧗ B. When someone criticizes you, how do you usually respond?

_____

_____

⧗ C. Can you give an example from your life where you listened carefully to criticism and grew from it? If so, share.

_____

_____

A mature rose can usually handle the shock of loving confrontation from a close friend and will grow more lovely, but an alligator will open her jaws and devour you.

ACTION ASSIGNMENT

■ Read through 1 Samuel 18–21. In your Bible, mark in green (or with the word *alligator*) evidences of a pattern of destruction in Saul toward David. What do you learn about alligators from Saul?

_____

_____

NOTE: A passage which has confused many is 1 Samuel 18:10, which says, "An evil spirit from God came forcefully upon Saul." Radio Bible Teacher Dr. M.R. De Haan says: "God is also the Lord of the spirits, and of the entire creation. While the Lord is sovereign, He permits Satan to do certain things . . . The expression, therefore, "an evil spirit from the Lord," does not mean that this spirit came directly from the Lord, but rather that He permitted it" (Dr. M.R. De Haan, *Dear Doctor, I Have A Question. . .*, Zondervan, Grand Rapids, 1963, p. 169-170).

Personally, it helps me to know that for some reason God is allowing Satan to rule for a time. The child or the woman who is abused, for example, by an "alligator" is still loved by God. One day all tears will be wiped away, Satan will be cast into hell, and justice will be served. But for now, Satan is the Prince of this Earth, and we must trust that the God who created the Universe and sent His Son to die for us knows what He is doing.

SCRIPTURAL REFLECTION

⧗ **Time-conscious Groups share only two or three highlights.**

8. Read the following passages from 1 Samuel and list what you learn about responding to alligators from David.

A. 18:11

_____

_____

B. 20:1-10

_____

_____

C. 22:1-5

_____

_____

D. 23:8-18

_____

_____

E. 24:1-22

_____

_____

F. 26:1-25

_____

_____

If you are married to an alligator, I recommend reading *Tough Love* by James Dobson, who recommends, in cases of repeated infidelity or substance abuse, that you separate from your husband and encourage him to get help. Alligators are in their own quicksand and very seldom get out without professional help. A separation may cause him to get the help he needs.

SCRIPTURAL REFLECTION

9. What else do you learn about Saul from the following passages in 1 Samuel?

A. 28:7

_____

_____

B. 31:1-6

_____

_____

C. How did David remember Saul in his eulogy in 2 Samuel 1:17-27?

_____

_____

⧖ D. Summarize what you have learned about alligators and responding to them from Saul and David.

_____

_____

_____

_____

ALLIGATORS

The difference between a rose and an alligator is that a rose may never hurt you, but an alligator is likely to destroy you. Alligators demonstrate a *pattern of destruction*. Every rose has a few thorns, but an alligator is covered with them. His smile reveals jagged teeth, lining his long snout. From the back of his neck to the muscled whip of his tail run rough, dangerous barbs. Your chances of escaping major injury if you cozy up to an alligator are slim.

Saul was an alligator. Repeatedly, he tried to pin David to the wall with his spear. When this failed, he sent David into battle with the Philistines, demanding one hundred Philistine foreskins for the hand of his daughter, Michal, in marriage. (If I had been Michal, I would have preferred a diamond ring.) This plan of murder failed as well, because the Lord was with David.

Jonathan, in defense of his friend, tried to confront Saul. Saul seems remorseful, as alligators sometimes are, and even takes an oath of good behavior, but eventually he slips into his destructive pattern again and tries to kill not only David, but also Jonathan.

Some people believe that alligators are always of the female gender, but alligators come in either sex. Others believe that alligators are always non-Christians, but unfortunately that doesn't seem to be true either. There is evidence that Saul was a believer (1 Sam. 10:1, 6-9), but he was certainly living a life of disobedience.

The thorns of an alligator, unlike the thorns of a rose, are life threatening. Alligators put your spiritual, emotional, or physical life in jeopardy. Experts testify that three acts of violence in an abuse situation is evidence of a pattern. In the same way, if a "friend" has demonstrated a pattern of destruction, you would be wise to flee. Connie told me:

I've worked as a secretary in four different offices. I'd never had any serious problem with coworkers until Lorraine. Lorraine had been the executive secretary for fifteen years, and she had Mr. Johnston wrapped around her finger. I'd heard her discredit the other secretaries to him. She never failed to seize an opportunity to mention if someone had come in late, or misplaced a document, or whatever—half of the things she said just weren't true. One time three other secretaries and I confronted her, together. She seemed surprised, even sorry. But then her viciousness became intense. She stabbed us in the back, one by one. The firings began and the women left with poor references. I hadn't been fired, but I wondered how long I'd be able to keep my job with Lorraine on the loose. When I felt Mr. Johnston's attitude toward me growing wary and cold, I suspected Lorraine. So before he fired me, I quit. It was the right decision. I'm much happier—and safer—where I am now.

Connie's decision to flee was a good one. This is what David did, and it's the best way to deal with alligators. In a book entitled *Becoming a Christian Friend*, Kristen Ingram inspired me with the idea of recognizing some people as being alligators. Mrs. Ingram says, "It would be foolish to go wading barefoot in the Everglades where alligators are lurking."[4] We should stay away from alligators, but we must be sure we are dealing with an alligator, and not a rose.

I treated a rose like an alligator once. I fled when I should have confronted. April was sending her toddlers over to our house every day, *all* day. After six months of this, I began to plead with Steve to move to another part of the city. He finally agreed. It was a very expensive and unnecessary solution, because April wasn't an alligator. April was not trying to destroy anyone. It was just that toddlers drove her crazy and she knew I loved kids. I'd told her so! What I never had the courage to tell her was that I also needed to have some time with my children by themselves, but I would love having her children sometimes. I think she would have been agreeable to working out a schedule. Instead of being clear, I dropped hints—which she didn't catch. My failure to confront led to flight, a dropped friendship, and large moving bills. I handled it poorly. (And my sister Sally wisely said, "Don't you realize what you've done? Your failure to confront encouraged April in her sin.")

Alligators, not roses, call for flight. Flight doesn't mean a lack of forgiveness, however. I asked Peg, who had been married to a man who left her for another woman, how she was able to keep bitterness from taking hold. The man shows no remorse, and in fact blames Peg for their failed marriage. Peg said, "I forgive him for me. I have seen how bitterness destroys people, and I'm not going to let that happen. So I forgive him for me."

SCRIPTURAL REFLECTION

10. What do you learn about forgiveness from the following verses?

⧗ A. Luke 17:3-4

_____

_____

⧗ B. Ephesians 4:32

_____

_____

_____

11. What has the Lord taught you through experience about forgiveness?

_____

_____

ARE YOU AN ALLIGATOR?

If you recognize that you have a pattern of destruction toward others, get help from Christian professionals. In their series of radio broadcasts on abuse, Karen and David Mains stressed that you cannot break free without help. Behavior patterns can be like quicksand: the more you struggle, the deeper you go. You need someone to extend a hand. I would recommend beginning with a pastor from a Christ-centered, Bible-preaching church. How do you find a church like that? Some good questions to ask are: Are the adult Sunday School classes studying the Bible? Do most people bring and use their Bibles in church?

Although there are a myriad of reasons people become alligators, ranging from genetic temperament to childhood abuse to depression, there is one sin that has proved to be especially fertile soil for growing alligators.

JEALOUSY

Marie, Ann, and Leslie had become close while touring one summer with the Continentals, a Christian singing group. Marie was the most gifted, musically, of the three women: she had a lilting soprano voice with a breathtaking range. Congregations were enthralled with her solos. Ann and Leslie also were given solos, but not so frequently. Ann accepted Marie's brighter light. Leslie tried, but as the adulation for Marie grew, Leslie found herself increasingly uncomfortable in Marie's company. She began to sit far from Marie and Ann on the bus, to ask to be placed with someone other than Marie for overnight arrangements, and grew generally noncommunicative with her formerly close friend. Marie was hurt, and approached Leslie, asking her to explain why she was avoiding her. Marie told me:

> My question opened a floodgate of feelings. For hours Leslie poured out the bitterness she felt toward me. I think the time might have been well spent had she repented of her problem. She admitted she didn't want to have these feelings of jealousy, but all she did was confess them, she didn't repent. I think her "confession" was designed to hurt me back—and it did. I became very uncomfortable singing solos. I thought, How many other

people from this group are feeling hurt, anger, and jealousy while I am singing? When I would be chosen for a solo, I felt regret, because I knew there was nothing Leslie wanted more. Then, while I was singing, despite my effort to concentrate on the Lord, I would find myself thinking of Leslie and those like her. I became stiff and joyless.

Novelists often portray women as being more jealous, more back-biting, than men. Perhaps we are. Perhaps our low self-esteem makes us more vulnerable, for example, to the sin of rejoicing over another's misfortune. How unlovely! I suspect that both men and women struggle with feelings of jealousy, but that women are more apt to express them. The expression of emotion is a right-brain function. This is a strength with emotions such as affection and compassion, but devastating with jealousy. Solomon says: "Anger is cruel and fury overwhelming, but who can stand before jealousy?" (Prov. 27:4) If you've ever been the victim of envy, you've tasted its cruelty. Dr. Madonna Kolbenschlag says that envy says, "I could forgive you anything, except what you are; except that I am not what you are."[5]

Envy diminishes both parties: it hurts the victim and gives a hard and bitter spirit to the perpetrator. "Envy rots the bones" (Prov. 14:30). It destroyed Saul, and it will destroy you and me if we don't root it out as soon as we recognize it.

It is interesting to see how differently Saul and Jonathan reacted to David's popularity, because he was a threat to both of them. Saul was the reigning king, and Jonathan was next in line. Yet Saul kept a jealous eye on David and tried to destroy him, whereas Jonathan did all he could to exalt David. What made the difference?

Saul had his eye on pleasing people, so he couldn't bear it when the women of Israel came out to meet him with tambourines and lutes, dancing and singing: "Saul has slain his thousands, and David his tens of thousands" (1 Sam. 18:7). Jonathan, however, had his eye on pleasing God. He felt God's pleasure with him when he exalted David. In a lesson on overcoming rivalry, Karen Mains said, "I think that when we feel the intimate pleasure of God, it doesn't matter how He chooses to work with our brothers and sisters."[6] I believe this is the key.

God is pleased when we can overcome our knee-jerk reaction of envy and rejoice with a successful friend. In an article entitled, "When True-Blue Turns Green," Mary Alice Kellogg tells the following story:

Helen sounded upset: "Could we meet for lunch?" For years, we had been through all the crises that crop up when you've been friends for a long time. I was prepared to lend as much emotional support as I could and went to the restaurant expecting that something bad had happened. As it turned out, Helen did need support; she had just been named president of a hot new public relations firm, with double her previous salary and glamour to spare. A dream job. So why was she upset?

"There are so few people who can hear this kind of news and truly feel glad for me," she sighed. "You're about the only friend I can genuinely share the happy news with." We toasted her success, and I reassured her that I was still her friend, even in the best of times.[7]

Gayle told me of how she and her best friend each had two sons and shared a longing to have a little girl:

She got pregnant first, and had a third son. Then I got pregnant. When my daughter was born I was almost afraid to tell her. But when I called her, she was so excited. She brought over sacks of clothes that she had been saving for her little girl and her attitude was pure joy. I'll never forget her reaction.

REFLECTION

12. Proverbs 14:30 says: "Envy rots the bones." What do you think this means?

_____

_____

13. What sort of situations tend to make you feel jealous?

_____

_____

14. How could you change your feelings in those situations from jealousy to rejoicing with your friend?

_____

_____

I don't want to be an alligator. I want to be a rose. In fact, I long to be like Jesus, the Rose of Sharon, who had absolutely no thorns. In order for that to happen, I need to be responsive to God's still, small voice.

Mary and Elizabeth were both incredibly sensitive to God, and He blessed them with a beautiful friendship. Their story has some deep truths to teach us.

WINDING DOWN

■ If time permits, close by having each woman share one thing which she has learned from the discussion.

GROUP PRAYER

■ Write down an area of concern in your life for which you would like your sisters in Christ to pray.

_____

_____

_____

_____

Pray in twos or use popcorn prayer.

NEXT WEEK'S ASSIGNMENT

■ When you get home, while the group experience is still fresh, complete the journaling assignment in this chapter.

■ Complete the next chapter and exercises.

PERSONAL JOURNAL

■ What did God impress on your heart as a result of the group discussion and prayer?

_____

_____

■ How is God leading you to apply what you've learned?

_____

_____

Chapter 10
God Knows Our Needs Better than We Do

Personal Prayer

Quiet your heart before God. Before you begin to read and journal, become aware of God's presence! In preparation for the opening discussion question, make a list of friends God has brought into your life at crucial times. Spend some time thanking Him for those friends. (This might be a good time to divide this chapter into five quiet times for the coming week.)

_____

_____

Group Prayer

■ Before you begin to discuss together, quiet your hearts before God. Using popcorn prayer, have group members share sentences of thanks for specific needs God has met in their lives. Then the leader can close, asking God for help with this lesson.

Warming Up

Remember! If you are a Time-concious group, discuss only those questions marked ⧗ throughout.

⧗ 1. Tell the group briefly about one of the friends from the above list and why you feel God was involved.

_____

_____

⌛ 2. What needs did God meet in Ruth's life through Naomi? In Naomi's life through Ruth? In David's life through Jonathan?

_____

_____

When she [Elizabeth] heard Mary's greeting, the unborn child stirred inside her and she herself was filled with the Holy Spirit, and cried out, "Blessed are you among women, and blessed is your child! What an honour it is to have the mother of my Lord come to see me! As soon as your greeting reached my ears, the child within me jumped for joy! Oh, how happy is the woman who believes in God, for His promises to her come true!" (Luke 1:41-45, PH)

LUCI SHAW BELIEVES we have abandoned Mary in an "evangelical limbo."[1] Convinced that many Catholics erroneously worship Mary, many Protestants fall into the opposite error: they ignore her, except at Christmas when she is dusted off and placed in their nativity scenes. I am eager to bring Mary out of the shadows, for she has so much to teach us.

MARY SAID YES TO GOD

Jesus tells us, "For out of the overflow of the heart the mouth speaks" (Matt. 12:34). Perhaps the truest test of our character comes when our container is jostled unexpectedly. What spills out?

The angelic visit came upon Mary unawares. The announcement was one of good news and bad news: the highest honor possible for a woman, intertwined with the risk of rejection by her family and fiance. Death by stoning was the fate for a woman caught in adultery. She was no adulteress, but would people believe her story?

What is this teenager's immediate reaction? One question— "How?" Hers is not a doubting "How can I be sure of this?" as Zechariah asked when Gabriel told him Elizabeth was to be with child (Luke 1:18), but simple curiosity. "I am a virgin, so how are You going to do this, Lord?" (Who wouldn't be interested?) And then, when told, she doesn't ask for time to think about it, time to consider, she simply says, "May it be to me as you have said" (Luke 1:38). Remarkable. In an article in *Christianity Today*, Luci Shaw says, "Mary said yes to God. Perhaps God chose her . . . because He knew it was her habit of life to say yes to her father and her Father."[2]

In a moment of crisis Mary, like Ruth, desired to do what pleased God. The risks were extremely high for both of them, but in an instant they decided for God. God was pleased, and one of the ways He blessed them was through the provision of godly, earthly friends.

SCRIPTURAL
REFLECTION

3. While God does not always bless those who trust and obey at the time and in the way they might like (Elizabeth was "blameless" in her child-bearing years, yet she was barren), and while He can bless those who are disobedient (Christ died for us when we were yet sinners), there does seem to be a frequent link between faith/obedience and blessing.

A. Do you see a link between faith/obedience and the blessing of earthly friends in Ruth's life? In David's life? In Mary's life? If so, explain.

_____

_____

B. Have you seen a link between faith/obedience and the blessing of earthly friends in your life? If so, give a brief example.

_____

_____

4. Read Psalm 34. State the principle that you find in each of the following verses from Psalm 34:

⌛ A. 34:4-7

_____

_____

⌛ B. 34:8-10

_____

_____

⌛ C. 34:11-16

_____

_____

ACTION
ASSIGNMENT

⌛ ■ Choose a passage to memorize from Psalm 34. Write it out on an index card now. Spend ten minutes now memorizing. I like to memorize word by word. Choose whatever method works best for you.

■ What passage did you memorize? Share it with the group. Why did you choose it? What did you learn from memorizing it?

_____

_____

_____

GOD'S PROVISION OF SPECIAL FRIENDS

God knows our needs for friendships better than we do ourselves. Isabel Anders writes in a lovely article in *Partnership* of how she became friends with a woman while she was alone on a three-day visit in London.

Isabel had been seeing a play a day, alone. She said, "I didn't realize how lonely I was, mingling with crowds and speaking only to waitresses, cab drivers, clerks, and ticket agents. I certainly wasn't looking for a friend on my last afternoon before returning home."[3]

Before the play, Isabel had lunch in the theatre tea shop. The shop was crowded, so the host asked Isabel if she would mind sharing her table with Sibyl, whom Isabel described as a sweet-faced English-woman. They chatted and sipped tea companionably, each enjoying the other's company. Then they parted, each to find her theatre seat.

When Isabel found her seat, she was startled to see that Sibyl had the seat next to her! Sibyl seemed very glad, saying it was "fated." Isabel wrote, reflectively: "I tend to be solitary and had not realized my own need to interact with someone deeply. I began to catch on that God was giving me the gift of a friend."[4] Though Isabel was younger than Sibyl (as Mary was younger than Elizabeth), that didn't prevent her from recognizing that God might be initiating this friendship.

The play was an intensely moving one, the subject being commitment in marriage and the perils of a lack of commitment. It was a meaningful theme to each woman: Isabel was then dating the man who would be her future husband, and Sibyl was married to a "man who had been (and had put her) through much grief."[5] Touched by the play, each woman glanced at the other occasionally. Sibyl was close to tears.

After the play, Isabel and Sibyl waited in the lobby for a violent storm to subside. The play and their sensitivity to God's hand helped them to share their lives vulnerably with each other. They discovered many threads binding them together, including the fact that they were sisters in Christ. Isabel was encouraged by the beauty of Sibyl's faith over adversity. Her thoughts may have been similar to those that Mary had about Elizabeth and the circumstances that drew them together:

The beauty of Sibyl's faith illuminated her. The triumph of grace over adversity and God's care for her as an individual shone through, as sweetly as I've ever seen in a human face. I felt renewed strength for the life that was ahead of me—whatever it might be.

. . . How calmly we walk into the miracles of our lives—and to me, friendship is one of those miracles! How, out of all the people of the streets of London, should Sibyl and I encounter each other? God knew my needs and Sibyl's better than we had known ourselves.[6]

FOR PERSONAL REFLECTION ONLY

■ What do you think your needs for friendship are at this time in your life? What is the longing of your heart?

_____

_____

■ Do you think that God would agree that those are your deepest needs?

_____

_____

■ Have you asked God to meet the friendship needs in your life? Is there any sin in your life that might keep Him from listening?

_____

_____

God knew the needs of Mary and Elizabeth better than they did themselves. Our gracious Lord made certain that Mary knew: "Even Elizabeth your relative is going to have a child in her old age, and she who was said to be barren is in her sixth month. For nothing is impossible with God" (Luke 1:36-37). And what is Mary's reaction? She recognizes God's provision of a friend in her time of need, so she *hurries* to go see Elizabeth, and then spends *three months* with her providential mentor. Despite great obstacles, Mary is determined to follow through on God's leading and go to see Elizabeth.

Elizabeth was not nearby. We're told she lived in the "hill country of Judah" (Luke 1:39), which most scholars believe was probably the hills surrounding Jerusalem. This was almost *one hundred miles* from Nazareth. How did Mary get there? Perhaps she walked, perhaps she took a donkey. It seems she went alone. This was a long trip for Mary, and she was pregnant. Was she tired as one so often is early in pregnancy? Did she have morning sickness? (I slept fourteen hours a day during the first three months and would swoon at the sight of a hair in the sink!) But despite the distance and her pregnancy, Mary seems to have been compelled to take the trip.

Did she talk to Joseph first? I imagine so, as it's unlikely she would leave him for three months without a word. But the angel had not yet appeared to him, confirming her story that this child had been, indeed, conceived by the Holy Spirit. I suspect their parting conversation was an unsettling one, one that would further spur Mary on her arduous journey, for she knew Elizabeth would understand.

SCRIPTURAL REFLECTION

5. On the basis of the following passages, describe some of the fears or challenges Mary might have faced. Then describe how a friend or a mentor might have helped her face them.

   A. Leviticus 20:10

   _____

   _____

   ⧗ B. Matthew 1:19

   _____

   _____

   ⧗ C. Matthew 1:25

   _____

   _____

   D. Matthew 2:13

   _____

   _____

   E. Luke 2:34-35

   _____

   _____

✖ 6. How was Elizabeth uniquely suited to be Mary's friend and mentor?

_____

_____

_____

ELIZABETH

God knew Elizabeth's needs as well. She had been barren all her life, and she was "well along in years" (Luke 1:7). God knew how important it was to her for this pregnancy to go well and how comforting it would be to her to see that He had done the impossible with Mary as well.

It was a disgrace to be barren in those days. Dorothy Pape, author and missionary with China Inland Mission (now Overseas Missionary Fellowship), gives us some insight on the disgrace of barrenness:

> *Until very recently, in most parts of the world, a woman has been seen mainly as a baby-producing machine, as someone to perpetuate the family line of the father. . . . Even Martin Luther, great Christian that he was, stated, "If a woman becomes weary, or at last dies from child-bearing, that matters not; she is there to do it." For a woman not to become pregnant has usually been taken as a sign that she is displeasing to the gods and has been regarded as just grounds for divorce or the taking of a concubine.*[7]

I have friends who have struggled with infertility. Often the unfulfilled longing to have a child of their own consumes them. One woman said:

> *I'm always, always, dwelling on it. Every month I hope my period won't come, and then I must bear the crushing disappointment when it does. For that week and the week following I think, We will never, never have a baby of our own. And then, from deep inside of me, hope springs up again, and climbs, as I think, Maybe this month it will really happen!*

I sympathize with their pain, for my children are the delight of my life. But people today don't look upon infertile women as being without value, as they did in Elizabeth's day. A barren woman then had to bear not only the sadness of not having a child of her own, but also the cultural condemnation that she had missed her life's calling, perhaps because of disobedience! This, of course, was not God's point of view, but man's. We know that *God* was pleased with Elizabeth, for we are told that she was upright in His sight (Luke 1:6). Still, it was difficult for Elizabeth to bear the townspeople's clucking tongues. That's why she says, "The Lord has done this for me. . . . He has . . . taken away my disgrace among the people" (Luke 1:25).

Not only did Elizabeth need to see the power of God as evidenced in Mary, she needed someone to talk to! Elizabeth's husband, Zechariah, had been struck dumb in the temple as discipline for not believing Gabriel's announcement. Therefore Elizabeth was deprived of intimate conversations with her husband in which they anticipated the birth of their child, of a sounding board for the questions that must have come to mind, and of a prayer partner.

We are also told that Elizabeth went into seclusion for the first five months of her pregnancy. Seclusion! I like a day to myself—but five months without friends or family? Certainly during this five-month retreat Elizabeth must have drawn near to God, and perhaps that was why God led her to impose this discipline upon herself. Perhaps He wanted to mature her, to teach her to depend on Him alone, to refine her through the fire of solitary confinement. Our Father knows how easily we women fall into dependent relationships. He wanted Elizabeth to trust in Him alone. After all, He had chosen her for two crucial roles: to be a mother to John the Baptist and to be a mentor to the mother of Jesus Christ, our Lord.

Considering all this solitude, how glad Elizabeth must have been to have a visit from Mary! Mary—who could speak, who could identify closely with Elizabeth's circumstances, and who had believed God immediately! The Scripture makes it clear that Elizabeth was overjoyed to see her relative. God knew that Elizabeth and Mary would need each other, and in His mercy, in His unfailing love, He gave them to each other. And each seemed to recognize that He was giving them the gift of friendship.

Their friendship seemed part of a providential plan. Consider all the links that bound them together. Mary and Elizabeth were

- *women living devoutly religious lives*
- *relatives, descended from King David*
- *experiencing miraculous pregnancies*
- *told their sons' names through Gabriel*
- *to be mothers of sons who would be great, linked in history, and destined to die horrible deaths*
- *each dealing with the unbelief of her husband or future, husband*

SCRIPTURAL REFLECTION

7. On the basis of the following passages, describe what some of Elizabeth's needs for friendship might have been. Then describe how a friend might have helped her with those needs.

A. Luke 1:18-20

_____

_____

⧗ B. Luke 1:24

_____

_____

⧗ C. Luke 1:36

_____

_____

D. Luke 1:59-61

_____

_____

E. Luke 1:76-79

_____

_____

F. Matthew 14:1-13

_____

_____

⧗ 8. Now describe how Mary was uniquely suited to be the friend that would meet many of Elizabeth's friendship needs.

_____

_____

When we consider these links, we understand why the greeting scene between Mary and Elizabeth is perhaps the most meaningful greeting scene in all of Scripture.

THE GREETING SCENE

Walter Wangerin wrote: "Faith is work. It is a struggle. You must struggle with all your heart. . . . And on the way, God will ambush you."[8] I identify with Wangerin's play on words, for there have been times when I have been so surprised by God's response to my mustard seed of faith! Certainly it was a hard act of faith for Mary to travel one hundred miles alone to see Elizabeth, and she obviously expected some encouragement, but, oh my, what an overwhelming scene!

Can you imagine Elizabeth's emotion when she saw Mary in the doorway? No letter or phone call had warned her—this was truly a joyous surprise! And at the sound of Mary's greeting the Holy Spirit caused two additional surprises. First, John the Baptist literally leapt in his mother's womb in recognition of his Messiah in Mary's womb. This was no small stirring! Second, Elizabeth was filled with the Holy Spirit and began to prophesy. God, through Elizabeth, gave Mary the blessing she so desperately needed.

In their inspiring book, *The Blessing*, Gary Smalley and John Trent tell of the great problems that befall children who grow up with parents who withhold what the Bible calls "the blessing."[9] The authors outline ways we can encourage our children, spouses, and friends with blessings. In a true blessing, a high value is attached to the person along with picturing a bright future. See how Elizabeth does this.

• "Blessed are you among women" (Luke 1:42). What higher value could be placed upon Mary? And if the friends around Mary were murmuring about her morality, how these words must have warmed her spirit!

• "And blessed is the child you will bear!" (Luke 1:42) Most unwed mothers are thinking primarily of the difficulty of their circumstances. If Mary's thoughts needed to be lifted beyond her temporary distress to the treasure she was carrying, Elizabeth does it here.

• "But why am I so favored, that the mother of my Lord should come to me?" (Luke 1:43) Though Elizabeth, because of her age, would normally be given more reverence than Mary, here she is bowing her knee to Mary. ("Bow the knee" is what the Hebrew word for blessing means.)

• "Blessed is she who has believed that what the Lord has said to her will be accomplished" (Luke 1:45). Elizabeth knows through the Holy Spirit that Mary, unlike Joseph and unlike Zechariah, immediately believed God! And this *blessed* is a Greek word meaning satisfied, fulfilled, full of God. Elizabeth is saying, "Good for you, Mary, you believed! And because of that, your future is going to hold joy and fulfillment."

This was a blessing that Mary would forever treasure in her heart. In response, Mary sings her hauntingly lovely "Magnificat." Some commentators cannot believe she composed this song. It is loaded with Old Testament references, and they say that it is too brilliant for a woman, so Luke must have written it! Others believe Elizabeth sang it.

But Scripture clearly states that Mary was the singer! The joy, the ecstasy, and the praise for her Savior that flowed from her lips give us one of the clearest portraits of just how godly Mary was.

Mary says, "His mercy extends to those who fear Him, from generation to generation" (Luke 1:50). The Greek word translated "mercy" is as close as you can get in the Greek to the Hebrew word *hesed* (unfailing love). And haven't we seen the truth of Mary's words? God's unfailing love has flowed from Naomi to her daughter-in-law, Ruth; from Ruth to her descendant David; and from David to his descendant, Mary! They feared God, and He blessed them, mightily, from generation to generation!

SCRIPTURAL REFLECTION

9. Meditate on Elizabeth's greeting to Mary in Luke 1:39-45. Make as many observations as you can on this *blessing*, asking such questions as: What thoughts might Mary have had before she knocked on the door? How do you think Elizabeth felt when she saw her? Why did Elizabeth say what she did in each verse? What did she mean? How do you think each phrase impacted Mary?

_____

_____

_____

10. What principles about blessing others do you learn from this passage?

_____

_____

11. Read Mary's Magnificat in Luke 1:46-55. One of the evidences of a spiritually mature friendship is that the friends help each other find strength, not in each other, but in God. Find evidences from Mary's Magnificat that Elizabeth's blessing helped Mary find strength in God.

_____

_____

ON-THE-SPOT
ACTION
ASSIGNMENT

For In-depth Groups Only
■ Keeping these principles in mind, take a few moments to think about how you might verbally bless the woman on your right. Then go around the circle and hear each woman's blessing.

_____

_____

NEVER IS HEARD A DISCOURAGING WORD

I can imagine a very different scenario, had Mary and Elizabeth not been the godly women they were. When I was first married, I was surprised to find that some women commonly disparaged their husbands to other women. (I wasn't a Christian at that time, and neither were my friends.) Perhaps that was due, in part, to the fact that many of my friends were wives of medical students, and were weary of their husbands' schedules. Together they would augment their husbands' weaknesses in their minds, chipping away at the foundations of their marriages. No wonder Scripture admonishes wives to respect their husbands!

NOTE: My sequel to _The Friendships of Women_ (_And Then We Were Women_) explores how maturity in our friendships can strengthen the family. I was encouraged to discover that research demonstrates that women's friendships generally have a stabilizing effect on marriages, for women engage in what sociologists term "marriage work." If a woman is upset with her husband, her friend often will diffuse her anger through humor, or through reminding her of her husband's strengths, or by helping her friend to see the situation through a man's perspective. However, if a woman is immature, or if she herself is unhappy in her marriage and would like some company, she may join her friend in a general harping on the weaknesses of men.

Had Mary and Elizabeth not been women who loved and feared God, they might have commiserated about the lack of spirituality of men and about the lack of faith Joseph and Zechariah had demonstrated.

When we were studying Mary and Elizabeth during a Bible study, one woman had the following insight into her own behavior:

> _I'm not likely to criticize a friend's husband, but I am not so gracious when it comes to my brother-in-law, Jeff. Though Jeff is really quite a nice chap, I'm extremely protective of my little sister and I want the very best for her and my nephews. The Lord has been showing me through this study that my criticism has actually hurt my sister's marriage more than any of Jeff's flaws, because I've encouraged her to think less of her husband._

Elizabeth undoubtedly had protective feelings for her young cousin, but she doesn't utter a discouraging word about Joseph. As friends (and as mothers-in-law) we have a choice: we can either encourage women to think well of their husbands, or we can help them to be like the foolish woman of the proverb, who tears down her house with her own hands (Prov. 14:1).

REFLECTION

12. Do you help your friends think well of their husbands? Do you strengthen their marriages—or tear them down?

_____

_____

MARY TREASURED UP ALL THESE THINGS

Both Elizabeth and Mary had a great deal of pain coming in their futures. If Elizabeth was still alive when John the Baptist was an adult, she had to relinquish him to the wilderness and then bear the pain of his murder, for he was beheaded for speaking out against the adulterous relationship Herod had with his brother's wife.

Mary too was going to be facing more heartache than most of us will ever know. Her name is derived from a Hebrew word meaning "bitterness." Luci Shaw writes:

> From the hour of Announcement on, dark pain lay ahead—friends' incredulity, lack of understanding, accusations of promiscuity and her son's illegitimacy, to begin with.[10]

After her visit with Elizabeth, Mary made the long trip home to Nazareth, only to turn around several months later to trek back to Judea, to Bethlehem. Luci continues:

> She and Joseph were poor, and even if they had a donkey to ride, a blanket on the back of an ass is no easy seat for a woman nine months pregnant, her body cold and stiff from sitting on the plodding animal for hours at a time.
>
> Bethlehem, in turn, seemed so harsh and unwelcoming in the winter night. Perhaps her first uneasy cramping of labor had begun, and the panic of helplessness as the busy innkeeper turned them away.[11]

Mixed with these moments of fear and pain were moments of absolute exaltation—her time with Elizabeth, the star above the manger, and the visit of the Magi! Luci says that Mary needed "the exhilaration of these days to balance the pain of the next thirty-three years and beyond."[12] Wisely, Mary "treasured up all these things and pondered them in her heart" (Luke 2:19). Life is mixed with moments of pain and joy. If we have been keeping a treasure chest (perhaps in the form of a journal of answers to prayer), we can dig it out during bleak times. Peg said:

> When my husband was planning to leave me, and then when he did, the Lord seemed so very near to me, showing me His unfailing love in amazing ways day after day. Through the love of friends, through the ways He was obviously trying to get my husband's attention, and through His presence, so unmistakably real, so strong.
> . . . But now, sometimes, the road seems so lonely, and I question: "Was God really with me? Or was I imagining it?" I need to go back to my treasure chest and look over those moments of epiphany again.

I believe that during those three months that Mary spent with Elizabeth, each gave the other moments for their treasure chests. By sharing their joy, they doubled it. God knew that each would need these moments to remember and treasure, for He could see the dark road ahead. God knows our needs better than we do ourselves.

REFLECTION

⧖ 13. If you were to pull three memories out of your treasure chest of times when God was particularly near to you, or when you were overwhelmed because of an evidence of His care, what would they be? (Share one with the discussion group.)

_____

_____

Review your memory work from Psalm 34. Are you ready to say it for the group when you meet?

GOD KNOWS HOW MUCH WE CAN CARRY

My friend Pat is a missionary with International Students Incorporated and a wonderfully warm and strong Christian woman. One day she said, with a twinkle in her eye, "Dee, I'm not going to ask God to give me friends anymore."

"But, why?" I inquired.

"Because I've done that three times, and three times the Lord has given me a friend who needed me a whole lot more than I needed her!"

I laughed, because I realized (as did Pat) that God knew exactly what He was doing. He knew Pat had the strength and wisdom to help hurting women. God may lead us to disheartened friends, for He knows what we can handle and what we can't. (And then we have the choice to follow through in obedience or to flee.) God knows our strengths and our needs better than we do.

God knows if you or I have the ability to be a friend to a younger woman, as Elizabeth was to Mary, and to give her light for the dark road ahead. And though the desire of our hearts may be to have a friend who is a peer, it may be the desire of God's heart for us to be a mentor to a younger friend, and He may bring her across our path. Isn't it at least interesting that both of the models of feminine friendship in Scripture are between women of different generations? And though we seem to assume that the benefit would be largely on the younger woman's part, that isn't necessarily so. Elizabeth was greatly blessed by Mary, as was Naomi by Ruth.

Let's consider the idea of finding or being a mentor, for it is one of the basic concepts in Scripture concerning the friendships of women, and it is a concept that, if applied, could dramatically change your life.

WINDING DOWN

■ If time permits, close by having each woman share one thing which she has learned from the discussion.

ACTION ASSIGNMENT

Match Spiritual Mothers and Daughters
This assignment is inspired by Susan Hunt's Spiritual Mothering Leader's Guide (Christian Education and Publications). Decide on an age division for your group which will put approximately half of the women in the younger division and half in the older. If you choose the age of 40, women over 40 should take a white slip of paper, write their names, and put it back in the basket. Women under 40 should do the same with pink slips. Then pass the basket and have women take out the opposite color. (If there are more younger women, some older women should take two names. If there are more older women, some younger women should take two names.) The older woman is to spiritually mother her "daughter" for the next week. (Then the tables will be turned and the daughter should nurture the mother the following week.) She should find ways to encourage her: prayer, notes, small gifts, an invitation to lunch or to walk together.

GROUP PRAYER

■ Write down an area of concern in your life for which you would like your sisters in Christ to pray.

_____

_____

Pray in spiritual mother/daughter pairs.

NEXT WEEK'S ASSIGNMENT

- When you get home, while the group experience is still fresh, complete the journaling assignment in this chapter.

- If you are a "spiritual mother," remember to mother your daughter!

- Complete the next chapter and exercises.

PERSONAL JOURNAL

- What did God impress on your heart as a result of the group discussion and prayer?

  _____

  _____

- How is God leading you to apply what you've learned?

  _____

  _____

Chapter 11
The Mentor Relationship

PERSONAL PRAYER

Quiet your heart before God. Before you begin to read and journal, become aware of God's presence! Read Mary's song of praise (Luke 1:46-55), aloud to the Lord, putting some of the phrases in your own words to make it more personal. Then ask God "to be mindful" of you and to help you with the lesson and with applying the concept of mentoring. (This might be a good time to divide this chapter into five quiet times for the coming week.)

GROUP PRAYER

■ Before you begin to discuss together, quiet your hearts before God. Whoever is leading the discussion should ask for the Lord's help for herself and for all the women as they share and interact.

WARMING UP

Remember! If you are a Time-concious group, discuss only those questions marked ⧗ throughout.

⧗ 1. If you were a spiritual "daughter," how were you nurtured this week?

ACTION ASSIGNMENT

■ On a scale from 1 to 10, with 10 being the best, rate your abilities in the following areas:

French-braiding hair _____   Making homemade soup _____

Personal devotions _____   Family devotions _____

Calligraphy _____   Finding my niche as a single _____

Administering a women's   Raising respectful children who
ministry in church _____   love the Lord _____

Politics (writing letters,   Making a difficult marriage
helping promising   work _____
candidates) _____

Gardening _____   Sharing my faith clearly and
                                 effectively _____

Keeping a house neat   Hospitality to international
and clean in minimum   students, newcomers, new
time _____   Christians _____

■ The following is an area that isn't mentioned, but God has given me some ability and wisdom in:

_____

REFLECTION

⌛ 2. Choose two or three of your highest rated abilities to share with the group. What are they? (Group members—be ready to take notes if there's an area where you'd like guidance!)

_____

On Christmas Eve, a deep San Francisco-style fog kept our car crawling blindly along the road. Suddenly another car pulled onto the road right ahead of us. Because we were now following a set of beautiful twin taillights, we could safely increase our speed from fifteen to twenty-five miles an hour. A mentor is someone further on down the road from you who is going where you want to go and who is willing to give you some light to help you get there.[1]

MY SISTER BONNIE was nineteen; I was fifteen. We were walking back to our family's cottage from the village of Ephraim, Wisconsin, a picturesque resort town of white buildings nestled in a hill overlooking the gleaming waters of Green Bay. A black '55 Thunderbird flashed by, and then suddenly my sister became unhinged: "That was Jim Rock's car! I'm sure it was! He's driven all the way up here to see me and he's trying to find our cottage—I know it, I know it!" We dashed madly through the wooded road so that Bonnie could comb her hair and put on fresh lipstick. Bonnie was right. Jim Rock, whom she'd met only once, was coming for an extended visit.

As the days passed, Bonnie worried that our parents might think Jim's visit was too long. Out of concern that Jim might outwear his welcome, Bonnie told her suitor what Benjamin Franklin had said: "Fish and visitors smell in three days." Jim decided to leave promptly! But, he was not deterred from his intentions, for he eventually married my sister—and, I should add, has good-naturedly listened to the telling of this tale for twenty-five years!

With this memory from my childhood, my initial reaction to the discovery that Mary spent three months with Elizabeth was *"Three months!* Perhaps someone should have given Mary a nudge about her manners!"

I asked Win Couchman, who is a retreat speaker on the subject of cross-generational relationships, what she thought about Mary's three-month visit. She told me that having a Filippino daughter-in-law has helped her to understand the story of Mary's visit to Elizabeth. Win said,

> *Lengthy visits and visits away from fiancé or husband seem so natural to her. And especially natural would be the visit between two pregnant relatives. There is an extremely open sharing between women in a family that I have been learning, to my delight, from this precious provincial woman. Her view of time is so different. Three months? A short visit.*

Now, as I am growing in my appreciation of the value of mentors, I realize that God planned this lengthy visit to help Mary prepare for the dark and uniquely obstacled road ahead.

SCRIPTURAL REFLECTION

■ Memorize Titus 2:3-4. Often there is a link between mentoring women and hospitality. One of the best ways to observe a good wife, mother, and homemaker is by spending time in her home. In Susan Hunt's excellent book, *Spiritual Mothering* (Crossway), she shares the following testimony from a woman named Karen Grant who tells of how, in her youth, she approached a godly woman named Linda with a request for mentoring.

> *One day after church, fumbling for words, I simply blurted out that I wanted her to teach me to be like her. . . . I'll forever love her for her positive response. She invited me to meet with her once a week in her home. The first week we went over what we wanted to accomplish, beginning from Titus chapter two. . . . we spent part of each "session" in prayer, part in study, and a very large part in questions I had for her. . . . She also knew I had to observe her in action. . . . She and her husband Ted often invited my husband and me for dinner. Her simple, yet nutritious and elegantly-served meals inspired me. I observed as she mothered her two girls and greeted her husband at the end of the day....Linda would periodically invite me to participate in an*

evangelistic coffee she was hosting in her home. . . . Now separated by many miles and many years, I still remember Linda gratefully and in awe. Because somehow, in my youthful desire to be like her, she guided me in my discovery to be like Him.

⏳ 3. Can you think of a time when a woman invited you for a meal or a visit in her home and, in so doing, taught you something through her example? If so, share specifically what and how she taught you.

_____

_____

⏳ 4. Using your imagination, what are some things you think Mary might have learned by being a guest in Elizabeth's home?

_____

_____

Time-conscious Groups share highlights only.

5. State the principle in each of the following proverbs. Then ask yourself: If I invited a younger woman to come to my home, over time would she see the positive aspect of this proverb in my life?

A. Proverbs 12:4—"A wife of noble character is her husband's crown, but a disgraceful wife is like decay in his bones."

Principle:_____

_____

How might she see it in me?

_____

_____

B. Proverbs 14:1—"The wise woman builds her house, but with her own hands the foolish one tears hers down."

Principle:_____

_____

How might she see it in me?

_____

_____

C. Proverbs 15:16—"Better a meal of vegetables where there is love than a fattened calf with hatred."

Principle:_____

_____

How might she see it in me?

_____

_____

D. Proverbs 29:17—"Discipline your son, and he will give you peace; he will bring delight to your soul."

Principle:_____

_____

How might she see it in me?

_____

_____

E. Proverbs 31:26-27—"She speaks with wisdom and faithful instruction is on her tongue. She watches over the affairs of her household and does not eat the bread of idleness."

Principle:_____

_____

How might she see it in me?

_____

_____

FOR PERSONAL REFLECTION ONLY

■ If many of the above proverbs are true in your life, I would especially encourage you to be given to hospitality to younger women! As you are still before the Lord, are there any younger women whom God impresses on your heart to invite over for a meal or visit?

ELIZABETH, MARY'S MENTOR

Elizabeth means "worshiper of God." We are told she led a blameless (blameless!) life. Jill Briscoe noted that Elizabeth is the kind of woman who, as you stand before her, convicts you by her life, challenges you by her faith.[2]

Mary would soon be a wife, so she watched with interest just how a godly couple related to each other in marriage. She and Joseph would not have the balm of a sexual relationship to soothe them during their first months of marital adjustment. (There was an interesting debate in England in 1985 concerning giving contraceptives to teenagers. The negative side was headed by an eloquent English mother. She said that encouraging teens in premarital sex uses up their "balm." She explained that during the difficult first year of marriage, when a couple is adjusting to each other, they need that balm of tremendous sexual excitement to soothe the hurts they unintentionally inflict on each other.) Mary and Joseph had not used up their balm, but they would not be using it, as there were to be no sexual relations until after Jesus was born. Mary and Joseph were going to need, instead, the balms of kindness, tenderness, and trust in God. And I believe God built up this balm in Mary by providing her with a mentor, by having her spend three months with a devout older woman who showed respect and love for her husband.

NOTE: When speaking in California, I referred to "the balm" of tremendous sexual excitment which God has given to newlyweds. Afterwards, a glowing little lady in her nineties came up and fairly shouted to me: "I LIKED YOUR POINT ABOUT THE BOMB!"

"The bomb?" I was confused.

"YES!" She repeated emphatically! "I REMEMBER! IT WAS A BOMB!"

Mary knew the Scriptures, as evidenced by her Magnificat. Elizabeth had just come out of five months of seclusion with the Lord. Both must have been eager to feast on the other's knowledge of prophecy. Can you imagine what it would be like to be pregnant with a child whose destiny was predicted in Scripture? And how caring of God to provide this sharpening time for Mary and Elizabeth to prepare for a future filled with joy and sorrow.

Elizabeth probably gave Mary help in practical matters as well.

How delightful it must have been to be with a friend who was pregnant, as you were, and to know you were both carrying sons! I can picture them dyeing material blue together, sewing a layette, and talking, all the time, about how to rear boys!

And finally, before Mary headed back to Nazareth, it's possible she helped in the delivery of John the Baptist. She did not know, at this time, that she would be giving birth in a stable. But God knew, and I'm convinced He provided her with this hands-on experience.

SCRIPTURAL
REFLECTION

For In-depth Groups Only

6. In *Matthew Henry's Commentary on the Whole Bible* (Henrickson), Matthew Henry says that some scholars believed Mary stayed for the birth, despite the fact that Luke mentions her return before he describes the birth. They believe that the evangelist would finish the passage concerning Mary before he proceeded with the story of Elisabeth but that Mary was there in order to help and to see the promise fulfilled. This is what makes the most sense to me—I think that's why she stayed three months! I can't imagine her leaving just before she was needed the most. However, there are others who believe she left in order to avoid the neighbors who came when John was born. Matthew Henry says this view is more widely held.

A. Do you think Mary stayed for the birth? Why or why not?

_____

_____

B. Read Luke 1:57-68. Using your imagination, list everything you can glean about Elizabeth from this passage.

_____

_____

C. In what ways was Elizabeth also a mentor to her neighbors? To her husband?

_____

_____

D. In your daily life, God may bring someone across your path who could benefit from nurturing: the hairdresser who seems stressed; the new mother who lives across the street; the friend of your teenage daughters who lingers in the kitchen while you are cooking. . . . What kind of questions would occur in the mind of a woman who is very sensitive to the Holy Spirit when God brings someone across her path?

_____

_____

THE VALUE OF MENTORS

Karen Mains reminisced about a seventy-year-old nun who cleaned her house when Karen was a young mother. The only payment Theresa would accept was that of bus fare. Every time the clock hit the quarter hour, Theresa would pray—threads of prayer were so woven into the fabric of her life. Karen says, "I think of her now with tears. I am certain that she built something into my life that I'm beginning to reap and see the benefit of now."[3]

Steve and I came to Christ while he was going through medical school, so we experienced great spiritual riches simultaneously with material poverty! During that time I became pregnant, and an older woman from our church (she was probably in her thirties—but she was older to me) stopped by to visit. Having met Bev only briefly, I was curious about the reason for her visit. Bev told me she wanted to make maternity clothes for me. I had trouble comprehending that she didn't want money or anything else in return but simply wanted to serve me in Christian love. I had never experienced this kind of friendship! Bev provided me with a vital model that the Christian life was much more than Christ meeting our needs, but it was a commitment to serve Him daily.

An older woman who is truly living the Christian life can be a tremendous model to a younger woman. If they spend time together, the younger woman can pick up, as if by osmosis, how she should live. Win Couchman tells about observing Mary Lou, who has been a mentor to Win:

> At Mary Lou's eightieth birthday party, I noticed that she was in very dignified black and white tweed. I decided to tease her a little about being so dignified now that she's eighty. Mary Lou stuck a finger under my nose and said, "You're not very observant today, Win! Take a look at the purse and the shoes!" I looked, and behold, red patent leather! . . . Then she took me in the back room and, dimpling, said, "Now, Win, there has to be a balance. Yes, I must be dignified. I am eighty. But I'm myself too!" And she flipped up just enough of the corner of her skirt to let me see the over-the-knee red underwear.[4]

Win says Mary Lou has been a beacon to her, that she has modeled a tenderness toward God, and yet also a fun in life—so many things that Win wants to be, further on down the road.

FOR PERSONAL REFLECTION ONLY

■ What are some areas in your life where you feel you are driving through a fog? (Do you struggle with gaining victory over having a quiet time, developing healthy eating habits, finding a ministry?)

_____

_____

■ Can you think of someone who has done well in this area and might be willing to give you some light?

_____

_____

_____

■ How sensitive are you to the "younger women" God puts in your path? How approachable are you?

_____

_____

_____

MENTORS IN THE CAREER WORLD

In *Mentors and Protéges*, Linda Phillips-Jones gives many examples of experienced career women who were eager to encourage less experienced women. She tells of Katherine S. White, the late fiction editor of *The New Yorker*, who was known for the unshakeable faith she had in her writers and who nurtured them on to better writing. "When White died, the magazine was deluged with letters that praised her and described the profound effect that her deep sense of caring had on people's lives."[5]

Grace, a young, dynamic, black lawyer, said of her mentor, "Her rules of personal behavior keep her ethically way above those around her. It really helps me to have her around as a kind of mirror."[6]

Successful, godly women in the career world are rare, but nothing is impossible for God, so pray persistently for a mentor. He knows your needs better than you do.

MOTHERS-IN-LAW

In your family, a mother, an older sister, an aunt, or even a mother-in-law can serve as a mentor. Now that I'm in my forties, I'm no longer amused by mother-in-law jokes—and I'm distressed, as the mother of two sons, that they are usually targeted at the mother of the son. I've pondered: *What are some of the root problems that create ugly, mother-in-law situations?*

Dr. James Dobson says that one of the reasons a woman feels more anxiety about letting a son go than a daughter is because the son is less apt to keep close contact. There's some sad truth in the saying, "A son is a son 'til he takes a wife, but a daughter's a daughter the rest of her life."[7] Because women have a gift for nurturing relationships, they're less likely to emotionally abandon their parents: they're more faithful in writing, calling, visiting, and expressing affection.

A mother is also going to feel more replaced by a daughter-in-law than she would by a son-in-law. It seems to me that the key is following Naomi's model. I have determined in my heart to remember how much Ruth and Orpah loved Naomi. If Naomi had feelings of jealousy when her sons married, she rooted them out and loved Ruth and Orpah as if they were her very own. What a beautiful, inspiring relationship! As a future mother-in-law, I gain hope from Naomi. (Since the original release of this book I've become a mother-in-law to a wonderful young woman. How I thank God for a Christian daughter-in-law who walks in faith and obedience. Julie makes being a mother-in-law a cinch!)

I've also been encouraged by the relationship my sister Bonnie had with her mother-in-law. I didn't realize how much Lillian meant to her until after Lillian's death. Bonnie is a blithe spirit, energetic and cheerfully eager about each day, seldom heavy-hearted. The exception, which surprised us all, was the year following her mother-in-law's death. My sister was devastated. Seven years later, as Bonnie and I sat on the beach together, I asked her to tell me why she loved Lillian so much. Her words tumbled out, and even then, after so much time, tears welled up in my normally dry-eyed sister:

> *Everybody loved Lillian! Just being near her was a comfort and a lift. Her humor, her joy in life, her attentiveness to your thoughts and feelings, her quiet faith. Lillian spent three months living with us one time. My friends raised their eyebrows and said, "Three months? Three months with your mother-in-law in the same house?" But it wasn't a difficult time. It is a joyous, precious memory in our lives. It helped that she was sensitive to both my need for privacy and my need for help. She would take long walks. She would completely stay out of the kitchen during preparation time. She said two cooks was one too many—so instead she would talk to the kids. I liked that. Then, afterward,*

she would insist on cleaning up by herself. But I think I was drawn to her because of the way she loved me. I didn't feel like a daughter-in-law but like a beloved daughter. Her actions, her eyes, and her smile told me—but if I didn't know, she wasn't hesitant to express it. If she sensed I was troubled she would say, "I hope you know how very much I love you." . . . I miss her so much.

As daughters-in-law, we need to become as vulnerable as Ruth. She told her mother-in-law everything! Jill Briscoe said that the biggest problem she sees in the relationships between mothers-in-law and daughters-in-law is lack of communication. We go so far, but hold our mothers-in-law at arm's length, unwilling to be like Ruth and go all the way to Bethlehem.[8]

SCRIPTURAL REFLECTION

7. Reflect again on the close relationship between Naomi and Ruth. Based on the following passages, answer these questions:

   A. Ruth 1:4-10—Naomi's sons married unbelievers. How do you think Naomi treated these girls during these first ten years?

   _____

   _____

   B. Ruth 1:5—What were some of the difficulties in Naomi's life? If you have a mother-in-law, how is her life difficult?

   _____

   _____

   C. Ruth 1:16–2:2—How was Ruth a mentor to Naomi during Naomi's time of high-tide grief? Is there an application for you? If so, what is it?

   _____

   _____

   D. Ruth 3:1-6—Sometimes this relationship is hampered by a daughter-in-law who holds her mother-in-law at arm's length. How is Ruth an example here? Is there an application for you?

   _____

   _____

⌛ E. What qualities do you think make a good mother-in-law? How can a mother-in-law go about helping her daughter-in-law to feel loved and accepted?

_____

_____

⌛ F. What qualities did you see in Ruth which made her an exceptional daughter-in-law? How can a daughter-in-law go about helping her mother-in-law to feel loved and accepted?

_____

_____

G. If a woman has a mother-in-law who is critical and disparaging, how might she win her over? (Consider Ruth.)

_____

_____

H. If a woman seems unable to win her mother-in-law over, what kind of Plan B do you think would be most pleasing to the Lord?

_____

_____

ACTION ASSIGNMENT

■ Write a note of encouragement to your daughter-in-law, mother-in-law or, if you have neither, to a mother or daughter or a spiritual mother or daughter.

■ Review your memory work of Titus 2:3-4.

MENTORING IS INFORMAL

In discipling, you meet with someone regularly to learn how to study the Bible, pray, and serve—but while mentoring may include some of this, it tends to be much less formal. It's not to be a dependent relationship, but simply a friendship as you spend time with a woman who is further down the road, at least in some areas of her Christian life. Win Couchman says, "Mentoring works very nicely over a cup of coffee."[9] I frequently had tea with Miriam, my ninety-year-old neighbor in Seattle. What a woman of God she is: given to diligent prayer, hospitality, and nurturing children into the kingdom. She showed me how to seize the tremendous opportunity of caring for others' children. Our daughter, Sally, who was then just a toddler, loved Miriam. (Sally still receives letters from her.) Whenever Sally would come back from a visit with Miriam, she'd have a verse of Scripture memorized and a lemon drop. (I think there was a connection.)

I was also impressed with how thankful, how content, Miriam was with her small home. I identified with the feelings expressed from a young woman in a letter to Win Couchman:

> *Your love of homemaking freed me to indulge my lifelong desire to be a homemaker. You demonstrated creativity in recipes, menus, and decoration of your modest home. This encouraged me not to covet bigger and better home and furnishings, but to express my personality and creative ideas in my home.*[10]

THE YOUNGER WOMAN SHOULD TAKE THE INITIATIVE
Win believes that it's best if the younger woman takes the initiative in asking to spend time, in asking to observe. It may begin with a simple request such as asking for help in making an apple pie or in balancing a budget. It may begin by the younger woman asking the older woman to share some of her wisdom. As a young mother, I asked a woman in Oregon how she had managed to raise her three teenage boys so that they loved the Lord so passionately. Her sons stood apart from their peers in the steadfastness of their walk, and I was particularly impressed because I knew their father was an atheist. She answered me carefully, and I'll never forget her words: "Dee, I can't say anything at home. I've never been able to. So I pray. Oh, do I pray! For an hour on my knees, every morning."

My friend Maureen Rank, author of *Free to Grieve*, sat with me at a writer's conference where we heard Karen Mains comment that she divides herself up and has several mentors. Maureen whispered, "That seems much healthier than having just one mentor who becomes God to you." I agree. One woman excels in raising children, another in hospitality, another in Bible knowledge. I can have a composite mentor by asking questions and taking the initiative to spend time with each of several women.

REFLECTION   ⧖ 8. How is mentoring different than discipling?

_____

_____

⧗ 9. Do you agree that it might be healthier to have a "composite" mentor rather than just one woman? Why or why not?

_____

_____

10. Do you agree that it is better if the younger woman takes the initiative? Why or why not?

_____

_____

Susan Hunt agrees the younger woman should take the initiative because it's difficult for an older woman to say, "Come spend time with me and I'll teach you how to be godly." However, I think that an older woman can reach out in friendship to a younger woman and that mentoring will take place without a formal declaration.

⧗ 11. What fears might keep a younger woman from reaching out to a woman she admires? How could she overcome those fears?

_____

_____

⧗ 12. What fears might keep an older woman from responding enthusiastically? How could she overcome those fears?

_____

_____

_____

The spring after the winter of her husband's death, Luci Shaw was the speaker at a poet's workshop in Seattle. Margaret Smith was one of her students, and longed to develop a more personal friendship with this woman with whom she had corresponded. But because Luci was a generation older than Margaret, and well known, Margaret was unsure how Luci would respond to an overture of friendship. But Margaret decided to risk inviting Luci to spend a few days at her Oregon home following the conference.

Margaret told me, with obvious delight, "Luci said yes!" Why did Luci agree? Partly because she liked Margaret and had hoped to know her better, but also because Luci is aware of her responsibility to young and promising poets. We need more women like Luci who, having succeeded in their fields (whether writing poetry, climbing the corporate ladder, or raising children who love the Lord) and are willing to have a mentor relationship with a younger woman. Margaret calls Luci, "Wise One." Luci said, laughing, "So I'm working on being wise."

A mentor relationship is obviously of great value to the younger woman, but it can be equally rewarding to the older woman. It is reciprocal. Ruth certainly was a blessing to Naomi, standing by her, empathizing with her sorrow. I believe that Margaret similarly blessed Luci, who, like Naomi, had just been widowed in midlife. One night during Luci's stay, Margaret, in an exercise of her gift for empathy, marked the following lines from a poem by George Herbert:

> And now in age I bud again;
> After so many deaths I live and write;
> I once more smell the dew and rain,
> And relish versing. O my only Light,
> It cannot be
> That I am [s]he
> On whom Thy tempests fall all night.

Believing the passage would minister to her grieving friend, Margaret left the book of Herbert's poetry open on Luci's bedside table. Through the medium of the poem, she was recognizing Luci's pain, acknowledging the tempest that had fallen on her, and affirming the truth of renaissance, of new life and growth after bereavement. The poem not only showed empathy, it gave wisdom and encouragement as it pointed to the truth that God, our "only Light," is the source of renewal and comfort.

Margaret found a pensive Luci walking behind the house early next morning, looking out beyond the stretch of rhododendrons and sea oats to the spruces that lined the Skipanon River. Margaret wrote a poem about this moment in their friendship:

> I found her out
> by the garden,
> watching the river and woods—
> I called her
> from hard dreaming . . .

Margaret went and stood beside Luci. Together they watched the flashes of indigo in the woods as stellar jays darted among the spruces. Luci said, "Those lines from Herbert—that's just it."

Empathizing, Margaret wrote further:

Someone should be able
to hold her
grief, take it
like a knapsack of rocks,
let her tiptoe
give wings to
fly with no gravity.

Margaret longed to hold some of Luci's pain. And she did, in part, by understanding. Such empathy erases the boundaries of age. Margaret said, "Although Luci is my mother's age, she's not like a mom. She's just a friend."

INTERGENERATIONAL FRIENDSHIPS:
Ruth 1:2-4; Luke 1:7

OLDER WOMEN AREN'T SO VERY DIFFERENT

My cousin Diane was disillusioned with the single life in Los Angeles. Remembering the beauty of her childhood summers in Ephraim, Wisconsin, she uprooted herself and moved there. Life was much quieter in this town that boasted "Population: 319." Because there weren't any women her age, Diane was forced to develop friendships with older women. I asked her what it was like. Reflectively, she said:

Once I got over the fact that these women were older, I stopped seeing that. They simply became my friends. I'm amazed, sometimes, how close we are. Because I am single, and have no children, I have actually found that there is a bigger division between married women who are my age than there is between married women who are a generation older. Since their children are grown, they are not so caught up in their children. We can talk about other subjects.

Wrinkles, gray hair, and a matronly figure should not obscure the reality that these women have been where you are going, and in their struggles with sin, with the joys and difficulties of sex, and with careers and relationships, they have gained some valuable wisdom. If you are aware of an older woman whom you admire for her walk with Christ, ask her if you could spend some time with her informally. Be careful not to take advantage, be careful to respect her commitments, but ask for permission to observe.

OLDER WOMEN NEED TO BE OPEN

Karen Mains says, "It is time for those of us in our forties and fifties to begin being responsible for our own adult spiritual age. We need to set ourselves aside in order to become so filled with God that He will make us women of great spiritual power."[11]

It's not optional on the older woman's part to be willing, for Scripture commands it. She may have to limit the number of younger women she can mentor at any one time, but she needs to be approachable. Paul mentions several things the older women should be modeling for the younger women. He stresses that the older women should be reverent in the way they live, not to be slanderers, or addicted to much wine, and they are to teach what is good. What is good? Paul spells that out clearly:

> They should be examples of the good life, so that the younger women may learn to love their husbands and their children, to be sensible and chaste, home-lovers, kindhearted and willing to adapt themselves to their husbands—a good advertisement for the Christian faith (Titus 2:4-5, PH).

Some churches permanently divide adult Sunday School classes according to age. This makes it difficult for the older women to teach the younger. If this is your situation, become involved in a Christ-centered Bible study group that doesn't have artificial age divisions. In these, older women often will teach younger women "to love their husbands and their children," as Titus 2 commands them to do. Phyllis held the younger women spellbound when she shared:

> When our children were young, my desire for sexual intimacy with my husband waned. It felt like a duty and I was resentful that after all day with the kids he would ask one more thing of me, and I was resentful of the Scripture that said I shouldn't deprive my husband of sexual relations (1 Cor. 7:3-5). But one day, in my quiet time, I saw that Scripture in a new light. The reason we aren't to deprive each other was so that Satan wouldn't get a toehold in our lives. I began to repent—not just by agreeing physically, but in my spirit. I was amazed at how God poured out the blessings on our marriage, renewing me, and

giving me more joy and energy for all I had to do. We can be to our husbands like the Shulamite maiden in the Song of Solomon was, if we just choose to be!

Though it may be best for the younger woman to initiate the mentor relationship, the older woman can demonstrate that she is open. Beryl, a woman in her sixties, sends cards and notes of encouragement to younger women. One young woman told me, "I have a stack of cards from Beryl, encouraging notes with timely Scriptures, which lifted me up at needy times in my life."

The first time I met Beryl was on the telephone. We were new in town and Steve had just begun his medical practice here. Beryl called and asked if I was Dr. Brestin's wife. When I answered affirmatively, she said, "I want you to know I'm in love with your husband." Then she broke into my shocked silence with her warm, loving laugh. "I also want you to know I'm old enough to be his mother." She then went on to explain that she had fervently prayed, as she sat in the ambulance next to her mother, for a tender, compassionate, patient doctor. "Your husband was God's gracious answer to my prayer." Beryl was teaching me to love my husband. She also showed me the door was open for friendship, and in walking through I have been tremendously encouraged by her model. Beryl has shown me God's love, joy, and patience as I've watched her delight in her twenty-eight-year-old son, who has Down's syndrome.

SCRIPTURAL REFLECTION

Time-conscious groups share highlights only.
- Meditate on the phrases in Titus 2:3-4. What principle do you find in each of the following, and how might you personally apply it?

13. First, mentors should be:

A. "reverent in the way they live"

Principle:_____

Application:_____

B. "not slanderers"

Principle:_____

Application:_____

C. "or addicted to much wine"

Principle:_____

Application:_____

D. "but to teach what is good"

Principle:_____

Application:_____

NOTE: The meaning here is to teach what is better, thus helping to choose the best priorities.

14. Then they can train the younger women to:

A. "love their husbands and children"

Principle:_____

Application:_____

B. "be discreet and chaste" (KJV)

Principle:_____

Application:_____

C. "to be keepers at home" (KJV)

Principle:_____

Application:_____

The above phrase is translated many ways: homelovers, domestic, busy at home. I think the KJV comes the closest as the word *keepers* or *homelovers* is derived from the word *guard*. When I think of a guard over the home, I think of someone who protects those who are within by creating a haven (thus homemaking) and by being acutely aware of ways to protect the inhabitants from outside threats: the destructive impact of the media; a society that fails to value a quiet life; and a myriad of worldly stresses and temptations.

D. "be good" (KJV)

Principle:_____

Application:_____

Again, note the connotation of choosing the higher road. This word is used when Jesus said, of Mary and Martha, "Mary has chosen the good portion" (RSV) and again in Ephesians 4:29, when we are told,

"Let no corrupt communication come out of your mouth, but that which is good to the use of edifying" (KJV).

   E. "be subject to their husbands"

   Principle:_____

   Application:_____

   F. Finally, this famous passage closes with the additional admonition, "so that no one will malign the word of God."

   Significance:_____

   _____

   We can sing sing with feeling, "What a Friend We Have in Jesus!" But it is also true, especially in the model of an older woman who has allowed God to spin her on His potter's wheel, to say with feeling, "What a Jesus We Have in a Friend!"

WINDING DOWN

■ If time permits, close by having each woman share one thing which she has learned from the discussion.

GROUP PRAYER

■ Write down an area of concern in your life for which you would like your sisters in Christ to pray.

   _____

   _____

   _____

   _____

Pray in spiritual mother/daughter pairs.

NEXT WEEK'S ASSIGNMENT

■ When you get home, while the group experience is still fresh, complete the journaling assignment in this chapter.

■ If you are a "spiritual daughter," the tables are turned this week. Do something to nurture your mother!

■ Complete the next chapter and journaling exercises.

PERSONAL
JOURNAL

■ What did God impress on your heart as a result of the group discussion and prayer?

_____

_____

■ How is God leading you to apply what you've learned?

_____

_____

Chapter 12
Reflections of Christ:
Review, Part One

Quiet your heart before God. Before you begin to read and journal, become aware of God's presence! Using the anacronym of ACTS:

- Adoration: Sing a song of praise to the Lord.
- Confession: Confess any known sin in your life and turn from it.
- Thanksgiving: Thank God for two blessings.
- Supplication: Ask Him for wisdom with this lesson—to particularly make you sensitive as you read through the questions. (This might be a good time to divide this chapter into five quiet times for the coming week.)

GROUP PRAYER

- Before you begin to discuss together, quiet your hearts before God. Using popcorn prayer, have the women ask for God's help in applying the truths learned in this book. The leader should close.

WARMING UP

Remember! If you are a Time-concious group, discuss only those questions marked ⌛ throughout.

1. If you were a spiritual mother, how were you nurtured this week?

_____

_____

2. Think about one truth or principle from Scripture that is repeated over and over again. What is it? How does the repetition of this truth impact you?

_____

_____

Salutation
(St. Luke 1:39-45)

Framed in light,
Mary sings through the doorway.
Elizabeth's six month joy jumps,
a palpable greeting,
a hidden first encounter
between son and Son.

And my heart turns over
when I meet Jesus
in you

Luci Shaw[1]

IN THE STORY of the wise man who built his house upon the rock and the foolish man who built his house upon the sand (Matt. 7:24-27), I've found it intriguing that both the wise man and the foolish man *heard* God's Word. The difference between them is that the wise man put it into practice, and the foolish man did not.

REFLECTION

3. Give an example of a truth from God's Word that you have put into practice in your life. Is there also a truth which you are struggling to put into practice?

_____

_____

4. For you, what disciplines increase the probability of going beyond hearing the Word to putting the Word into practice?

_____

_____

As you put God's friendship pattern into practice, a transformation will take place in you: because each of the characteristics in God's pattern are actually characteristics of Christ, you will become Christ's reflection in the world, as were Ruth, David, and Mary. We've looked at eleven threads that have wound their way through the tapestry of the three scriptural models of friendship we've examined, and I'd like to review each of these threads (five this week, six next week) and give you an opportunity to reflect on how you might apply them, specifically, in your life.

GREETING SCENES

By "greeting scenes," I mean the sensitivity to realize, on meeting someone, that God may be involved. God knows our needs better than we do and wants us to be alert to the people we meet.

Ruth, Jonathan, and Mary were alert to the friends God placed in their path. All crossed high hurdles to establish those friendships because they believed God was leading.

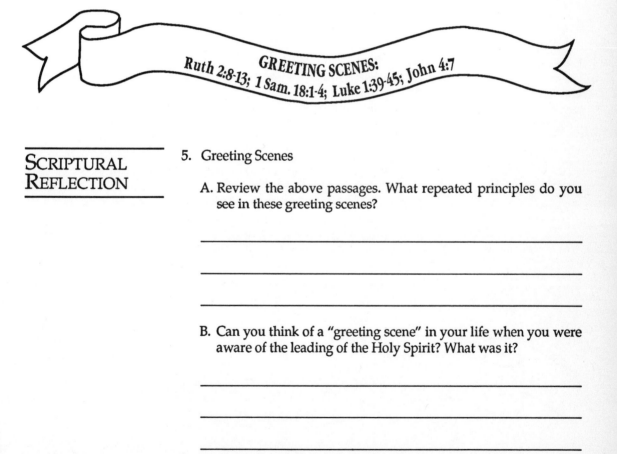

GREETING SCENES:
Ruth 2:8-13; 1 Sam. 18:1-4; Luke 1:39-45; John 4:7

SCRIPTURAL REFLECTION

5. Greeting Scenes

A. Review the above passages. What repeated principles do you see in these greeting scenes?

_____

_____

_____

B. Can you think of a "greeting scene" in your life when you were aware of the leading of the Holy Spirit? What was it?

_____

_____

_____

C. How sensitive are you to those you meet for the first time? Do you ask, when you meet them, whether it could be that God has a reason for bringing this person across your path?

_____

_____

DEPENDENCE ON GOD MORE THAN A FRIEND

Rachel said that the root problem leading to lesbianism is "worshiping" a person rather than God, developing a dependency on another person. Likewise, Naomi expected men to fulfill her needs, and when the men were gone, she was devastated.

As women, our tendency toward dependency on people is our Achilles' heel. We forget that our only real security is in God, and we trust instead in each other. In our desire to secure our bond, we are tempted by sins such as gossip and betrayal. When we or a soul mate moves, we feel like our foundation is crumbling.

When Steve told me were going to leave Seattle, I sobbed out my misery to my sister Sally on the telephone.

Sally said, "Dee, calm down. Do you know where your real home is?"

"Seattle!" I sobbed. "My friends are here, my church is here, my home is here."

"Your real home, Dee," my sister wisely said, "is in heaven. You are just passing through and Seattle was a temporary tent stop." As Sally lifted my eyes beyond the horizons of this earth to heaven and my real home, I realized she was speaking the truth. The temporal things will pass away, and we need to place our feet securely on the solid rock of Jesus Christ. It's important to love our friends and to be committed to them. But we need to be dependent on God, because He's the only One who will never leave us.

It should encourage us to see how Ruth, David, and Mary depended on God and found Him absolutely faithful.

DEPENDENCE ON GOD MORE THAN A FRIEND:
Ruth 2:11-12; 4:16; 1 Sam. 23:16; Luke 1:38; John 2:24

SCRIPTURAL REFLECTION

6. Dependence on God

A. Review the above passages. How is dependence on God rather than on a friend modeled in each? What principles do you see?

_____

_____

B. (Share only if you choose.) Consider this: Are you willing to share a soul mate? To refuse to gossip? To trust that God will provide when your best friend moves?

_____

_____

C. If this particular Bible study was regularly having twelve or more in attendance, would you be willing to put the names in a hat, divide the group, and make a concerted effort to invite new members to join? Why is this difficult? Why is it important?

_____

_____

D. Have you grown in this area of your life? If so, give evidence for your dependence on God instead of people.

_____

_____

AN INTERTWINING OF INTUITION WITH HOLY SPIRIT POWER

Intuition is a right-brain function and most women are blessed with it. Obviously, there are times when we're going to be wrong, but if we check our hunches by leaning on the Holy Spirit (by being immersed in the Scriptures and sensitive to His quiet voice), we will be wise to move ahead when something seems "good to the Holy Spirit and to us" (Acts 15:28).

I believe this is what Ruth did when she read between the lines of Naomi's rejection and stood by her side. Likewise, Mary seemed to know that it was important to take the hundred-mile trip to see Elizabeth.

INTERTWINING OF INTUITION WITH HOLY SPIRIT POWER:
Ruth 1:16; 3:5; 1 Sam. 18:1-4; 23:16; Luke 1:39-56

SCRIPTURAL REFLECTION

7. Holy Spirit Power and Intuition

A. In the above passages, what action did the individuals take based on "what seemed good to the Holy Spirit and to them?" What principles do you see here?

_____

_____

B. Can you share a time in your life when you took action because of a "hunch" that seemed in keeping with the leading of the Holy Spirit?

_____

_____

C. In order to use your gift for intuition wisely in friendship, let me ask you: Are you reading through the Bible regularly? Are you memorizing Scripture regularly?

_____

_____

_____

RISK TAKING
Risk taking is essential for finding friends and bonding with them. Ruth, Jonathan, and Mary took tremendous risks in initiating friendships and then in making themselves vulnerable. Christ risked dying on the cross, even though many would not respond.

Ruth 1:16; 2:2; 3:5; 1 Sam. 18:1; 19:4; 20:4; Luke 1:39; Matt. 26:42

RISK TAKING:

SCRIPTURAL REFLECTION

8. Risk-Taking

A. In the above passages, how do you see the models taking risks? What principles do you see?

_____

_____

B. Tell about a risk you've taken in friendship or in this group that you are glad you took.

_____

_____

C. Will you risk becoming involved with a hurting, bleeding friend? Will you risk reaching out to someone you admire? And if someone does not at first respond to you, will you try again?

_____

_____

UNFAILING LOVE

Naomi prayed that God would show Ruth unfailing love (Ruth 1:8), and Jonathan said to David, "Show me unfailing kindness like that of the Lord" (1 Sam. 20:14).

We are living in a time of impermanence and easy good-byes. It takes discipline to show unfailing love when a friend is needing a great deal of help, or when she moves away, or when she hurts you with unkind words. But how like Christ, who shows us His faithfulness morning by morning, we become if we can show steadfast kindness in these situations!

UNFAILING LOVE:
Ruth 1:8, 20; 1 Sam. 20:14; 2 Sam. 9:1-13; Luke 1:50; 1 John 3:16

SCRIPTURAL REFLECTION

■ Take some time with this most important of principles! How do you learn about unfailing love from the above passages? What principles do you see?

9. Unfailing Love

A. Share a time when a friend gave unfailing love to you.

_____

_____

B. With long-distance friends, how do you know to whom God would have you be true? How will you discipline yourself to show steadfastness to those long-distance friends?

_____

_____

C. How will you discipline yourself to remain true to your real connections nearby?

_____

_____

_____

D. How will you respond if a close friend lets you down?

_____

_____

_____

WINDING DOWN

■ If time permits, close by having each woman share one thing which she has learned from the discussion.

GROUP PRAYER

■ Write down an area of concern in your life for which you would like your sisters in Christ to pray.

_____

_____

Pray, using popcorn prayer.

NEXT WEEK'S ASSIGNMENT

■ When you get home, while the group experience is still fresh, complete the journaling assignment in this chapter.

■ Complete the next chapter and exercises.

PERSONAL JOURNAL

■ What did God impress on your heart as a result of the group discussion and prayer?

_____

_____

■ How is God leading you to apply what you've learned?

_____

_____

Chapter 13
Reflections of Christ:
Review, Part Two

PERSONAL PRAYER Quiet your heart before God. Before you begin to read and journal, become aware of God's presence! Using the anacronym of ACTS:

- Adoration: Sing a song of praise to the Lord.
- Confession: Confess any known sin in your life and turn from it.
- Thanksgiving: Thank God for two blessings.
- Supplication: Ask Him for wisdom with this lesson—to particularly make you sensitive as you read through the questions. (This might be a good time to divide this chapter into five quiet times for the coming week.)

GROUP PRAYER

- Before you begin to discuss together, quiet your hearts before God. Using popcorn prayer, have the women ask for God's help in applying the truths learned in this book. The leader should close.

WARMING UP

Remember! If you are a Time-concious group, discuss only those questions marked ⧗ throughout.
1. What is an incident that embarrassed you or made you feel badly in childhood, but now that you look back on it, you realize that it wasn't a big deal! (This is a warm-up to sharing vulnerably!)

SHARING VULNERABLY

After her night with Boaz, Ruth told Naomi "everything." Jonathan and David bared their souls to each other, and Elizabeth didn't tone down her ecstasy in seeing Mary.

In Gethsemane, Jesus vulnerably told Peter, James, and John that He needed their support and prayer. He said, "My soul is overwhelmed with sorrow to the point of death" (Mark 14:34).

Do you remember Ann Kiemel's observation? She found that "being vulnerable actually draws people to us, because the world is full of people . . . that are bleeding and hurting."[1]

SHARING VULNERABLY: Ruth 1:11-21; 2:13; 3:9, 16; 1 Sam. 18:4; 20:3, 14, 41-42; Luke 1:43; Matt. 26:38

SCRIPTURAL REFLECTION

2. Sharing Vulnerably

A. How did the models in the above Scriptures share vulnerably?

_____

_____

B. What principles do you see?

_____

_____

_____

C. Can you think of a time in this group where you saw bonding taking place because of an individual's willingness to share vulnerably? If so, when?

_____

_____

_____

D. What are some ways to measure if a friend will be trustworthy with your confidences?

_____

_____

E. Would you be willing to confess an area in your life where you are struggling with sin, or doubt, or worry and share vulnerably with the group for prayer?

_____

_____

Now pray for those who shared, using popcorn prayer.

SCRIPTURAL
REFLECTION

F. How could you better strip away pretense with trusted friends?

_____

_____

G. Are you trustworthy with confidences when a friend shares vulnerably with you?

_____

_____

_____

WHATEVER YOU ASK ME TO DO, I'LL DO IT

Ruth spoke these words to Naomi when Naomi proposed her daring plan (Ruth 3:5). And Jonathan said the same thing to David when David asked him to risk his life to find out Saul's true motives (1 Sam. 20:4). And Christ has said to us, "You may ask Me for anything in My name, and I will do it" (John 14:14).

This pattern intrigues me: it shows me how careful I should be in making requests of soul mates, but also how responsive I should be when a close friend asks for help from me. It is particularly hard for a hurting friend to ask for help, but if she even hints, we should respond with, "Whatever you ask me to do, I'll do it."

"Whatever you ask me to do, I will do for you."
Ruth 3:5; 1 Sam. 20:4; John 14:14

SCRIPTURAL
REFLECTION

3. Whatever You Ask Me To Do . . .

A. What do you learn from the above models about responding to soulmates who ask for help? What principles do you see?

_____

_____

B. Can you think of a time in your life when a friend responded to your request for help enthusiastically? If so, share what happened and how you felt.

_____

_____

C. Will you respond cheerfully and eagerly, despite great personal sacrifice, when a soulmate asks for help?

_____

_____

WORDS OF BLESSING OR ENCOURAGEMENT

Repeatedly, our scriptural friends "blessed" one another verbally. Note the pattern in the following examples: the high value that is attributed to the friend and the bright future that is pictured, often through prayer, because of God's faithfulness.

Naomi to Ruth and Orpah: "May the Lord show kindness [unfailing love] to you, as you have shown to your dead and to me" (Ruth 1:8).

Boaz to Ruth: "All my fellow townsmen know that you are a woman of noble character" (Ruth 3:11); "May you be richly rewarded by the Lord, the God of Israel, under whose wings you have come to take refuge" (Ruth 2:12).

Jonathan to David, when he "helped him find strength in God" at Horesh: "Don't be afraid. . . . My father Saul will not lay a hand on you. You will be king over Israel, and I will be second to you" (1 Sam. 23:17).

Elizabeth to Mary: "Blessed is she who has believed that what the Lord has said to her will be accomplished!" (Luke 1:45)

WORDS OF BLESSING OR ENCOURAGEMENT:
Ruth 1:8, 16; 2:12-13, 20; 3:11; 4:15; 1 Sam. 19:4; 20:16-17, 42; 24:17; 2 Sam. 9:1-13; Luke 1:42-45; John 14:1

SCRIPTURAL REFLECTION

4. Blessing Others

A. What do you learn from the above models about blessing or encouraging others? Which "blessing" particularly stands out to you? Why?

_____

_____

B. What principles do you see?

_____

_____

ACTION ASSIGNMENT

■ On individual index cards or notes, write two sentences of encouragement to each of the members of your group, using what you've learned about blessing others. Read them to them in front of the group. When everyone is done reading their cards, give the cards to the individuals to take home.

INTERGENERATIONAL FRIENDSHIP

Although David and Jonathan were peers, the friendships between Ruth and Naomi and between Mary and Elizabeth were intergenerational friendships. This should speak to us, as should God's command that the older women teach the younger. It is likewise interesting that in both cases the friends were also relatives, though mentors aren't limited to relatives.

INTERGENERATIONAL FRIENDSHIPS:
Ruth 1:2-4; Luke 1:7

SCRIPTURAL REFLECTION

5. Intergenerational Friendship

A. What was the value in the above models of the friendship to the younger women? To the older?

_____

_____

B. Have you been blessed by an intergenerational friendship? If so, share something about it.

_____

_____

C. God may have someone older and someone younger than you in mind for a friendship. As you are still before Him, who might they be?

_____

_____

PARTING SCENES

God zoomed His camera in on parting scenes between Ruth and Naomi and then again with David and Jonathan. As we watch them weep and cling to each other, we understand Shakespeare's words "Parting is such sweet sorrow."[2]

Likewise, Scripture shows us that Christ did not shrink from saying good-bye to those He loved. He began saying good-bye very early in His three-year ministry, warning them that He would be crucified. His words "Let not your heart be troubled" (John 14:1) remind me of Jonathan's parting words to David. Words and emotions that are expressed in parting scenes come to our remembrance again and again. Parting scenes, though painful, are not wasted sadness.

PARTING SCENES:
Ruth 1:8-14; 1 Sam. 20:41-42; John 19:26

SCRIPTURAL REFLECTION

6. Parting Scenes

A. What do you learn from the above models? What principles do you see about parting?

_____

_____

_____

B. Can you share a memorable "parting scene" from your life? What was it?

_____

_____

_____

C. Will you endure the pain of a parting scene in order to give future comfort? Will you go to the airport? Sit at the bedside of a dying friend? And will you learn, from parting scenes, the value of expressing your affection before a move or death prompts it?

_____

_____

_____

_____

COMMITMENT

Ruth's vows take my breath away: "Whither thou goest, I will go." These were not empty promises. *Ruth followed through.*

And David and Jonathan promised each other unfailing love, renewing their covenant to keep themselves true. It is in the account of the keeping of David's promise that we see perhaps the clearest reflection of Christ.

Jonathan has been killed in battle and David is king of Israel. He asks, "Is there anyone still left of the house of Saul to whom I can show kindness [literally, "unfailing love"] for Jonathan's sake?" (2 Sam. 9:1) And they bring before him Jonathan's son, the lame Mephibosheth.

When Mephibosheth comes into David's presence, he is terribly frightened. But David, in a reflection of Christ, says, "Don't be afraid . . . for I will surely show you kindness for the sake of your father Jonathan. I will restore to you all the land that belonged to your grandfather Saul, and you will always eat at my table" (2 Sam. 9:7).

And God says to us, though we are crippled in both feet, "Don't be afraid . . . for I will surely show you kindness for the sake of My Son Jesus, and I will give you a place in heaven forever, and you will always eat at My table." That's the promise, the commitment. All we need to do is come in the attitude of Mephibosheth and the promise is ours.

Ruth, Boaz, David, and Jonathan kept their promises, and Christ will keep His promise to us.

COMMITMENT/PROMISES:
Ruth 1:16-17; 1 Sam. 20:42; 2 Sam. 9:1-13; Matt. 28-20

SCRIPTURAL
REFLECTION

7. Commitment/Promises

A. What from the above passage particularly impresses you? Why?

_____

_____

_____

B. What principles do you see repeated in the above passage?

_____

_____

C. What is the value of a friendship promise? The danger?

_____

_____

D. Has this concept been meaningful in your life? If so, share something about it.

_____

_____

E. Might you make a solemn vow of friendship to a soul mate as you would to a marriage partner? How faithful are you being to the promises, spoken or implied, that you have made?

_____

_____

ONE LAST STORY—TIPAWAN

Several threads from God's friendship pattern can wind their way through every friendship, adding depth and beauty. When I met Tipawan the Lord kept reminding me of different threads from His pattern.

"Foxy!" is how a man in our church described this slender, doe-eyed beauty from Thailand. "Trouble!" was the word that came to my mind.

Tipawan had been so eager to escape difficult living conditions in Thailand that she agreed to come to Los Angeles with an American man she barely knew. Tipawan thought he intended to marry her, but he intended to be her pimp, not her husband. When she refused, he put her on a plane back to Thailand. The plane stopped briefly in San Francisco, and Tipawan got off! She was determined to stay in America, though she had but twenty dollars. A man she met in the San Francisco airport had compassion on her and brought her back to his apartment. She lived with him and they became sexually involved.

Tipawan knew only one other person in the United States, and that was a childhood friend from Thailand who had married an American and moved to Kearney, Nebraska. Her name was Chinda, and Chinda is my friend as well. Tipawan called Chinda one day and Chinda encouraged her to take the bus to Nebraska. Chinda told me, "I wish she wasn't living with that man, Dee. Maybe if she come here, I can help her." Chinda's obedience impressed me. New to the Lord, Chinda was taking a great risk to become involved with a woman who had visa, financial, and deep spiritual problems.

My first meeting with Tipawan, our "greeting scene," occurred when Chinda brought her to Sunday School. Tipawan asked searching questions revealing a spiritually hungry heart. It wasn't difficult to see that God had brought her across my path for a reason. Despite the fact that she was almost young enough to be my daughter, I realized that God often uses intergenerational friendships for His glory. I was hoping to become involved with her through Sunday School, and perhaps I would have her over for dinner. My plan was limited commitment! Chinda had other plans. She said to me, "Tipawan very mixed up. I need you to talk to her, Dee. So I bring her over to your house much times, drop her off, and come back much hours later."

As I considered refusing Chinda, several thoughts came to mind. One was the words of Ruth and of Jonathan: "Whatever you ask me to do, I will do it." It's hard to ask for help, and we should respond willingly when a friend is in need.

Next, I considered what a great risk this was going to be: Tipawan had so many needs, I feared she would swallow me alive! But I realize the value of risks, especially when you have a hunch God is leading. And God confirmed it by bringing a verse I'd memorized to mind: "whosoever . . . seeth his brother have need, and shutteth up his compassions from him, how dwelleth the love of God in him?" (1 John 3:17, SCO) My *natural* inclination when I see someone in need is to shut up my compassions! But if I'm going to use my gift for friendship redemptively to bless the world, I'm going to have to take risks based on my intuitive sense that God is leading and not step over the broken and bleeding people in my path. So I agreed to Chinda's plan.

During my afternoons with Tipawan, we slowly became acquainted. She was charming me with her gradual smile, her gentleness, her seeking heart. Because she spoke broken English, it took time for her to communicate and for me to understand. But slowly and surely we were bonding. Sometimes we'd take a break from our earnest discussion and get out the sled and slide down our snow-covered hill. Tipawan was fascinated by snow!

One day after sledding, we sat by the fire warming our hands with steaming mugs of cocoa. Risking vulnerability, Tipawan tearfully told me that she had had seven abortions. I was shocked, but I knew my immediate response had to be compassion. I put my arms around her and she wept. I told her Christ could forgive her for taking the lives of her babies if she would come to Him and turn from her sin. I knew that because she was from a Buddhist culture, the Gospel message was new to her. I continued talking to her about Jesus, but I sensed she wasn't comprehending.

The weeks passed, and so did our meetings. One day Tipawan rang the doorbell and rushed in excitedly. With animated gestures, she relayed a dream to me. She said, "First this dream scare me, then make me so happy."

> *I dream I walk in a big dark cave. Buddha standing there, and flying around his head are the parts of babies. Arms. Legs. Faces. They crying. Crying. It very terrible. I want to get out. But the door shut and I can't get out. "Please, Buddha," I cry, "let me go!" Then, Buddha raise his hand. [She raised her hand, to show me, in a peace sign.] The cave open and I free!*

"What do you think your dream means, Tipawan?" I asked. "Why did it make you happy?"

"I think it means Buddha forgive me about all those babies I killed."

I was quiet. I got up, walked over and sat beside her on the sofa. Taking her hands in mine, I said, "I know how badly you want to be forgiven. From the very first day I met you, I could see how heavily this burden has weighed upon your heart." She nodded, the tears were coming. "I want to see you forgiven too, but, Tipawan, Buddha doesn't have the power to forgive you." She looked up with fear in her eyes.

"Buddha was just a man. A wise man. A strong leader. But he died and he can't help you. But there is someone who can help you. God sent His only Son, Jesus, to come to earth and to die on a cross to pay for your sin."

I brought out pictures, hoping to help her understand. First, I showed her a picture of Jesus on the cross. She touched it, tenderly. I kept explaining. "The way that Jesus is different from Buddha is that He wasn't just a man. He is God, but He came to earth and lived, for a while, as a man. He never sinned, and after He died, He rose from the dead! He alone has the power to forgive sin." Then I showed Tipawan a picture of the risen Christ with 500 witnesses. I also showed her a picture of Him with Thomas, who wanted to touch His nail-pierced hands. She was pensive. As I shared my testimony with her, I sensed that the Holy Spirit was drawing Tipawan. I told her that coming to Jesus would mean a turn in her life: she would need to stop living for herself and start living for Him.

I prayed fervently that next week, as did Chinda. We prayed that the Spirit would teach Tipawan and lead her into truth. Chinda and Tipawan burned the midnight oil many a night talking about spiritual truths. Tipawan was still coming with Chinda to Sunday School and church, and seemed eager to know the one true God.

One Sunday Tipawan said to me, "I come to your house tomorrow—you help me become God's daughter." She did, and she prayed one of the most beautiful prayers I'd ever heard, full of understanding and repentance. And God changed her. The fear in her eyes was replaced by peace and inextinguishable joy!

I would like to tell you that this story ended with Tipawan living wholeheartedly for the Lord. I wish that for Tipawan's sake and because, I admit, it would make a lovely ending to this book. But that isn't what happened. Despite my protests, and an offer of room and board from a lovely Christian couple in our church, Tipawan eventually went back to California and her live-in boyfriend. Her plan was to live with him but not sleep with him.

I called a few weeks later to check on her. She said, "I had to sleep with him, Dee. He so sad. But I not smoking!"

Consternated, I paused. After a moment, I asked hopefully, "Have you found a Bible study? Are you going to church?"

"I did, Dee. But I stop. I know the people there think it bad for me to live with a man not my husband."

I am not without sympathy for Tipawan, for I realize from my study of Naomi how easily women fall into depending on a human relationship rather than on God. I pray that as Tipawan grows in her trust of God, she will have the strength to change her lifestyle. My natural response at this point is to give up. I put so much time into our friendship, and I am frustrated. But then the Lord reminds me of how He has loved me with an everlasting love, of how, though I don't live up to His wishes for me, His mercies are new morning by morning. He doesn't give up on me, and I can't give up on my friend Tipawan.

As a long-distance friend, I can pray for her, I can write to her, and I can show her the kind of unfailing love that the Lord has shown me. I need to let her know the right path and not condone her sin, but I must not abandon her.

NOTE: My contact with Tipawan continued for five years after the release of *The Friendships of Women*. At this point I have lost contact with her. In some ways this is discouraging, but I also know that we belong to a faithful God who brings good things out of our obedience. One of the most amazing things that has happened, and I believe that my friendship with Tipawan played a part, is that we have adopted a young girl from an orphanage in Thailand. I tell this amazing story in *And Then We Were Women*, the sequel to this book.

MY PARTING SCENE

The Lord has taught me some profound truths about friendship, and I hope that His teachings have flowed through me to you, my reader, and now, my friend. So we are bound together in His truth and in His Spirit. It's painful to close this book; it's hard to say good-bye, but I am encouraged by C.S. Lewis' great shout, "REMEMBER! CHRISTIANS NEVER SAY GOOD-BYE!"[3] I will meet every one of you who has personally trusted Christ for her salvation—one day, in eternity!

So I ask you to go in peace and to practice, as I will, God's friendship pattern. God promises us that, as we obey His Word, His love will truly be made complete in us (1 John 2:5). We will experience greater and greater fellowship with one another (1 John 1:7) and we will become Christ's reflection in the world. I am coming to understand, more and more, what the Apostle John meant when he said, "For we realize that our life in this world is actually His life lived in us" (1 John 4:17, PH).

In His Unfailing Love,

Dee

WINDING DOWN

■ A year from now, what do you think you will still remember from this book and this study?

_____

_____

■ How are you different because of this study?

_____

_____

GROUP PRAYER

■ Write down an area of concern in your life for which you would like your sisters in Christ to pray.

_____

_____

Pray, using popcorn prayer.

RECOMMENDED RESOURCES FOR WOMEN

WOMEN'S FRIENDSHIP MINISTRIES

Dee is a popular seminar speaker. She speaks often on friendship as well as falling more deeply in love with Jesus. She seldom speaks to groups of less than 350, because she limits her engagements. For more information, she can be contacted in the following ways:

> Dee Brestin
> 11 Lakeview Drive
> Kearney, NE 68845
> 308-237-7572 weekdays 8:30 – 4:00 cst
> 308-234-3993 fax
> dbrestin@kearney.net
> www.deebrestin.com

If you are interested in purchasing The Focus on the Family audio-cassette featuring Dr. Dobson's interview with Dee, Call 1-800-A-Family and request tape CS439 Women and Friendships. Suggested donation $7.00.

OTHER STUDIES BY DEE BRESTIN

We Are Sisters (Victor)

This is a sequel to *The Friendships of Women* and deals with how maturity in our friendships can strengthen the family. In addition to looking at how our friendships impact us as wives and mothers, this book looks within the family at mothers and daughters; sisters; and the volatile relationship between an ex-wife and the new wife. Some of the scriptural women you will be studying are Jochebed and Miriam; Rachel and Leah, and the Daughters of Jerusalem in the Song of Solomon. Study questions included.

THE DEE BRESTIN SERIES OF BIBLE STUDIES FOR WOMEN (VICTOR)
Thousands of women are discovering these practical Bible study guides geared specifically to women. These are not books, but Bible study guides, with lots of additional helps through quotations from various authors, action assignments, and probing discussion questions:

Women are hungering for Bible studies designed specifically for them by other women. Partly in jest and partly in absolute seriousness, Vickie Kraft, a graduate of Dallas Seminary and a trailblazer in the area of women's ministries, said: "Men can teach the Word beautifully, but when it comes to appying it to women, they haven't a clue!" The following studies are designed to meet that need.

The Joy of Women's Friendships
This material is different than the material in *The Friendships of Women.* Some of the Scriptural models examined are Rachel and Leah, the daughters of Jerusalem in the Song of Solomon, and Miriam and Jochebed.

The Joy of Hospitality
Women can use their homes to make an enormous difference in the lives of family, friends, unbelievers, new Christians, and those who are hurting. Scripture abounds with examples of women who did so!

The Joy of Eating Right (co-authored with Peggy Johnston)
While support groups and programs for women abound, most fail to realize that the central problem in poor eating habits is spiritual. Rather than a diet, this guide will help you to change your lifelong eating habits, based on spiritual and nutritional principles.

A Woman of Value (Proverbs)
The Book of Proverbs stresses characteristics that God values in women. This guide will examine eight of those characteristics in depth and also look at women in Scripture who possessed them and women who did not!

My Daughter, My Daughter (Chariot Victor)
God is calling out to women (My Daughter, My Daughter) to understand and pass on their holy heritage. Biblical women will spring to life as they are compared to the lives of contemporary women. Miriam is compared to Sandi Patty, a leader in song who fell, repented, and was given grace. The Hebrew midwives are compared to Kathy Troccoli, a woman of faith who is saving the lives of innocents. Eve, and then Sarah, is compared to Lori Beckler, a woman who was tempted by the world to ignore God's voice, but then, through faith, overcame the temptation and went on to found the women's conference, Heritage Keepers. Each chapter closes with an in-depth Bible study that can be done individually or with a small group of women.

A Woman of Insight (Ecclesiastes)
Pearls of wisdom for women will be uncovered in this fascinating book. How badly we need the wisdom of this book today when so many women, even Christian women, are losing their eternal perspective.

A Woman's Journey through Luke (Chariot Victor)
12 lessons on the Savior. Luke is the gospel most sympathetic to women and this guide looks carefully at passages and stories that are of particular interest to women. You'll look carefully, for example, at the women who traveled with Jesus, at Mary and Martha of Bethany, and the women at the cross and the empty tomb.

A Woman's Journey through Ruth (Chariot Victor)
8 lessons on love. Ruth's name means "a woman" friend and she shows us the height of which we are capable as women. In addition to a wonderful friendship story, it is a love story, and provides a beautiful symbolic portrait of our relationship with Jesus, our kinsman-redeemer.

A Woman's Journey through Esther (Chariot Victor)
8 lessons on faith. This fascinating and controversial book will delve into such questions as: Was Vashti right to disobey her husband? Was Esther right to participate in a beauty contest that involved sleeping with the king? What was the secret to Esther's successful women's ministry?

A Woman's Journey through 1 Peter (Chariot Victor)
8 lessons on confidence. Even if you are married to an unbeliever, or facing persecution, or a terminal illness, Peter shows us how to face life with confidence. This guide is laced with lovely illustrations from John Bunyan's classic, *Pilgrim's Progress*, which also shows us how to sojourn through this life.

OTHER SMALL GROUP STUDIES FOR WOMEN

What Happens When Women Pray (Cook)
by Evelyn Christenson (group study guide included)

Spiritual Mothering (Christian Education and Publications)
by Susan Hunt
This book and accompanying leader's guide deals with women mentoring women. The phone number of Christian Education and Publications is 1-800-283-1357.

The Cynthia Heald Series (NavPress)
   Becoming A Woman of Excellence
   Becoming A Woman of Purity
   Becoming A Woman of Purpose

Many of the above are guides which gear into a particular topic. This is great, but don't limit yourself to topical guides. To stay balanced, alternate with guides which will take you through whole books of the Bible. Dee has written many book studies for the *Fisherman Series* (Harold Shaw) and also recommends those published by InterVarsity, NavPress, and Cook.

**OTHER CHRISTIAN BOOKS WHICH
DEAL WITH WOMEN'S FRIENDSHIPS**

The Seasons of Friendships (Zondervan)
by Ruth Senter
Not a "How-To" book, but a lovely look at friendship in the different seasons of our lives. Mrs. Senter takes an honest look at the painful and delightful friendships of her childhood, adolescence, and adulthood.

In the Company of Women (Multnomah)
by Brenda Hunter, Ph.D.
A helpful at women's relationships. Dr. Hunter is a psychologist with the Minirth-Meier New Life Clinic and also the founder of the organization "Mothers at Home." About half of this book is dedicated to the mother/daughter relationship and the other half to other women's relationships, including some insightful chapters on women's friendships.

The Gift of Feeling (John Knox Press)
by Paul Tournier
The noted Swiss physician examines a women's gift for intimacy and how she can impact the world—not only her own friendships, but the world at large.

Can I Afford Time for Friendships? (Bethany House)
by Stormie Omartian, Ruth Senter, Colleen Evans
Editors of *Today's Christian Women* interview these three authors concerning women's friendships.

FOR THOSE WHO ARE STRUGGLING WITH OVERCOMING A LESBIAN LIFESTYLE

Dee highly recommends Exodus, International. They have seminars, support groups, and a helpful list of reading materials including testimonies of women have found victory. Their address is P.O. Box 77652, Seattle, WA 98177-0652. Their phone number is 206-784-7799. One particularly good pamphlet available from Exodus is:

Emotional Dependency, A Threat to Close Friendships
by Lori Thorkelson
A pamphlet available from Exodus International to help you recognize and respond to this danger.

SECULAR BOOKS WHICH DEAL WITH WOMEN'S FRIENDSHIPS

Just Friends (Harper and Row)
by Lillian Rubin
Dr. Rubin, a social scientist and pyschotherapist draws on interviews with 300 men and women. Their reflections on friendships of men women, and men and women are fascinating. Dr. Rubin's own reflections are insightful as well. She deals with the fact that we don't have any ceremony or covenant to recognize friendship, as we do with marriage. Hence, the title, *Just Friends.*

You Just Don't Understand: Women and Men in Conversation (William Morrow)
by Deborah Tannen, Ph.D.
This fascinating book, while not about women's friendships directly, helps us to see why women need women, but also how to understand and be less hurt by a man's very different style of communication.

Endnotes

CHAPTER 1: FROM GIRLHOOD ON, GIFTED FOR INTIMACY

1. Elliot Engel, "Of Male Bondage," *Newsweek* (June 21, 1982), p. 13.
2. Janet Lever, "Sex Differences in the Games Children Play," *Social Problems*, 23 (1976), pp. 478-87.
3. Zick Rubin, *Children's Friendships* (Cambridge, Mass.: Harvard University Press, 1980), p. 108.
4. Judith Bardwick, *Psychology of Women* (New York: Harper and Row Publishers, 1971), pp. 126-27.
5. Paul D. Robbins, "Must Men Be Friendless?" *Leadership* (Fall 1984), p. 26.
6. Richard Cohen, "Men Need Liberating from Repressed Feelings," *Male-Female Roles* (St. Paul, Minn.: Greenhaven Press, 1983), p. 96.
7. Joel D. Block, *Friendship —How To Give It—How to Get It* (New York: MacMillan, 1980), pp. 57, 80.
8. Lillian B. Rubin, *Just Friends: The Role of Friendship in Our Lives* (New York: Harper and Row, 1985), p. 63.
9. Ladd Wheeler, Harry Reis, and John Nezlik, "Loneliness, Social Interaction and Sex Roles," *Journal of Personality and Social Psychology*, 45/ (1983), p. 951.
10. William Shakespeare, *Romeo and Juliet*, Act 2, Scene 2, *Great Books of the Western World*, Vol. 26 (Chicago: Encyclopaedia Britannica, Inc., 1952), p. 296.

CHAPTER 2: WOMEN ARE FRIENDLIER

1. Joel D. Block and Diane Greenberg, *Women and Friendship* (New York: Franklin Watts, 1985), p. 3.
2. Lillian B. Rubin, *Just Friends* (New York: Harper and Row, 1985), p. 105.
3. Letha Scanzoni, "On Friendship and Homosexuality," *Christianity Today* (September 27, 1974), p.11.
4. Stuart Miller, *Men and Friendship* (Boston: Houghton Mifflin, 1983), p. 2.
5. C.S. Lewis, *The Four Loves* (San Diego: Harcourt Brace Jovanovich, 1960), p. 90.

6. Sondra Enos, "A New Kind of Father," *Ladies Home Journal* (June 1986), p. 47.

7. Rubin, *Just Friends*, p. 161.

8. Barbara Eakins, R. Gene Eakins, *Sex Differences in Human Communications* (Boston: Houghton Mifflin, 1978), pp. 67–69.

9. Dr. Donald Joy as interviewed by Dr. James Dobson, Cassette #CS099, "The Innate Differences Between Males and Females" (Broadcast of "Focus on the Family" from Arcadia, California).

10. "Just How the Sexes Differ," *Newsweek* (May 18, 1981), p. 78.

11. Joy, "The Innate Differences."

12. "Just How the Sexes Differ," p. 78.

13. Gary Smalley on "Focus on the Family" (Broadcast from Arcadia, California on September 29, 1986).

14. Joy, "The Innate Differences."

15. Dr. Gabriele Lusser Rico, *Writing the Natural Way: Using Right-Brain Techniques to Release Your Expressive Powers* (Boston: Houghton Mifflin, 1983), p. 69.

16. Lori Andrews, "How Women Think," *Parents* (April 1986), p. 74.

17. Rico, *Writing the Natural Way*, p. 78.

18. Paul Tournier, *The Gift of Feeling* (Atlanta: John Know Press 1981), p. 29.

19. Ibid., p. 27.

20. Ibid., pp. 27–28.

21. Andrews, "How Women Think," p. 74.

22. Tim Hackler, "Biology Influences Sex Roles" (St. Paul, Minn.: Greenhaven Press, 1983), p. 17.

23. Ibid.

24. Joy, "The Innate Difference."

25. Dobson, "The Innate Differences."

26. Smalley, on "Focus on the Family."

27. Dr. Seuss, *Horton Hatches the Egg* (New York: Random House, 1940).

28. Elliot Engel, "Of Male Bondage," *Newsweek* (June 21, 1982), p. 13.

29. Hackler, "Biology Influences Sex Roles," p. 17.

30. Marian Sandmaier, "When A Woman Smiles, Nobody Listens," *Mademoiselle* (July 1986), p. 139.

31. Carol Gilligan, *In a Different Voice: Psychological Theory and Women's Development* (Cambridge, Mass.: Harvard University Press, 1982), p. 10.

CHAPTER 3: THE DARKER SIDE OF BEING CRAZY-GLUED

1. C.S. Lewis, *The Four Loves* (San Diego: Harcourt Brace Jovanovich, 1960), p. 113.

2. Eva Margolies, *The Best of Friends, the Worse of Enemies* (New York: Doubleday, 1985), p. 16.

3. *Detroit Free Press*, March 3, 1966.

4. Judy Blume, *Blubber* (Scarsdale, N.Y.: Bradbury Press, 1974).

5. John White, *Eros Defiled: The Christian and Sexual Sin* (Downers Grove, Ill.: InterVarsity Press, 1977), p. 120.

6. Jay Adams, *Competent to Counsel* (Grand Rapids, Mich.: Baker Book House, 1970), p. 139.

7. Dr. John Stott has an excellent article explaining why a lifelong and loving homosexual partnership is not a Christian option in *Christianity Today*, November 22, 1985.

8. Dr. Jan Flax as interviewed by Eva Margolies, *The Best of Friends, the Worst of Enemies* (New York: Doubleday, 1985), p. 83.

9. Maxine Hancock and Karen Mains, *Child Sexual Abuse* (Wheaton, Ill.: Harold Shaw Publishers, 1987), p. 38.

10. Karen C. Meiselman, *Incest: A Psychological Study of Causes and Effects with Treatment Recommendations* (San Francisco: Jossey-Bass, Inc., 1978), p. 188.

11. Lori Thorkelson, *Emotional Dependency: A Threat to Close Friendships* (San Rafael, Calif.: Exodus Int'l, 1984), p. 3.

12. John White, *Eros Defiled*, p. 111.

13. Ibid., p. 119.

14. Darlene Bogle, *Long Road To Love* (Grand Rapids, Mich.: Zondervan, 1985).

15. There are many active ministries available for the person who longs for release and help in overcoming homosexuality. They have newsletters, cassettes, and retreats. Here are two:

> Exodus,
> P.O. Box 2121,
> San Rafael, CA 94912

> Spatula Ministries (for families of homosexuals),
> P.O. Box 444,
> LaHabra, CA 90631

16. Colette Dowling, *The Cinderella Complex* (New York: Summit Books, 1981), p. 110.

CHAPTER 4: CINDERELLA IN THE CHANGE OF LIFE

1. Luci Shaw quoted in an interview by LaVonne Neff, "The Meaning of Faith in the Face of Death," *Christian Life* (June 1986), p. 44.

2. Luci Shaw, "Beauty For Ashes," *Christian Life* (June 1986), p. 44.

3. Daniel Levinson quoted in an article by Steven Hamon, "Closer Than a Brother," *Christianity Today* (Jan. 1, 1982), p. 31.

4. Dr. Beth Hess, "The Good a Friend Can Do," *Changing Times* (April 1981), p. 63.

5. Dr. Joel D. Block and Diane Greenberg, *Women and Friendship* (New York: Franklin Watts, 1985), p. 4.

6. Jan Titterington, "Insights from the Book of Ruth," *His* (January 1976), p. 3.

7. Ibid., p. 4.

8. Block and Greenberg, *Women and Friendship*, pp. 29–30.

9. Titterington, "Insights," p. 3.

10. Roy Hession, *Our Nearest Kinsman* (Fort Washington, Penn.: Christian Literature Crusade, 1976), p. 8.

11. The Targum, *Clarke's Commentary* (Nashville: Abingdon, 1824), p. 192.

12. Hans Christian Andersen, "The Snow Queen," *Fairy Tales* (New York: Grosset and Dunlap, 1981).

13. Dr. James Dobson, *What Wives Wish Their Husbands Knew About Women* (Wheaton, Ill.: Tyndale House Publishers, 1975), p. 143.

CHAPTER 5: BINDING UP THE BROKENHEARTED

1. Paula D'Arcy, *Song for Sarah* (Wheaton, Ill.: Harold Shaw Publishers, 1979), p. 62.

2. Carin Rubenstein, Ph.D., and Margaret Jaworski, "When Husbands Rate Second," *Family Circle* (May 5, 1987), p. 105.

3. Barbara Eakins, R. Gene Eakins, *Sex Differences in Human Communication* (Boston: Houghton Mifflin, 1978).

4. Jay Adams, *Competent to Counsel* (Grand Rapids, Mich.: Baker Book House, 1970), p. 140.

5. Louis McBurney, "Treatment for Infidelity Fallout," *Leadership* (Spring 1986), p. 113.

6. Ibid.

7. For marital problems, I recommend *Rekindled* by Pat Williams (Revell) and *Love Must be Tough* by James Dobson (Word). For unexpected pregnancy, I recommend *Just Like Ice Cream* by Lissa Johnson (Ronald N. Haynes Publishers) and *Beyond Choice* by Don Baker (Multnomah Press).

8. Lorraine Hansberry, *A Raisin in the Sun* (New York: New American Library, Inc., 1958), p. 125.

CHAPTER 6: THE RISK OF LOVE

1. Luci Shaw, "Perfect Love Banishes Fear," *Listen to the Green* (Wheaton, Ill.: Harold Shaw Publishers, 1971), p. 40.

2. Vance Packard, *A Nation of Strangers* (New York: Pocket Books, 1974), p. 146.

3. Randolph Bourne, *Youth and Life,* quoted in "Celebrating Friendship," *Saturday Review* (October 1961), p. 6.

4. Gordon MacDonald, *Ordering Your Private World* (Nashville: Thomas Nelson, 1984), p. 105.

5. C.S. Lewis, *The Four Loves* (San Diego: Harcourt Brace Jovanovich, 1960), p. 103.

6. Ann Kiemel Anderson and Jan Kiemel Ream, interviewed by Rebecca Powell Parat, "Our Search for Acceptance," *Christian Life* (March 1986), pp. 26–30.

7. Gail MacDonald, interviewed by Ruth Senter, "Joined Hands in Ministry," *Partnership* (January/February 1984), p. 54.

8. Adam Clarke, "Ruth," *Clarke's Commentary* (Nashville: Abingdon, 1824), p. 198.

CHAPTER 7: BEST FRIENDS

1. L.M. Montgomery, *Anne of Green Gables* (Boston: L.C. Page and Publishers, 1940), p. 75.

2. Lillian Rubin, *Just Friends* (New York: Harper and Row, 1985), p. 63.

3. bid., p. 63.

4. Dr. Donald Joy as interviewed by Dr. James Dobson, Cassette #CS099, "The innate Differences Between Males and Females" (broadcast of "Focus on the Family" from Arcadia, California).

5. Letha Scanzoni, "On Friendship and Homosexuality," *Christianity Today* (September 27, 1974), p. 11.

6. Thornton Wilder, *Our Town,* in *Three Plays* (New York: Harper and Row, 1938), p. 100.

7. Dee Brestin, *Finders Keepers* (Wheaton, Ill.: Harold Shaw Publishers, 1983).

CHAPTER 8: PROMISE ME UNFAILING LOVE

1. Lesley Dormen, "Good Friends Are Not Like Family," *Glamour* (September 1986), p. 162.

2. Lillian B. Rubin, *Just Friends* (New York: Harper and Row, 1985), p. 175.

3. Anita Moreland Smith, "My Sister, My Friend?" *Today's Christian Woman* (Nov/Dec 1986), p. 41.

4. Ibid., p. 42.

5. Mary Brown Parlee, "The Friendship Bond," *Psychology Today* (October 1979), p. 43.

6. Eva Margolies, *The Best of Friends, the Worst of Enemies* (New York: Doubleday, 1985), pp. 148–149.

7. Dr. Joel D. Block and Diane Greenberg, *Women and Friendship* (New York: Franklin Watts, 1985), p. 260.

CHAPTER 9: ROSES AND ALLIGATORS

1. Kristen Johnson Ingram, *Being a Christian Friend* (Valley Forge, Penn.: Judson Press, 1985), pp. 61–62.
2. Gini Kopecky, "Betrayals (Just Between Friends)," *Redbook* (September 1983).
3. Dawson Trotman, as quoted by Gordon MacDonald in *Ordering Your Private World* (Nashville: Thomas Nelson, 1984), p. 106.
4. Ingram, *Being a Christian Friend*, p. 63.
5. Madonna Kolbenschlag, *Kiss Sleeping Beauty Good-bye* (New York: Doubleday, 1979), p. 58.
6. Karen and David Mains, "Don't Give Me That Guilt Trip" (Wheaton, Ill., The Chapel of the Air, Tape 648a).
7. Mary Alice Kellogg, "When True-Blue Turns Green," *Savvy* (May 1986), p. 28.

CHAPTER 10: GOD KNOWS OUR NEEDS BETTER THAN WE DO

1. Luci Shaw, "Yes to Shame and Glory," *Christianity Today* (Dec. 12, 1986), p. 22.
2. Ibid.
3. Isabel Anders, "The Unexpected Gift," *Partnership* (Jan/Feb 1984), p. 42.
4. Ibid.
5. Ibid.
6. Ibid, p. 43.
7. Dorothy Pape, *In Search of God's Ideal Woman* (Downers Grove, Ill.: InterVarsity Press, 1976), p. 27.
8. Walter Wangerin, Jr., as quoted by Bruce Buursma, *The Chicago Tribune*, Aug. 8, 1986.
9. Gary Smalley, John Trent, *The Blessing* (Nashville: Thomas Nelson, 1986), pp. 24-25.
10. Shaw, "Yes to Shame and Glory," p. 23.
11. Ibid.
12. Ibid., p. 22.

CHAPTER 11: THE MENTOR RELATIONSHIP

1. Win Couchman, "Cross-Generational Relationships," speaking at Women for Christ, 1983, Winter Break (tape available from Domain Communications, Wheaton, Ill.).
2. Jill Briscoe, "Woman Power," tape #7 (tape available from Bible Believers Cassettes, Springdale, Arkansas).
3. Karen Mains, "An Interview with Karen Mains: Our Search for Spiritual Mentors," *Virtue* (October 1985), p. 73.

4. Couchman, "Cross-Generational Relationships."

5. Linda Phillips-Jones, *Mentors and Proteges* (New York: Arbor House, 1982), p. 37.

6. Ibid., p. 40.

7. Dr. James Dobson, "Turn Your Heart Towards Home" film series.

8. Briscoe, "Woman Power," tape #3.

9. Couchman, "Cross-Generational Relationships."

10. Ibid.

11. Mains, "Spiritual Mentors."

CHAPTER 12: REFLECTIONS OF CHRIST: REVIEW, PART ONE

1. Luci Shaw, "Salutation," *The Secret Trees* (Wheaton, Ill.: Harold Shaw Publishers, 1976), p. 32.

CHAPTER 13: REFLECTIONS OF CHRIST: REVIEW, PART TWO

1. Ann Kiemel Anderson and Jan Kiemel Ream, interviewed by Rebecca Powell Parat, "Our Search for Acceptance," *Christian Life* (March 1986), pp. 26–32.

2. William Shakespeare, *Romeo and Juliet*, Act 2, Scene 2, *Great Books of the Western World*, Vol. 26 (Chicago: Encyclopaedia Britannica, Inc., 1952), p. 296.

3. Sheldon Vanauken, *A Severe Mercy, Davy's Edition* (San Francisco: Harper and Row, 1977), p. 230.

PRAYER REQUESTS

PRAYER REQUESTS

PRAYER REQUESTS